Contents

1 The Nature and Role of Operations   **1**

Defining operations management; classifying operations; operations management as a key organisational function; the input-transformation-output model; product vs service operations; capacity management and demand management; customer service

2 Recent Influences on Operations Management   **19**

Improvements in transport; improvements in communications technology; the convergence of consumer preferences

3 Strategic Aspects of Operations Management   **33**

The supply chain process; relationships with other business functions; key performance objectives; strategic outsourcing

4 The Design of Products and Services   **49**

The design process for products and services; design evaluation and improvement; environmentally sensitive design; design tools

5 The Design and Management of the Operations Network   **73**

Network design and investment; product and process design; process layouts

6 Job Design and Work Organisation   **93**

Jobs and job design; the scientific management approach; motivational approaches; the socio-technical systems approach; empowerment and self-managed systems

7 The Planning and Control of Resources   **115**

Operations planning and control; the planning and management of capacity; loading, scheduling and sequencing

8 The Management of Demand   **137**

Dependent and independent demand; methods of forecasting demand; materials requirements planning and manufacturing resources planning; enterprise resource planning

9 Just In Time Manufacture   **161**

Push systems and pull systems; the definition and philosophy of just in time; lean manufacturing; detecting and preventing failure

10 Project Management   **179**

The nature of project work; the project management process; creating a project network

CIPS Study Matters

Level 5

Advanced Diploma in Purchasing and Supply

Ope...nent

© Profex Publishing Limited, 2010

Printed and distributed by the Chartered Institute of Purchasing & Supply

Easton House, Easton on the Hill, Stamford, Lincolnshire PE9 3NZ

Tel: +44 (0) 1780 756 777

Fax: +44 (0) 1780 751 610

Email: info@cips.org

Website: www.cips.org

First edition July 2006
Second edition February 2008
Third edition April 2009
Reprinted with minor amendments October 2010

Preface

Welcome to your new Study Pack.

For each subject you have to study, your Study Pack consists of three elements.

- A **Course Book** (the current volume). This provides detailed coverage of all topics specified in the unit content.

- A small-format volume of **Passnotes**. For each learning objective, these highlight and summarise the key points of knowledge and understanding that should underpin an exam answer. Use your Passnotes in the days and weeks leading up to the exam.

- An extensive range of **online resources**. These include a **Quick Start Guide** (a rapid 40-page overview of the subject), practice questions of exam standard (with full suggested solutions), notes on recent technical developments in the subject area, and recent news items (ideal for enhancing your solutions in the exam). These can all be downloaded from the study resources area at www.cips.org. You will need to log in with your membership details to access this information.

For a full explanation of how to use your new Study Pack, turn now to page xv. And good luck in your exams!

A note on style

Throughout your Study Packs you will find that we use the masculine form of personal pronouns. This convention is adopted purely for the sake of stylistic convenience – we just don't like saying 'he/she' all the time. Please don't think this reflects any kind of bias or prejudice.

October 2010

The Exam

The format of the paper

The time allowed is three hours. The examination is in two sections.

Section A – case study scenario, with two application questions based on the case study, each worth 25 marks.

Section B – questions to test knowledge and understanding. Candidates will be required to answer two questions from a choice of four. As with Section A, questions will be worth 25 marks each.

The unit content

The unit content is reproduced below, together with reference to the chapter in this Course Book where each topic is covered.

Unit characteristics

This unit is designed to enable those who work in purchasing to assess the efficiency and effectiveness of an organisation's operations. This is the process of converting input resources into output products and services that occurs in all types of organisation, whether in manufacturing or services, public sector or private.

Students should be able to understand how operations staff add value to its inputs through the effective management of production and delivery. Operations staff are likely to be the most important internal customers of purchasing and supply chain managers.

By the end of this unit students will be able to analyse and evaluate an operations environment and implement a strategic plan that allocates resources in terms of materials, labour and machinery. In addition they will be able to consider the infrastructure requirements of the management control systems, as applied to different process types and technologies, and select the right approach.

Statements of practice

On completion of this unit, students will be able to:

- Compare the challenges facing operations managers who operate in increasingly complex global markets for goods and services

- Formulate an operations strategy that will integrate with the product requirements of a marketing function.

- Advise on the benefits of make or buy/outsourcing decisions associated with specific components and services

- Assess the relationship between design and procurement and propose potential design tools that will ensure cost effective development of new products and services

- Plan and manage an operations function and advise on the optimum layout for specific types of products and process work flows

- Formulate effective resource plans and schedules that will deliver products in a cost effective manner

- Propose philosophies, tools and techniques for continuous improvement and be able to apply these approaches within an operations function in order to improve the overall competitiveness of the business

Learning objectives and indicative content

		Chapter
1.0	**The concept of operations** (Weighting 20%)	

1.1 Define operations management and assess the influences on operations management in the broader competitive environment

	Chapter
• Definitions of the term operations management	1
• Distinguishing operations management as one of the key functions in an organisation	1
• Improvements in transport and communications technology	2
• The convergence of consumer preferences	2
• Increased competition and implications of shorter product lifecycles	2

1.2 Evaluate the input-transformation-output model and explain how it relates to operations management

• The varied resource inputs to the input stage	1
• The meaning of transformation and how this applies to manufacturing and business processes	1
• The different types of output from the transformation processes	1

1.3 Compare the different characteristics of products and service operations and analyse how they impact on operations management practice

• Aspects of tangibility	1
• Quality and specification issues	1
• Demand management	1, 8
• Training and development	1
• Capacity management	1, 7
• Service quality and managing the customer	1

1.4 Evaluate the strategic relationship between the operations function and other main functions within the business.

• Marketing	3
• Finance	3
• Purchasing and supply chain	3
• Human resources	3
• Information technology (IT)	3

1.5 Analyse key performance objectives, their relationship with the order winning criteria and how they contribute to the success of a business.

• Cost	3
• Quality	3
• Responsiveness and speed	3
• Flexibility	3
• Dependability	3

How to Use Your Study Pack

Familiarisation

At this point you should begin to familiarise yourself with the package of benefits you have purchased.

- Go to www.cips.org and log on. Then go to Study and Qualify/Study Resources. Browse through the free content relating to this subject.

- Download the Quick Start Guide and print it out. Open up a ring binder and make the Quick Start Guide your first item in there.

- Now glance briefly through the Course Book (the text you're reading right now!) and the Passnotes.

Organising your study

'Organising' is the key word: unless you are a very exceptional student, you will find a haphazard approach is insufficient, particularly if you are having to combine study with the demands of a full-time job.

A good starting point is to timetable your studies, in broad terms, between now and the date of the examination. How many subjects are you attempting? How many chapters are there in the Course Book for each subject? Now do the sums: how many days/weeks do you have for each chapter to be studied?

Remember:

- Not every week can be regarded as a study week – you may be going on holiday, for example, or there may be weeks when the demands of your job are particularly heavy. If these can be foreseen, you should allow for them in your timetabling.

- You also need a period leading up to the exam in which you will revise and practise what you have learned.

Once you have done the calculations, make a week-by-week timetable for yourself for each paper, allowing for study and revision of the entire unit content between now and the date of the exams.

Getting started

Aim to find a quiet and undisturbed location for your study, and plan as far as possible to use the same period each day. Getting into a routine helps avoid wasting time. Make sure you have all the materials you need before you begin – keep interruptions to a minimum.

Begin by reading through your Quick Start Guide. This should take no more than a couple of hours, even reading slowly. By the time you have finished this you will have a reasonable grounding in the subject area. You will build on this by working through the Course Book.

Using the Course Book

You should refer to the Course Book to the extent that you need it.

- If you are a newcomer to the subject, you will probably need to read through the Course Book quite thoroughly. This will be the case for most students.

- If some areas are already familiar to you – either through earlier studies or through your practical work experience – you may choose to skip sections of the Course Book.

The content of the Course Book

This Course Book has been designed to give detailed coverage of every topic in the unit content. As you will see from pages vii–xiii, each topic mentioned in the unit content is dealt with in a chapter of the Course Book. For the most part the order of the Course Book follows the order of the unit content closely, though departures from this principle have occasionally been made in the interest of a logical learning order.

Each chapter begins with a reference to the learning objectives and unit content to be covered in the chapter. Each chapter is divided into sections, listed in the introduction to the chapter, and for the most part being actual captions from the unit content.

All of this enables you to monitor your progress through the unit content very easily and provides reassurance that you are tackling every subject that is examinable.

Each chapter contains the following features.

- Introduction, setting out the main topics to be covered
- Clear coverage of each topic in a concise and approachable format
- A chapter summary
- Self-test questions

The study phase

For each chapter you should begin by glancing at the main headings (listed at the start of the chapter). Then read fairly rapidly through the body of the text to absorb the main points. If it's there in the text, you can be sure it's there for a reason, so try not to skip unless the topic is one you are familiar with already.

Then return to the beginning of the chapter to start a more careful reading. You may want to take brief notes as you go along, but bear in mind that you already have your Quick Start Guide and Passnotes – there is no point in duplicating what you can find there.

Test your recall and understanding of the material by attempting the self-test questions. These are accompanied by cross-references to paragraphs where you can check your answers and refresh your memory.

Practising what you have learned

Once you think you have learned enough about the subject, or about a particular topic within the overall subject area, it's good to practise. Access the study resources at www.cips.org, and download a practice question on the relevant area. Alternatively, download a past exam question. Attempt a solution yourself before looking at our suggested solution or the Senior Assessor's comments.

Make notes of any mistakes you made, or any areas where your answer could be improved. If there is anything you can't understand, you are welcome to email us for clarification (course.books@cips.org).

The revision phase

Your approach to revision should be methodical and you should aim to tackle each main area of the unit content in turn. Begin by re-reading your Quick Start Guide. This gives an overview that will help to focus your more detailed study. Then re-read your notes and/or the separate Passnotes accompanying this Course Book. Then return to question practice. Review your own solutions to the practice questions you have had time to attempt. If there are gaps, try to find time to attempt some more questions, or at least to review the suggested solutions.

Additional reading

Your Study Pack provides you with the key information needed for each module but CIPS strongly advocates reading as widely as possible to augment and reinforce your understanding. CIPS produces an official reading list of books, which can be downloaded from the bookshop area of the CIPS website.

To help you, we have identified one essential textbook for each subject. We recommend that you read this for additional information.

The essential textbook for this unit is *Operations Management* by Slack, Chambers and Johnston, published by Pearson (ISBN: 978–027373–160–3).

CHAPTER 1

The Nature and Role of Operations

Learning objectives and indicative content

1.1   Define operations management and assess the influences on operations management in the broader competitive environment.

- Definitions of the term operations management
- Distinguishing operations management as one of the key functions in an organisation

1.2   Evaluate the input-transformation-output model and explain how it relates to operations management

- The varied resource inputs to the input stage
- The meaning of transformation and how this applies to manufacturing and business processes
- The different types of output from the transformation process

1.3   Compare the different characteristics of product and service operations and analyse how they impact on operations management practice.

- Aspects of tangibility
- Quality and specification issues
- Demand management
- Training and development
- Capacity management
- Service quality and managing the customer

Chapter headings

1   Defining operations management

2   Classifying operations

3   Operations management as a key organisational function

4   The input-transformation-output model

5   Product vs service operations

6   Capacity management and demand management

7   Customer service

1 Defining operations management

Overview

1.1 An operation is defined by the Collins English Dictionary as 'a process, method or series of acts especially of a practical nature'. The definition covers all human activity of a productive and organisational nature and is directly applicable to business operations. An operational activity may appear insignificant when viewed in isolation but it is the result of an integrated set of operations that together deliver effective operations or processes.

1.2 A process may be viewed as a particular course of action intended to achieve a desired result or more specifically a set of logically related tasks performed to achieve a defined business outcome.

1.3 A process exists to achieve a purpose. It is also useful to think of roles and responsibilities in this way. A person's job is not to carry out a process but to achieve a result. Michael Hammer, often called the father of business process re-engineering, defined process as 'a related group of tasks that together create a result of value to a customer'.

1.4 Operations or processes consist of a series of integrated single operations that take inputs, add value to them and deliver outputs. The process must be designed, formalised and linked to other processes in order to effectively deliver the desired operational activity.

- As an example one complaint to an organisation may be ineffective but if it is delivered via a call centre where calls are monitored and records kept, a pattern of problems can emerge and remedial actions put in place leading to an overall improvement.

- A delivery of components to form part of a production run requires other operations to enable it to reach the production line. The delivery must be recorded, notification of delivery must be available, storage must be available, location must be recorded, machinery is needed to move the components to the right point.

1.5 With the above examples (one a service, the other from manufacturing) the operations and operational activities are different but the effective integration of the operational links serves to form part of the value-adding activities that underpin organisational operations. It is the integration and effective co-ordination and management of the operational activities involved that together help form operations management.

Definitions of operations management

1.6 Operations management has its development roots during the manufacturing era. In consequence many definitions still allude to this period. This is not necessarily incorrect but the definitions must often be extended to modern day work practice, in particular the supply chain concept and the growing importance of services.

- 'Operations management consists of those activities which are concerned with the acquisition of raw materials, their conversion into finished product, and the supply of that product to the customer'. (R L Galloway).

- 'Operations management is concerned with creating, operating and controlling a transformation system that takes inputs and a variety of resources, and produces outputs of goods and services needed by customers'. (J Naylor)

- 'Operations management is the term used for the activities, decisions and responsibilities of operations managers who manage the production and delivery of products and services'. (Slack, Chambers and Johnston)

- Operations management is 'the direction and control of the processes that transform inputs into finished goods and services.' (Krajewski and Ritzman)

- Operations management is 'the management of any aspect of the production system that transforms inputs into finished goods and services.' (Jones, George and Hill)

1.7 Operations management concerns itself with the effective and efficient management of any operation. Although originally manufacturing based, the degree to which a physical component or product is involved is largely irrelevant. Operations management can be equally applied to a TV news programme, a hospital ward or a local authority where the objective is more toward service delivery than product delivery.

1.8 The role of operations management is crucial to the success of any organisation as it seeks to improve effectiveness, ie to ensure that operations are carried out so as to meet customer requirements and to improve efficiency.

1.9 Increasing effectiveness will increase profitability or contribution by making the organisation leaner, more responsive and more competitive. Improvements in efficiency will reduce costs but these cost savings must not be made at the expense of effectiveness. Measures must be put in place to evidence improvement gains achieved through increasing effectiveness. Measuring performance allows judgement by setting targets and evaluating feedback leading to discussions on future improvements, efficiency savings or approaches.

1.10 Efficiency can be defined as the relationship between inputs and outputs achieved. The fewer the inputs (both goods and services) used by an organisation to achieve a given output, the more efficient is the organisation.

1.11 Effectiveness is the degree to which an objective or target is met.

The 'restricted sense' and the 'broader sense'

1.12 Two interpretations of the term 'operations management' must be clearly understood.

- Operations management in the **restricted** sense concentrates on organisational aspects such as planning, organising and controlling the production process together with the management of interface functions in order to achieve organisational objectives. This is not necessarily restricted to production management but can equally apply for service or not-for-profit organisations, but these operational aspects are the core functions of operations management.

- Operations management in the **broader** sense sees a **wider** remit in every activity of the organisation. Above, we asked: 'Do you sense that many managers within your organisation could be said to have some operational management role?' The answer will usually be yes. Most management roles focus on the efficient use of resources to meet company goals. In the broader sense we need to consider the interface between the functions of the operation so as to achieve the best overall delivery of customer service irrespective of functional boundaries.

2   *Classifying operations*

The manufacturing sector

2.1   The role of operations has broadened as the scope of business has expanded. From its original remit of production management the broader term 'operations management' reflects the wider scope of the role and its importance across wider sector environments.

2.2   The conventional aspect of operations management is its production origins. In the manufacturing environment this involves the conversion of raw materials into a final product through a manufacturing (transformation) process. Discussed later in the chapter the input-transformation-output model is fundamental to operations management.

2.3   The input-transformation-output model takes inputs such as components and assembly items to be put into the transformation process where they contribute to the manufactured product then progress through to the output required to meet customer demands. The principal role of operations management is to increase productivity by reducing the amount of inputs, which can include costs, labour and processes while securing the same level of outputs.

The service sector

2.4   Services are the activities that influence the physical, emotional or intellectual condition of a customer and are an increasing aspect of the operations management role. As much of manufacturing has moved to overseas locations the economy has benefitted from a substantial increase in service provision.

2.5   Services include consultancy, retailing, dentistry, solicitors, public service areas etc. They can equally apply the input-transformation-output model taking ideas, people and/or concepts as inputs and transforming then through a series of processes to achieve a defined outcome. As an example the services provided by a local authority must not only be delivered but the reasoning behind them must be explained and justified to council taxpayers who derive no first-hand benefit from them. Delivery of the service is the first part of the definition and influencing the intellectual condition of the customer is explaining the reasoning.

2.6   Supply activities are those involved in the change of ownership of a physical product. Goods move and change ownership and make-up as they progress along the supply chain (raw material – refined material – component of first production process – delivery to be incorporated into manufacture of the final product) or as ownership is transferred as part of a wholesale or retail process. The supply chain has a direct relevance for the operations manager as they are reliant on the timing and quality of delivered goods inputs in order to progress to the transformation stage.

2.7   The service supply chain requires the same consideration from operations managers involved. As an example the production of a text book may require inputs from a number of different writers. These inputs need to be collated and transformed into the finished book before being bound and delivered to customers.

2.8   The role of logistics is a crucial contributor to successful operations. The role is the movement and storage of material in and out of the organisation in the most effective manner. The role of logistics personnel will vary greatly but can involve such areas as storage, stock control and distribution, with the objective of managing these operations in the most effective manner to meet company and customer needs.

2.9   Distribution activities are those involved in the movement and storage of goods including movement by sea, air, road and rail, warehousing, containerisation and all interlinked logistic considerations. These can equally have an operations function. Warehouses can take in bulk deliveries and transform them by braking the delivery into smaller quantities and adding value by arranging home deliveries.

2.10   The retail operations manager takes deliveries from a number of suppliers and organises the processes that display and support the sales process. Value is added by the transformation process of breaking large quantities and providing smaller quantities to individual customers. The advent of online retailers has demonstrated how effectively technology can be used to bring a fresh approach and reduce costs.

The not-for-profit sector

2.11   When considering not-for-profit organisations such as hospitals, local authorities or charities, increases in effectiveness can be viewed as the contribution these improvements bring to the overall organisation. This is the contribution that comes from better processes, systems and linkages that achieve equal or superior output without an increase in resources.

2.12   Measuring improvements can be more difficult in a service-orientated environment. Governments have introduced national targets, with mixed success, but they provide a target for bodies to aim for or exceed. The targets can also be used for similar organisations to benchmark their operations against more successful organisations. An example is local authorities where successful improvements and gains are published, along with league tables, on the internet.

2.13   The site allows public sector organisations to learn of successful improvements and how they were implemented, and then apply them to their own organisation in a manner that they find appropriate for their own circumstances.

2.14   It would be a mistake to consider different sectors as operating in isolation. Good operations management requires an interface (in terms of cross-functional teams, information flows and good communications) to be an ongoing feature of the business or service irrespective of the organisational structure used.

3 Operations management as a key organisational function

Introduction

3.1 The role of operations is concerned with any productive activity. Operations management is concerned with ensuring that these activities are carried out effectively and efficiently. In its broader sense operations management is about ensuring the efficient use of resources to meet customer expectations. These expectations are an amalgam of company history and tradition, company resources, company image, brand perception, customer services levels and a host of other related factors that come together and need to be met or exceeded.

3.2 Operations management concerns itself with the effective and efficient management of any operation. Although originally manufacturing based, the degree to which a physical component or product is involved is largely irrelevant. Operations management can be equally applied to a TV news programme, hospital ward or a local authority where the objective is more toward service delivery than product delivery.

3.3 The role of operations management is crucial to the success of any organisation as it seeks to improve effectiveness, ie to ensure that operations are carried out so as to meet customer requirements and to improve efficiency in the design and management of those operations so that they can meet customer service requirement in the most cost-effective and timely manner while maintaining customer service levels.

3.4 Irrespective of the changing nature of operations management the need to use resources effectively and efficiently is central to any organisation. The challenge for those involved is to ensure that this is possible and that resources are used to meet the needs of the organisation and customers, not only now but to meet planned future developments.

3.5 The increasing effectiveness will increase profitability or contribution by making the organisation leaner, more responsive and more competitive. Improvements in efficiency will reduce costs but these cost savings must not be made at the expense of effectiveness. Measures should be put in place to evidence improvement gains achieved through increasing effectiveness. Measuring performance allows judgement by setting targets and evaluating feedback leading to discussions on future improvements, efficiency savings or approaches.

3.6 Operations managers 'make things happen'. They take in goods, ideas and concepts and refine them to deliver the finished article. Many roles have an operations management perspective. Even if the role does not carry the operations management title the areas of operations management form part of many managers' roles.

Responsibility for cost

3.7 Operations management is concerned with managing the resources of an enterprise that are required to produce the goods and services to be sold or provided to consumers or other organisations. Operations managers have responsibility for the design of the operation and the systems and processes involved in making them.

3.8 The operations function involves managing a large cost centre with an overall responsibility for up to 80 per cent of all the costs incurred by a business. These comprise most, if not all, of the direct costs (employees and materials) and a proportion of overheads that are applicable to specific operations.

3.9 With the high level of costs involved, the operations function has a key role in managing the flow of money through the organisation. Costs are built up as a product or service moves from raw materials or information through processing to result in finished goods or service delivery. The purchase of raw materials, components and items for assembly, and the direct costs involved in the transformation process, must be well managed not only from an operational standpoint but also with regard to the cashflow implications.

Responsibility for activities

3.10 Operations managers have a degree of responsibility for all the activities of the operation that directly or indirectly contribute to the effective production of goods and services. The direct responsibility concerns all the activities involved in the input–transformation–output process. The indirect responsibility concerns the linkages between operations and the other functional areas of the business.

3.11 As organisations have changed to meet the needs and challenges of the modern business environment their management structures have also been altered, often to a flatter and more flexible structure that serves to encourage cross-functional team working. The role of operations managers involves an ongoing interface with other business areas such as design, purchasing and supply chain management, logistics and finance. This interface role will involve cross-functional team-working to ensure that all relevant areas linked to a project or issue are discussed and developed as appropriate.

Responsibility for performance

3.12 Operations management places responsibility on managers to continually improve the performance of their operation. The role involves the issue of managing complexity.

3.13 Even where individual tasks are not complex, the drawing together of these tasks in a way that is most appropriate and effective to deliver results may be a challenge. One part of the operation may involve a number of individual tasks that come together to produce the desired outcome but the operations manager also needs to consider how these individual tasks may impact different business areas if they are designed to meet just one operational requirement.

3.14 The need to continually improve, at least as fast as competitors, is a constant pressure across the organisation. As competitors work to improve systems and performance and customers' expectations continue to rise, organisations in a competitive environment must rise to meet the challenge or possibly risk seeing the competition make inroads into their business. The role of operations management is central to ensuring that the organisation is in a fit condition and responsive enough to meet these outside pressures.

3.15 To meet these needs it is essential that operations managers have a strategic plan in place. This operations strategy works within the corporate strategy of the organisation.

3.16 Operations managers must also try to ensure that problems do not occur in the first place. This responsibility involves operations management in product design, logistics, storage and distribution issues, design of production processes and systems, and quality throughout the organisation through the delivery of the goods or services.

3.17 The design of the operation, the products and the processes is an essential aspect of operations management. Although responsibility for product design may not be a direct operations management role, it is vital for operations managers to become involved in this area. This will ensure that, via cross-functional team-working, the product can be integrated into the stock management and production processes of the organisation in the most effective manner to deliver the desired outcome.

3.18 Operations managers have a direct responsibility for the planning and control of the operation. This area covers decisions relating to what the operation's resources should be doing and ensuring they are doing it effectively and efficiently. Areas covered include the objectives and activities of operations planning and control, system capacity and system efficiency, and demand and management strategies that serve to give a flavour of the complexity and essential nature of this crucial role of operations management.

4 The input-transformation-output model

Inputs and outputs

4.1 Operations management is a field of study that tries to understand, explain, predict and change the strategic and organisational effects of the transformation process. The design of a process should reflect what the customer wants and should be flexible enough to change when customers' preferences change.

4.2 Operations management is the systematic direction and control of the processes that transform inputs into finished goods and services. While purchasing is concerned with acquiring the right product at the right time, finance with providing the capital, marketing with creating and developing demand, operations produces and (in many cases) delivers the product/service.

4.3 The transformation of inputs to outputs is central to operations management. All operations produce goods and/or services by developing processes that transform the state of something to produce outputs. The transformation process will change the condition of a product and/or service by taking a set of input resources and transforming them (for example, by a manufacturing process) to produce a more refined output.

Figure 1.1 *The input–transformation–output model*

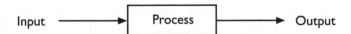

4.4 All operations are input-transformation-output processes. Inputs may be, for example, people, materials, energy, finance, or information. These are converted or aid conversion into a more refined or finished product or service via the transformation process to produce, as an output, the goods or services designed to meet customer needs.

- **People**: the workforce who provide the skills, knowledge and competencies that underpin the operation.

- **Materials**: the raw materials or the assembly items that form part of the finished product.

- **Energy**: the management of costs is central to operations management. Energy management represents just one area for consideration.

- **Finance**: the organisation must have adequate finance for buying and updating capital items (such as plant and equipment) and for working capital (to meet running costs such as wages, purchases and many other related areas of expenditure).

- **Information**: good information is essential to any operational activity in today's workplace. Data processing should be managed to deliver required information as and when required and in a meaningful form to the user.

Operating processes and management support processes

4.5 Processes fall into two distinct categories: 'operating processes' and 'management support processes'.

- **Operating processes** are those that add value to a product or service such as in the transformation process but can also include the addition of value through marketing, customer service and research and development.

- **Management support processes** are those that are needed to keep the operation running as efficiently and effectively as possible. This covers areas such as human resources, information technology and financial management.

4.6 Each is of equal importance in the sense that each requires the other to work effectively to maximise resources. The role of operations is clearly more linked with 'operating processes' but requires input from the 'management support processes' in order to work as effectively and efficiently as possible.

4.7 Within an operations environment the production/operation system would involve a number of process considerations that come together as facilitators of the transformation process.

- Capacity
- Type of production/operation
- Level of skills available
- Layout of plant and equipment
- Effectiveness of information technology
- Cost to be achieved

4.8 The transformation of resources is effected by using the combined effort of all the above factors, in a methodical way, to deliver the desired output. The method or design of the transformation process is central to producing the desired outcome.

4.9 The situation is similar in a services environment. Hotels, airlines, hairdressers and a range of other service providers take in inputs (ie people) and transform them by accommodating them, moving them or changing their physical appearance. These can be seen as customer process operations.

4.10 Accountants, market research agencies and news services transform data and information to deliver the required output. These roles can be viewed as predominantly information processors.

4.11 The output stage involves the delivery of the blend of goods and services to meet customer needs.

4.12 All processes will produce by-products or waste. By-products will sometimes have other applications in the production of other goods but in many cases the by-products need careful management and disposal in the appropriate manner.

4.13 'Waste' refers not only to physical waste. The subject has come under considerable scrutiny over the years firstly with Taichi Ohno, the architect of the Toyota Production System and the 'seven wastes', and more recently with Robert Smith's 'Triangle of Waste' which examines redundant stock, obsolete stock and returned stock as 'waste' areas that organisations are not managing well.

4.14 The 'seven wastes' of Taichi Ohno are particularly relevant at this stage.

- **Over-production**. From an operations perspective this requires sound stock management procedures and production techniques to ensure that the correct quantities are ordered and made.

- **Waiting time**. This adds no value, only cost and inconvenience. Machines that are not compatible and produce at different rates can cause waiting on the production line. Waiting for the telephone to be answered, the shop to open, the assistant to come back are all examples of service sector incidences of 'waiting'.

- **Unnecessary transporting**. Loads should be maximised, goods should be transported to the correct location and should not require additional transportation.

- **Inappropriate processing**. All processes must be appropriate to the required output, ie they must meet customer requirements.

- **Unnecessary inventory**. Inventory costs money. Except in the most refined just-in-time systems inventory still needs to be carried. The objective is to carry as little as possible to meet current requirements.

- **Unnecessary motions**. This concerns the design of movement within the working environment in order to ensure that every movement is minimised while still performing the required task.

- **Defects**. Products should be designed so as to build in quality from the outset through good use of design, materials and processes. Defects require an organisation to instigate post-manufacturing inspection processes with consequent costs and may involve re-working of an item or failure to meet customer service requirements.

4.15 The transformation process links a related group of tasks together to create a result of value to a customer (Michael Hammer). The role of the operations manager is to ensure the efficient and effective application of the transformation process. To achieve this will involve the operations manager outside the transformation area to have extensive involvement in both the prior inputs and later outputs.

5 *Product vs service operations*

The mix of goods and services

5.1 The outputs of a business may be either goods or services or a mix of the two. The proportions of goods and services in the mix will vary from industry to industry. Here are some examples (with percentages included for illustration only).

Table 1.1 *The mix of goods and services in different industries*

Operation	Goods	Services
Mining	95%	5%
Vending machines	95%	5%
Low-cost consumable goods	80%	20%
Home computers	75%	25%
Fast-food operation	60%	40%
High-quality restaurant meal	30%	70%
Car breakdown service	25%	75%
Local authority	25%	75%
Teaching	5%	95%

5.2 With mining the purpose is to extract raw materials. Little emphasis is placed on the delivery of support services with the exception of transportation to a port or for refinement.

5.3 A fast-food restaurant offers a mix of a limited product range with a standardised approach to service; a more upmarket restaurant provides better facilities and specialised advice; a local authority provides goods in terms of refuse collection, street cleaning etc, but concentrates more on offering a range of support services that meet the needs of the community.

5.4 This analysis demonstrates that most operations produce a mix of goods and services.

5.5 We are seeing major changes in two key areas that affect the goods-service mix.

- **Customer service requirements.** Customers are becoming more demanding and require better and consistently high levels of customer service. One approach is to use this to the supplier's benefit and 'add value' to the customer experience. Delivery in 24 hours, late product customisation, 'delighting' the customer with unexpected upgrades and improvements at no extra cost, are all examples. The reward can be better customer relationships and retention, leading to an improvement in the operation overall.

- **The impact of information technology.** Information and communication technologies can allow for the provision and standardisation of services in a way that can be easily understood by customers. A well designed website can provide company information, product information and purchase information together with a secure method of purchase and detail on subsequent delivery.

Aspects of tangibility

5.6 Products are tangible, which means that they have a physical presence (unlike services which have no physical presence). The essence of services is that they do not result in the ownership of anything.

Table 1.2 *Characteristics of goods and services*

Goods	Services
Tangible	Intangible
Can be inventoried	Cannot be inventoried
Little customer contact	Extensive customer contact
Standard customer contact	Flexible customer contact
Long lead times	Short lead times
Capital intensive	Labour intensive
Quality easy to assess	Quality very difficult to assess

5.7 Services have been defined by Kotler as: 'any activity of benefit that one party can offer to another that is essentially intangible and does not result in the ownership of anything. Its production may or may not be tied to a physical product'.

5.8 Service delivery differs from the operational aspects of goods delivery in a number of crucial ways. The operations and marketing roles, in particular, face a number of distinct problems that require different approaches to address the issues raised. The characteristics of services that make them distinctive are as follows.

- Intangibility
- Inseparability
- Variability (also referred to as heterogeneity)
- Perishability
- Ownership

5.9 **Intangibility** refers to the lack of substance that is involved in service delivery. Unlike goods there are no physical aspects, no taste, no feel etc. This can inhibit the choice of a customer to use a service, as they are not sure what they will receive.

5.10 **Inseparability**. A service often cannot be separated from the provider of the service. The creation or the performance often occurs at the same instant that a full or partial consumption of it occurs. Goods must be produced, then sold, then consumed (in that order). Services are only a promise at the time they are sold; most services are sold and then are produced and consumed simultaneously.

5.11 **Variability**. Many services face a problem of maintaining consistency in the standard of output. Variability of quality in delivery is inevitable because of the number of factors that can influence it. It may prove difficult or impossible either to attain precise standardisation of the service offered or to influence or control perceptions of what is good or bad customer service.

5.12 To minimise the impact there is a need to monitor customer reactions. A common way of addressing this problem involves applying a system or business format to deliver a service that can then be franchised to operators. The franchisor can set precise guidelines throughout its business in areas such as customer service, dress code and design and layout that can serve to standardise the offering.

5.13 **Perishability**. Services cannot be stored. Seats at a concert, provision of a lecture, services of a dentist consist of their availability for periods of time. Perishability presents specific marketing problems. Meeting customer needs in these operations depends on staff being available as and when they are needed. This must be balanced against the need for a firm to minimise unnecessary expenditure on staff wages. Anticipating and responding to levels of demand is a key planning priority.

5.14 **Ownership**. Services differ fundamentally from goods in that purchase does not result in a transfer of property. The purchase of a service only confers on the customer access to or rights to use a facility – not ownership. This may lower the customer's perception of the service's value.

5.15 Services involve a higher degree of customer contact and presentation than with the selling of a product. The physical delivery of a service is less of a problem as the service element is intangible. However, other areas take on a more important role.

- **People**: have a crucial role in providing service. Customer satisfaction can often depend on the person providing the service, because the service is inseparable from the person delivering it. As a result, there is an increased emphasis on staff training and development.
- **Physical evidence**: the ambience surrounding the service being provided. As an example the ambience surrounding a top hotel may serve to convey the nature of the product, reinforce the image of the hotel, engender rapport, imply qualities and transmit messages.
- **Process**: this refers to the methods used to provide the service and is directly related to the role of operations management. Procedures for dealing with customers and for supplying the service must be carefully planned and managed so as to reduce variability.

Quality issues

5.16 Quality is key to service delivery. Only the customer can judge quality.

5.17 Quality of service is an increasingly important performance measurement tool in both the public and private sectors. With the move to a more service-orientated economy and greater transparency and accountability being expected in the public sector, the area of service is increasingly being placed under scrutiny.

5.18 Quality of service to customers is, by its nature, subjective and qualitative. Gathering the information provides greater challenges than would be the case with a product, where measures such as rejection rates or percentage for scrap could be used. Questionnaires are commonly used (either by mail, email or over the telephone), although the response rate can be low.

5.19 Two categories of data are relevant.

- **Quantitative** (also known as hard data) based on figures (eg variances, profit, sales, costs, ratios, indices)
- **Qualitative** (also known as soft data) based on opinions and feedback

5.20 Judgement on quality of service provision can be formalised by linking feedback from questionnaires with some quantitative measures that can be used in connection with it. Ratios such as returns to sales or complaints per units sold are one tool. Delivery targets (eg 95 per cent delivery in two days) can be measured against actual achievement. Speed of service at supermarkets and calls waiting at call centres are all performance measures that together can give a realistic and rounded assessment of the quality of service being delivered.

5.21 The role of operations management must be measured to be fully evaluated in its effectiveness. Measurement highlights areas for improvement, permits benchmarking where appropriate and allows for the setting of realistic targets and objectives. The role needs to be fully appreciated at the strategic level of an organisation in order to reach full potential and should be fully supported as a strategic objective. The role is becoming more complex as business pressures continue to grow.

6 *Capacity management and demand management*

6.1 Capacity management involves matching the operating system with the demand placed on the system. Capacity management is a key requirement of operations management as all other operations plans and actions are dependent on the availability of capacity. Capacity is the ability to produce work in a given time.

6.2 Effective system capacity and system efficiency are measures of an organisation's ability to meet customer requirements.

6.3 Capacity management and demand management are mentioned at this point in your syllabus and again later. We defer our detailed coverage of these topics until Chapters 7 and 8.

7 *Customer service*

7.1 Increasingly companies are realising the importance of customer service in their relationship with customers. However, it is often difficult to ascertain exactly what customer service is or to provide a precise definition of customer service measures that should be put in place.

7.2 *The Essence of Services Marketing* by Adrian Buckley provides three definitions that together consider customer expectations, the complexity of customer service and the all-encompassing role of customer service.

- 'Timeliness and reliability of delivery of products and services to customers in accordance with their expectations.'

- 'A complex of activities involving all areas of the business which combine to deliver the company's products and services in a fashion that is perceived as satisfactory by the customer and which advances the company's objectives.'

- 'All the activities required to accept, process, deliver and fulfil customer orders and to follow up on any activity that has gone wrong.'

7.3 It can be seen from the scope of these definitions that effective delivery of customer service is far-reaching and complex to get right and deliver.

7.4 Customer service and customer service requirements will vary according to industry, companies, individual market segments and end users, amongst other factors. Identifying the main elements of customer service applicable to a particular business situation is a key first step in understanding the customer service requirements the organisation should be seeking to fulfil. Figure 1.2 should help.

Figure 1.2 *Influences on customer services*

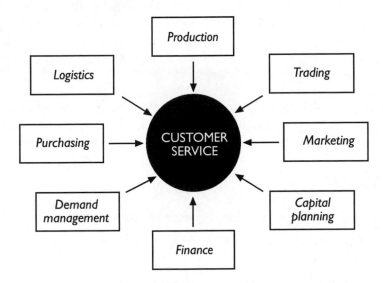

Adapted from Logistics and Transport Focus, Oct 2003

7.5 Martin Christopher detailed a four-stage approach to developing a customer service strategy.

- **Identify a service mission.** This is similar to creating a mission statement that serves to give the organisation a focus. A service mission will define the nature, purpose and direction of customer service. It should consider internal customers (users and deliverers) within the organisation as well as external users (customers).

- **Set customer service objectives**, such as:

  (i) Ascertaining customer's needs;

  (ii) Identifying where customer service fits in relation to other areas of the marketing mix;

  (iii) Deciding whether segmentation is necessary to meet the needs of individual customers or groups of customers;

  (iv) Prioritising among a range of possible objectives that will vary from company to company.

- • **Recognise that not all customers require the same level of service.** Segmentation is the process of dividing customers into different groups or segments, within which customers with similar characteristics have similar needs. By identifying each group a customer service programme can be developed to meet their needs.

- • **Develop an effective service package that meets the identified needs.** As with any customer service package, only customers can effectively judge it, so a feedback mechanism is crucial.

7.6 To ensure that a customer service strategy will meet the needs of customers a value proposition needs to be developed, implemented and controlled with a dedicated focus on meeting customer needs. Customer service has a key role to play in 'adding value' and enhancing the service offering.

7.7 Customer service is a team game, which does not respect artificial company or departmental boundaries. The customer knows that poor service has been delivered – they are not concerned about the problem areas. If the team plays well and excellent customer service is provided then the organisation has delivered what it set out to do. If one member of the team fails to do their job the organisation provides poor service. 'Team' applies to anyone who has the ability to impact the customer service of the business.

7.8 The role of the operations manager when involved in service delivery is to ensure that processes are sound and robust and that the delivery team is well motivated, trained and committed to achieving the high level of customer service required.

Chapter summary

- • The role of the operations function is concerned with any productive activity.

- • The role of operations management is less clearly defined than some other business functions.

- • Operations or processes consist of a series of integrated single operations that take inputs, add value to them and deliver outputs.

- • Measuring improvements can be more difficult in a service-orientated environment.

- • Operations management is the systematic direction and control of the processes that transform inputs into finished goods and services.

- • Operations management is a field of study that tries to understand, explain, predict and change the strategic and organisational effects of the transformation process.

- • Capacity is the ability to produce work in a given time.

- • Quality is key to service delivery. Only the customer can judge quality.

- • Customer service is a team game, which does not respect artificial company or departmental boundaries.

Self-test questions

Numbers in brackets refer to the paragraphs above where your answers can be checked.

1   Define operations management. (1.6)

2   What is the difference between the 'restricted sense' and the 'broader sense' of operations management? (1.12)

3   Can we apply the input – transformation – output model to services? (2.5)

4   Give four examples of inputs into the transformation process. (4.4)

5   What are the seven wastes of Taichi Ohno? (4.14)

6   How does Kotler define service? (5.7)

7   How do you minimise variability in service operations? (5.11, 5.12)

8   What four stage approach to forming a customer service strategy was given by Professor Martin Christopher? (7.5)

Further reading

- *Operations Management*, Slack, Chambers and Johnston, Chapters 1, 11

- *Production and Operations Management*, Muhlemann, Oakland and Lockyer, Chapters 1, 23

CHAPTER 2

Recent Influences on Operations Management

Learning objectives and indicative content

1.1 Define operations management and assess the influences on management in the broader competitive environment.

- Improvements in transport and communications technology
- The convergence of consumer preferences
- Increased competition and implications of shorter product lifecycles

Chapter headings

1 Improvements in transport

2 Improvements in communications technology

3 The convergence of consumer preferences

1 Improvements in transport

Modes of transport

1.1 The changing and increasingly integrated nature of logistics and the supply chain, together with a move to global operations, has meant that practitioners need a more detailed knowledge of transport modes in order to evaluate options available. Owing to this move to globalisation more product is moved over greater distances. Long-distance supply chains have been established by companies, which require careful co-ordination and planning to operate effectively.

1.2 The main transport modes (air, sea, road and rail) are long established but operate in the competitive world trading environment and are continually developing to meet customer needs. In common with all areas of international trade, transportation of goods has undergone considerable change in recent years. Developments in areas such as containerisation, intermodal transport, and the increasing effectiveness of information technology are driving the industry forward.

Sea freight

1.3 Many goods handled internationally are transported by sea freight. The industry has undergone considerable change in recent years but one of the major influences was the advent of containerisation introduced from the late 1970s onwards. Containerisation offers both benefits and disadvantages when compared with the more traditional between-deck/break-bulk stowage used in conventional non-container vessels.

Table 2.1 *Advantages and disadvantages of sea freight*

Advantages of sea freight	Disadvantages of sea freight
• The introduction of door-to-door movements.	• Huge initial investment in vessels, ports and facilities.
• Increased security due to containment and reduced handling.	• Costs of investing, maintaining, tracking and storing containers.
• Improved transit and turnaround times.	• Not all cargoes are suitable for containerisation.
• Cost savings from areas such as packing and better space usage.	
• Raised service quality.	

Road freight and rail freight

1.4 Within Europe, road freight still dominates and has seen major advances in the services offered by logistic companies in recent years with greater emphasis on strategically located warehouses, technology and timed deliveries. Rail freight is limited within the UK but is used more effectively in continental Europe.

1.5 The Channel Tunnel has had a more direct impact on road haulage, offering guaranteed crossing times for vehicles. The opening of the Channel Tunnel offers new opportunities for the movement of freight by rail. Rail economists cite various distances as the point where rail transport becomes profitable. The Channel Tunnel offers the prospect of more regular use of the tunnel by freight carriers and the potential growth of intermodal operations (see below).

1.6 Running between Folkestone and Coquilles in France the Channel Tunnel has added a new dimension to both the road and rail industry and has been a main catalyst in the development of intermodal transport throughout Europe.

1.7 The tunnel offers regular departure and arrival times that are virtually unaffected by the weather, allowing for better planning and optimum usage. Vehicles can drive on at one end and drive off at the other offering a seamless transition from road to rail and back to road. This conventional wagonload traffic together with commercial car traffic provides the main revenue stream for the Channel Tunnel.

Intermodal transport

1.8 The growth in intermodal transport has developed alongside the acceptance of containers. Intermodal transport is a system where goods are moved by the most economical mix of transport modes from place to place, utilising containers. Easy transfer for one mode to another is essential and many transport modes have developed vessels or vehicles to carry the standard sized loads.

1.9 The following is a definition of intermodal transport from the European Council of Transport Ministers:

The movement of goods in one and the same loading unit or vehicle, which uses successively several modes of transport without handling the goods themselves in changing modes.

1.10 The development has been rapid in recent years with a growth in specialised handling equipment to enable transfer between the different transport modes. Handling equipment needs to raise and lower containers. Such machines are large in size and require considerable investment.

1.11 A growing area of traffic comes from intermodal swap body traffic, loaded onto rail at UK Inland Clearance Depots (ICDs) from road vehicles and reloaded at a convenient point in Europe or *vice versa* to facilitate door-to-door delivery.

1.12 Intermodal transport is growing quickly in the area of rail-road transfer where it offers a number of cost and environmental advantages and enables containers to travel by rail where viable and then be offloaded and on-delivered by road. This offers the environmental benefits of using rail linked to the convenience of using road. It remains equally valid across all transport modes but has limited applicability with airfreight where, with the exception of the largest fright aircraft, goods are usually carried in purpose designed 'igloos'.

1.13 Alongside this growth and increased professionalism the role of transport has undergone a quiet revolution. We have seen the development of regional, national and global 'hub and spoke' distribution networks that allow for smaller consignments to be consolidated into full loads and considerable gains to be made by the application of technology to enhance the entire storage and distribution sphere of operations.

1.14 Vehicles have become more fuel-efficient as governments continue to raise duties but also because efficiency gains are at the heart of logistic thinking. Alternatives to the traditional diesel fuel such as liquid petroleum gas or liquid natural gas are being used where appropriate. Legal constraints on emissions drive higher environmental standards. ISO 14001 places environmental concerns on supplier and hauliers together and as the haulage industry works more closely on environmental issues with suppliers the gains should be more than worthwhile.

1.15 The use of technology supports the increasing complexity of transport operations by allowing for more accurate booking, loading, tracking and tracing of cargo. The *Storage and Distribution* module examines this in more detail but developments such as telematics, which enable comprehensive communications and tracking of vehicles, and radio frequency identification (RFID), where goods can be scanned permitting real-time inventory management, are just two examples of the increased efficiency and effectiveness that can be delivered when integrating IT systems.

2 *Improvements in communications technology*

Introduction

2.1 Computer-based technologies have revolutionised business over recent years. The growth, power, application and increasing refinement of information technology has offered a powerful tool that business has not been slow to exploit. The term information technology (IT) is generic and covers all forms of technology used to create, store and use information.

2.2 Information processing technologies include any devices that collect, collate, store or distribute information. Information is data that has been collected and refined into a meaningful form for the person receiving it.

The internet, intranets and extranets

2.3 The internet and the world wide web are an accepted framework for implementing and delivering information system applications. The internet is the infrastructure on which the web is based, ie the resources of the web are delivered to users over the internet.

2.4 The internet is a global collection of networks that are interconnected using a common networking standard. The world wide web is a collection of resources (programs, files and services) that can be accessed over the internet.

2.5 An **intranet** is a private network that utilises internet protocols but is usually only accessible to a number of users. These are usually within the same organisation or work group. Access is restricted by a number of means including passwords, firewalls and user group account names.

2.6 An **extranet** is an intranet that has been extended to include directly related business users outside the organisation. An example would be the CIPS website which is accessible to members via membership number and password but offers a level of accessibility to non-members. Other examples are suppliers, large customers and strategic business partners who can all be allocated differing levels of access, if required.

2.7 An extranet allows separate organisations to exchange information and coordinate their activities. This, in turn can lead to a virtual organisation that is a loosely linked group of people and resources that work together as though they were an organisation. Additional security can be provided by operating a virtual private network which is a network based on leased dedicated telephone lines that is built on top of the Internet infrastructure. This, when linked to entry protocols, serves to provide a higher degree of security.

2.8 Applications of this technology are discussed later in the text and are particularly relevant to approaches such as simultaneous engineering, computer aided design, the use of virtual teams in new product design, and project management.

2.9 The rapid growth in the use of internet-based technologies has allowed organisations to become more flexible in the way they operate. The speed and accuracy of communications brings with it a host of benefits to help improve the effectiveness and efficiency of an organisation.

2.10 There are a number of concerns that must still be borne in mind. Breaches of security of web-servers and the internet overall is widely known and organisations must seek to protect and keep their own system updated. Reliability of connections is a shortcoming. Internet protocols do not guarantee a minimum level of network throughput per customer nor that its intended recipient will receive a message. Standards are being developed but have yet to be universally accepted and adopted. It is worth bearing in mind the state of the internet ten years ago and its rapid growth to today's usage. Although fast developing there are still a number of growing pains.

2.11 Internet technologies offer a wide range of applications to operations management. The interaction between organisations can lead to data sharing, quotations and order management and an overall simplification of administrative procedures. Stock management can be integrated between supplier and manufacturers in order to schedule deliveries, particularly when just-in-time systems are being used.

Telecommunications

2.12 The telecommunications market is undergoing a period of major change with technological advances being developed at a prodigious rate. Mobile communication offers email, photo, video and internet access possibilities that are progressively being simplified and enhanced.

2.13 Telecommunications in the UK are among the cheapest in the world with real term falls of 37 per cent for local calls, 68 per cent for national calls and 56 per cent for international calls since 1984. The deregulation of the UK telecommunications market and the growth in competition within the market indicate that real term prices will remain competitive in the future.

2.14 As a result of the deregulation of the industry there are now over 200 public providers in the UK market with over 130 operators offering international services.

2.15 Investment in the UK communications infrastructure is approximately £6 billion per annum. BT alone invests £3 billion per annum. Cable networks have seen an investment of more than £7 billion since 1991 and broadband services reach nearly 12 million homes.

Electronic data interchange (EDI)

2.16 Electronic data interchange (EDI) can be most easily understood as the replacement of paper-based orders, invoices and declarations with electronic equivalents. A definition of EDI is given by Roger Clarke: 'the exchange of documents in standardised electronic form, between organisations, in an automated manner, directly from a computer application in one organisation to an application in another'.

2.17 The essential elements of EDI are as follows.

- The use of an electronic transmission medium (originally a value-added network but now more common over the internet).
- The use of structured, formatted messages based on agreed standards (that enable checking against pre-agreed criteria)
- Fast delivery
- Direct communication between applications

2.18 EDI can be contrasted with email. Email enables free-format, textual transmission of messages by electronic means between people. EDI contrasts with this with structured business messages to an agreed format transmitted electronically between computer applications.

2.19 EDI depends on a moderately sophisticated information technology infrastructure that must include data processing, data management and network capabilities. A common connection point is needed for all participants, together with a set of electronic mailboxes (in order that an organisation's computers are not interrupted by each other). Although the ability is there for organisation's to communicate directly with each other it is more common to route via a third-party provider.

2.20 EDI offers a number of practical benefits to users. Owing to its formatted structure EDI saves unnecessary time in the re-capture of data. This brings the benefits of faster data transfer and fewer errors and offers a more streamlined process. EDI offers easy and cheap transfer of structured information and is used extensively in areas such as inventory management, transport and distribution, administration and cash management, governmental communications, and between government agencies and their suppliers and clients.

Radio frequency identification (RFID)

2.21 **Radio frequency identification** (RFID) is a rapidly expanding technology that enhances stock management and control and offers the potential for real-time tracking and visibility of assets as it develops in the future. It is a fast developing technology that can offer considerable potential for supply chain and stock management, operations management and demand management.

2.22 Presently much stock management is carried out either manually or by using barcode technology. However the barcode is over 20 years old and, although it is effective for product recording and recognition, technology has moved on around it. Barcoding can serve many functions in operations management and storage such as verification of stock levels, identification of stock location, tracking and tracing the movement of goods and despatch details.

2.23 The Article Numbering Association (ANA) have identified the following as being the advantages of barcodes.

- Fast and accurate data capture at each stage of the supply chain
- Improved standard and quality of management information
- Less stockholding and less waste
- Improved responsiveness to customers
- The ability to automate warehousing
- Improved level of control over storage and distribution
- Improved levels of communication between organisations within the supply chain.

2.24 **RFID** is potentially the biggest change since the introduction of barcode technology. RFID tags can be embedded on each product allowing the data within the tag to be transmitted to a computer interface unit or readers at a distance. This is already established in a number of industries such as livestock identification and automated vehicle identification systems. The costs are now being reduced to the point where RFID tags can be cost effective at consumer level.

2.25 The tags can be 'passive' or 'active' ('smart').

- Passive RFID tags operate without a separate external power source and obtain operating power generated by the receiver. Passive tags are consequently much lighter than active tags, less expensive and offer a virtually unlimited operational lifetime.

- Active RFID tags are powered by an internal battery and are usually read/write (ie the tag data can be rewritten and/or modified).

2.26 This type of information in real time provides greater management information with the potential of visibility of the supply chain. This should give increased competitive advantage to those organisations adopting RFID technology first.

2.27 RFID systems are finding increasing acceptance in the area of transportation and distribution. Hauliers are using RFID systems to monitor access and egress from terminals. When combined with weigh-in-motion scales, the same systems can be used for transaction recording at refuse dumps, recycling plants, mines and other similar operations. Rail is utilising programmable tags to allow identification of each wagon by type, ownership and serial number. The main objective is effective fleet management and utilisation that allows reductions in fleet size and/or deferral of investment in new equipment.

3 The convergence of consumer preferences

Globalisation

3.1 The period since the second world war has seen a considerable growth in the numbers, size and spread of multinational companies who have benefited from factors such as the reduction in tariff barriers, the growth in technology, the impact of worldwide communications, the increasing standardisation of trade-related documentation and the harmonisation of customs tariff numbers among many others.

3.2 Organisations confront a challenging set of problems in the form of global competition, emergence of developing economies, formation of trade blocs, environmental neglect, economic stagnation and recessions, and low labour skills. Alongside this, new opportunities are being offered in the form of larger global markets, environmental clean-up operations, infrastructure regeneration and reconstruction, and the ongoing development of the worldwide financial and telecommunications markets.

3.3 The impact of technology and the development of new service markets, programmes for upgrading human skills and the survival of lean producers and lean marketers are all part of the modern trading environment. The ability to succeed in today's economic community will require much more awareness of global issues and the global market place than has previously been the case.

3.4 The globalisation of business has, in many ways, been permitted by the impact of enhanced communications. Systems can be integrated within organisations, ignoring international boundaries, and can add value to a firm's performance by reducing stockholding, ensuring efficient materials usage and cost effective manufacture, and saving on labour costs amongst other areas.

3.5   With developments in IT and communications, particularly the internet, smaller organisations can now cost-effectively start to view the world in a similar way, as a global market for their products or services. International communications and other developments enable marketing, in particular, to be viewed in the global context.

Marketing in a global economy

3.6   The convergence of global consumer markets has been emphasised by the widening of marketing from a national or pan-national approach to a highly developed global perspective being taken by organisations.

3.7   Factors that have enhanced this global approach include the following.

- **Branding:** customers want products or services they are familiar with and that they trust. The use of international media to establish a 'brand identity' and the status factor in using internationally established brands has led to branding becoming an important consideration for any company wanting to establish its identity in overseas markets.

- **Market positioning:** it is now easier to identify and target user/consumer segments in many international markets. For the international marketer this means that market planning can be more effective and that promotion can be better targeted.

- **Promotion:** developments in international media coupled with the speed and effectiveness with which messages can be relayed have led to a more global outlook on promotional campaigns. A global approach to advertising will influence whatever type of medium is being used (trade fairs, television, magazines etc), and will often stress the brand in using the brand logo, brand colours and brand identity to reinforce the image in the mind of users/consumers.

- **Distribution:** the increase in global trade has been aided by a growth in the number and efficiency of services for transporting goods internationally. In today's international trading environment there may be the need to site manufacturing in the most cost effective locations or to purchase components from different countries. An effective global physical distribution/logistics network is essential to underpin the globalisation of world trade.

- **Pricing:** the implications of pricing strategy are significant to the international company. Differential pricing (adopting different prices in different markets) can often lead to difficulties as importing from lower priced countries for re-selling in more expensive markets can be damaging to a company's brand integrity, may introduce legal problems and can result in loss of profit.

3.8   Global marketing requires a different approach from traditional exporting in that it aims towards economies of scale in production and distribution and towards a gradual convergence of customer needs and wants on a global basis.

3.9   The global corporation seeks competitive advantage by identifying worldwide markets and then developing a manufacturing strategy that supports the marketing strategy. Global marketing needs (according to Noonan in *Export Marketing*):

- an organised strategy
- active market management and policies
- a flexibility recognising local market differences.

3.10 To the operations manager within this global concept there is the need to gain competitive advantage in manufacturing. This advantage can then be used to underpin the global marketing strategy by delivering goods of the appropriate quality, on time and in a manner that meets customer's needs.

3.11 The Japanese writer Kenichi Ohmae coined the phrase 'Think Global – Act Local' as a way in which global corporations should view their markets. Organisations should always remain aware of local tastes and preferences, local culture and law, and should adapt the marketing mix to suit different needs while also being consistent in the approach to marketing strategy on a global scale.

Socio-cultural variety

3.12 The convergence of consumer preferences has occurred widely, particularly in regard to globally branded and technologically based products. However, wide socio-cultural differences and varying perspectives exist.

3.13 The socio-cultural environment consists of those physical, demographic and behavioural differences that influence business activities in different markets. Success will come from an understanding and knowledge of the country and the people you are dealing with. In today's competitive global economy you will need to fight hard for customers; appreciating their wants and needs is arguably more crucial in international trade than in any other area of marketing.

3.14 Culture has been defined as learned responses to recurring situations. Much of human behaviour is learned and cultural factors have a considerable influence on a customer's or business partner's values and attitudes. As individuals mature, their family, friends, school, religion, country and many other factors influence them. As they socialise they adopt sets of values, perceptions and preferences that influence the way they react to others or respond to events and which will strongly pattern their behaviour as adults.

3.15 Each country has its own values and customs – the dos and don'ts that make up the cultural pattern of the people. The international trader has to be able to recognise the similarities that bring customers together but must be sensitive to understand and value cultural differences. To work effectively in a variety of markets it is necessary to appreciate the need and be aware of and show respect to other cultures, in both attitude and behaviour.

3.16 Awareness of culture is an important element for any individual or organisation carrying out business overseas. Cultural appreciation helps you to assess the needs and wants of your customers. Differences in attitude and belief may affect:

- Attitude toward ownership of an item
- Strength and direction of attitude
- Reason for desire / antipathy
- Perception of appropriate style/ design
- Meaning of colours, symbols or words

3.17 It is clear there has been a convergence of consumer preferences in many areas. Using branding and telecommunications as examples there is the opportunity to either add value or reduce costs and an organisation must decide on the strategy appropriate to it.

3.18 For many organisations production and sourcing will be on a global basis looking not only at price but also location of manufacturing sites and quality of product as key areas. This approach widens the remit of operations to give an international perspective.

3.19 The operations management role, initially production based, has been extended to incorporate service delivery and can now be viewed within an international perspective with international manufacturing and sourcing contracts and decisions often forming an integral part of the operations role. This broadens the remit of the operations manager who needs to take existing skills into overseas operations and develop and refine them to ensure delivery often in multi-site and multi-country operations.

The impact of globalisation on operations management

3.20 Globalisation has been defined by Ruud Lubbers as 'a process in which geographic distance becomes a factor of diminishing importance in the establishment and maintenance of cross border economic, political and socio-cultural relations'. The definition highlights the way in which communications are reducing geographic issues and enabling an approach that can view the world as one market.

3.21 This view of the world extends to production as well as marketing. The industrialised world has over recent years seen much of its manufacturing base move to overseas markets. The reasons are often discussed but the reality is that many overseas countries offer lower production costs due to lower rates of pay and overheads and can often match or improve on quality.

3.22 Globalisation has affected operations management as the operations manager, whether in goods or services, needs to deliver the efficiencies and effectiveness called for in a diverse mix of markets.

3.23 The management of overseas operations, whether outsourced or company-owned, calls for a wider appreciation of cultural, ethical and communication issues than is the case when operating only in the domestic market.

3.24 Many organisations throughout the world are now taking a global perspective on their strategies to take advantage of the current situation. The globalisation of production has opened new opportunities for countries such as China and Indonesia. The globalisation of services has opened new opportunities for India, in particular as high computer literacy coupled with English language skills have led to a growing IT support and call centre industry.

3.25 World best practice demonstrates that organisations should take commercial advantage of these opportunities in order to meet the increasing demands of customers in terms of quality and cost.

3.26 The best overseas manufacturers and service providers are constantly in demand. The role of the operations manager may involve training and updating certain providers to ensure expected standards are met but in many cases the provider may be more advanced because of their ability to specialise and their knowledge of the requirements of global companies.

Increased competition

3.27   The globalisation of business coupled with the economic growth in global economies has combined to lead to a highly competitive global environment. Organisations must be sure of their strategies and be responsive to customer needs in order to survive.

3.28   Professor Michael Porter identifies five competitive forces in the environment of an organisation. The impact of globalisation is serving to widen the impact of these factors.

*   The threat of new entrants to an industry. A new entrant will bring extra capacity and poses a threat as established organisations may lose market share and economies of scale. With the increased globalisation of business new entrants may often mean established international firms looking for new markets.

*   The threat of substitute products or services. Substitutes pose a threat as they limit the ability of an organisation to charge high prices for its products so that demand for products becomes relatively sensitive to price

*   The bargaining power of customers. Customers will look for better quality products and services at lower prices. Factors such as differentiation by adding value in areas such as delivery or customer service, the ability to switch between products and the importance of the spend, can reduce this strength

*   The bargaining power of suppliers. This depends on a number of factors including the business relationship, the number of suppliers, the importance of the supplier's product and the cost of switching from one supplier to another.

*   The rivalry amongst current competitors in the industry. The intensity of competitive rivalry will influence the profitability of the industry as a whole.

3.29   The influence of Porter's Five Forces leads companies to consider their competitive position. Competitive position describes the market share, costs, price, quality and accumulated experience of an entity or product relative to its competitors.

3.30   Competition forces most organisations to look for cost savings or value-added activities that enhance marketability. One of the key roles of operations management is to make improvements in efficiency and effectiveness in order to increase productivity. Operations managers will seek to increase productivity but also to enable value-added production through areas such as design, flexibility in manufacture and late customisation of product.

Shorter product lifecycles

3.31   The product lifecycle (PLC) concept is based on the premise that products pass through various stages in their sales life. The basic principle of the PLC is that products have a finite life (although exceptions can be found to this rule). The length of the PLC will be different for all products. For example the length of the PLC for Mars bars will be different from specific models of mobile telephones.

Figure 2.1 *The product lifecycle*

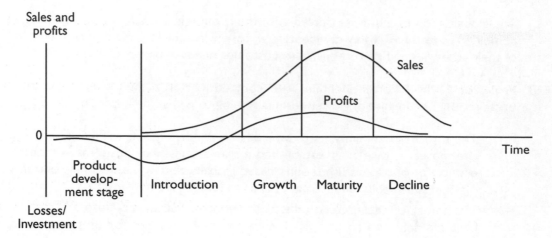

3.32 Increased competition, when linked to increasing customer demands, forces companies to review their product offerings more frequently. Product lifecycles are shortening in response to increased competition, advances in technology and customer demand.

3.33 The use of computer aided design and manufacture enables faster product development and manufacture. Organisations that can bring new and innovative quality products to market can gain a substantial competitive edge over the competition. CAD/CAM systems permit faster times (from concept through to manufacture) while permitting simulation of use where appropriate. Simulations means that, often, models and mock-ups are not required as computer-generated information can carry out testing on a virtual model. This not only saves money but also speeds up the product development to launch process.

3.34 Globalisation widens the remit of the operations role. Greater emphasis is placed on adopting world best practice. This can be achieved through monitoring technical developments and applying benchmarking where appropriate. The operations role is to understand the manufacturing and service developments needs of globalisation and apply the benefits to work practices.

Chapter summary

- Operations managers increasingly operate in a complex global market for goods and services.

- In the broader concept of operations management the role involves a proactive approach to management that demonstrates, and applies where applicable, the knowledge gained by monitoring competitive and global trends.

- Because of this move to globalisation more product is moved over greater distances. Long-distance supply chains have been established by companies, which require careful co-ordination and planning to operate effectively.

- The international freight market has changed out of all recognition over recent years with a wealth and variety of transport providers to meet the needs of international trading companies.

- Information processing technologies include any devices that collect, collate, store or distribute information. Information is data that has been collected and refined into a meaningful form for the person receiving it.

- The telecommunications market is undergoing a period of major change with technological advances being developed at a prodigious rate

- In recent years there is an acceptance of the impact of globalisation on both business and consumers

- The product lifecycle is shortening because of competitive pressures, advances in technology and increasingly demanding customers

- The operations management role, initially production based, has been extended to incorporate service delivery and can now be viewed within an international perspective with international manufacturing and sourcing contracts and decisions often forming an integral part of the operations role.

Self-test questions

Numbers in brackets refer to the paragraphs above where your answers can be checked.

1   What are the main advantages and disadvantages of sea freight? (1.3)

2   Define 'intermodal transport' (1.9)

3   What ISO accreditation places environmental concerns on suppliers and hauliers? (1.14)

4   Define the internet. (2.4)

5   What is the difference between an intranet and an extranet? (2.5, 2.6)

6   What does RFID stand for? (2.21)

7   How does Lubbers define globalisation? (3.20)

8   What are Porter's Five Forces? (3.28)

Further reading

* *Operations Management*, Slack, Chambers and Johnston, Chapters 8, 21.

CHAPTER 3

Strategic Aspects of Operations Management

Learning objectives and indicative content

1.4   Evaluate the strategic relationship between the operations function and other main functions within the business

- Marketing
- Finance
- Purchasing and supply chain
- Human resources
- Information technology

1.5   Analyse key performance objectives, their relationship with the order winning criteria and how they contribute to the success of a business

- Cost
- Quality
- Responsiveness and speed
- Flexibility
- Dependability

1.6   Analyse the significance of strategic outsourcing decisions in terms of:

- Span of control within an organisation
- Core competencies
- Impact on other functions

Chapter headings

1   The supply chain process

2   Relationships with other business functions

4   Key performance objectives

5   Strategic outsourcing

1   The supply chain process

The supply chain/supply network

1.1   The supply chain as understood by logistics and purchasing is often referred to in operations as the supply network. The 'network' in this context refers to the various tiers of suppliers who feed into the organisation and the tiers of middlemen or distributors who act as the interface between the organisation and its customers. The design of the demand/supply network is led by the strategic objectives of the organisation.

1.2   The supply chain consists of the various links that are formed together into an integrated network with the objective of providing customer satisfaction while minimising waste and operating in an efficient and effective manner.

1.3   The interface links begin with the production of raw material or growing of agricultural produce through the progression stages of refining or processing and forming to the stage where the item or component is in the form required by operations to enable the transformation process.

1.4   The supply chain approach differs from the traditional perspective in that, rather than each stage acting independently, the network now acts in an integrated manner that manages the flow from source through to customer.

1.5   The traditional route is characterised by separate organisations that operated independently and where relationships were frequently short-lived, price-focused and adversarial. The supply chain approach is more integrated, with longer-term business relationships being formed and a greater commitment to the reduction of waste and improvements in quality throughout the entire supply chain.

1.6   The supply chain approach requires a new way of thinking in organisations that moves away from separate departments and functions to a more cross-functional approach that looks at what is best for the supply chain (and, in consequence the customer) overall. A major benefit of the supply chain approach is that it helps by highlighting the areas of activity that can benefit from a closer integrated approach with business partners.

1.7   Russell Syson in *Improving Purchasing Performance* gives three reasons why a more integrated approach can benefit organisations.

   •   The need for each link to rise to the forecast demand of other links and consequently the holding by each link of stock as a means of anticipating demand. This effect can be exacerbated by falsely extended lead-times in order to cope with demand or by adding additional costs to the supply chain by means of the 'Forester effect' where each link manufactures in excess of anticipated demand in order to meet actual demand on-time.

   •   The policies and objectives of organisations together with the individual objectives of departments or functions can be uncoordinated leading to additional cost.

   •   Control systems do not interlink.

1.8   Supply chain management requires an investment in time and systems to operate effectively. In consequence the focus is on developing closer relationships with longer-term or strategic partners. To address the issues raised by Syson requires commitment and modern business thinking.

- Forecasting must be more accurate and information must be cascaded along the supply chain in an accurate and timely manner. The importance of accurate forecasting can be seen in the increased emphasis being placed on demand management where sophisticated computer systems can complement traditional statistical forecasting methods to increase forecast accuracy.

- Policies and objectives are extended outside the organisation to a linked approach with business partners. This increased commonality of goals enables the supply chain to work towards common goals in an agreed manner.

- Forecast demand, logistics information and costs can be made available to supply chain partners through IT systems. The interlinked approach allows supply chain partners to input relevant data and information that is then available to other supply chain partners. Common control measures can be put in place and deviations identified and discussed.

1.9   The objective of supply chain management is to improve the total performance of the supply chain. This will, in turn, lead to improvements in the total performance of an organisation through increased flexibility, better use of systems and overall reductions in the cost of supply.

The operations role

1.10   The operations role is central in this process. Operations take inputs from the supply chain and transform them through the manufacturing or service development processes into the outputs that progress through to customers. The key aims of operations are that inputs are delivered on time, in the right quantities and are of the right quality.

1.11   There is a need for a close relationship between purchasing and operations in order to facilitate these aims. Purchasing needs to work with supply chain partners by placing emphasis on the main delivered requirements of the chain. If quality has been identified as crucial (as in the case of just in time manufacture) then purchasing will work with suppliers to reach quality objectives. Suppliers will, in turn, place commensurate requirements on their suppliers enabling a quality focus to become integrated throughout the supply chain.

1.12   The role of purchasing has adapted to meet these changing requirements. The more traditional adversarial relationships on price, delivery and quality (although they still have their place) have given way to a tighter model where the number of suppliers is reduced and greater emphasis is placed on managing the relationship with the remaining, selected suppliers in such a way as to benefit the organisation and the supply chain overall. Operations needs to have an open and ongoing dialogue with purchasing as both functions need to adapt to a series of changing scenarios.

1.13   The interface with the logistics operations requires both good communications and the effective use of information technology. Production depends on goods being available, when needed, as core to the production process. The logistics chain must ensure that goods are available when required. This may be no easy task. With an increased emphasis on overseas sourcing and overseas manufacture logistics links could be to a domestic manufacturer or to an outsource provider in another country with deliveries from a series of international locations.

1.14　The role of logistics links with storage and distribution considerations where the primary aim is to reduce costs while adding value by aspects such as on time, full order deliveries or by the physical delivery of goods that meet customer requirements. The logistics function falls at both ends of the operations role in that it arranges both goods in (prior to manufacture) and goods out (following manufacture).

1.15　Stock control considerations form an integral part of the production process. Decisions must be made on inventory management and storage. The general aim of supply chain management is encapsulated in the just in time approach where high quality goods are delivered just in time for the manufacturing process. This approach does away with the need for inventory.

1.16　Many organisations use a more realistic approach to meet their individual needs such as materials requirements planning (MRP), examined later in the text, where forecasts and actual orders are combined to anticipate demand and stock is delivered in advance of production to ensure availability when production commences. It is a difficult balancing act to deliver as late as possible in order to minimise inventory costs yet have goods available when production commences.

1.17　The emphasis for operations is placed on quality goods being available when required. This is not achieved in isolation but requires sound inter-organisational communication via dialogue, cross-functional meetings and enhanced information technology. An understanding and appreciation of the strengths, limitations and constraints on other business areas must be combined with a commitment to continual improvement throughout the supply chain. Operations is dependent on other interfacing business areas to successfully deliver its objectives and in consequence needs to adopt a proactive stance in its relationships and in its contribution to supply chain considerations.

2　*Relationships with other business functions*

Organisational structure

2.1　Modern management thinking works toward breaking down the formal business structures to a more integrated organisation that allows staff to become empowered by the multi-skilling approach involved in team working.

2.2　The organisational structure of many organisations is undergoing a fundamental shift. The traditional management structure is based on functional divisions (see Figure 3.1 on the following page). This leads to a focused concentration of knowledge within the specific functional area with the objective of maximising the resources and skills base to deliver contribution to the required customer service levels.

2.3　The weakness of this traditional structure is becoming ever more apparent in today's fast moving business environment. The functional structure can be criticised as being short-sighted, too focused on meeting the needs of individual functional areas, rather than looking at the needs of the business as a whole and, in consequence, the needs of the customer.

Figure 3.1 *Functional organisation structure*

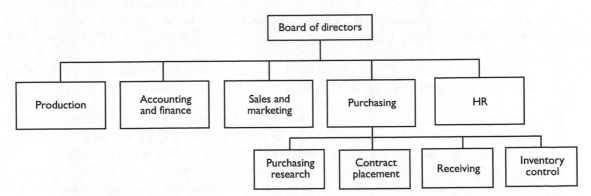

2.4   The functional structure represents a proven way of operation for many organisations and change to any existing management structure needs careful consideration and appraisal. However, as business circumstances change there will often be a need for a strategic review of any organisation and its operating structure and processes.

2.5   One structure, the matrix structure (see Figure 3.2), represents a shift in thinking that examines the effective and efficient use of resources not only in one functional area but also across the business as a whole. The emphasis is more to do with efficiency gains that can be made when functional areas adopt a closer team-working approach, in effect pooling their resources to maximise efficiency over the entire organisation.

Figure 3.2 *Matrix organisation (in an advertising agency)*

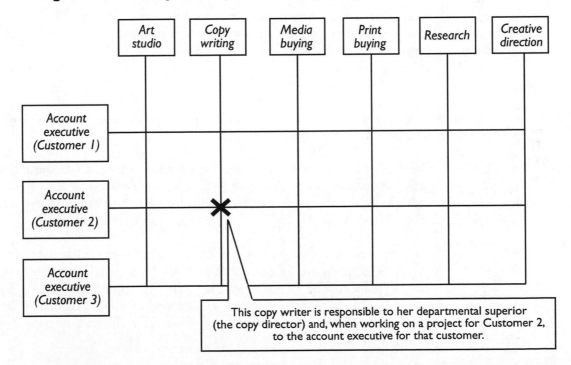

2.6   With the matrix structure there is more emphasis on cross-functional teamwork, earlier involvement of functional specialists and earlier involvement of outside specialists.

2.7   Matrix structures cause their own problems – most notably the blurring of reporting lines – but they can also serve to enhance the overall knowledge of employees and challenge and empower them to learn new skills. This in turn adds to the individuals' effectiveness within the organisation.

2.8   Operations management increasingly requires a more rounded business knowledge and a creative flair that can help drive a business or organisation forward.

2.9   That more rounded knowledge requires a more detailed understanding of the business areas that operations interface with. The broader business perspective enables the operations role to interface more fluently with other parts of the organisation by having a more detailed knowledge of the issues facing other functional areas and by being more able to have a rounded view of proposals and solutions that will better fit the organisation overall.

Marketing

2.10   The role of this department is to understand the 'needs and wants' of customers. The focus on 'customer service levels' is a measure of the importance of customers throughout all organisations and increasingly so in today's competitive global market.

2.11   The operations role will interface from the concept stage through to production. Marketing are looking for a product or service that will meet customer needs. Operations are looking at design and suitability for manufacture coupled with accurate demand management that will enable accurate advanced planning.

2.12   Marketing will often require flexibility in the production process. This may be met by adopting a flexible manufacturing system that can adapt to late changes and modifications or by designing a system that permits late customisation.

Finance

2.13   The role of the finance department is to evaluate the effectiveness of any changes proposed or made from a financial perspective.

2.14   Finance will require a business case to be presented and accepted before committing to expenditure. Capital expenditure, in particular, will be carefully scrutinised and options such as lower cost alternatives and outsourcing evaluated. Purchase options such as leasing, hiring or hire purchase will also be evaluated as options to purchase.

2.15   Finance have an interest in manufacturing costs as these will often represent a substantial amount of organisational expenditure. Systems such as MRP II (manufacturing resources planning) allow for detailed costing of manufacturing runs by apportioning costs for labour, machinery and overheads to individual jobs. The expenditure made by production forms an ongoing interface between finance and operations as reduction of costs is a common goal of both functions.

Human resource management

2.16 Human resource managers are responsible for ensuring that the workforce is meeting the needs of the organisation now and in the future.

2.17 Production is often a labour intensive function and requires that the human resource team understand the production process and the human resource needs of the operation. Production often requires a flexible workforce to meet fluctuating demand and requires that the workforce and associated employment contracts are designed in such a way as to meet this demand.

2.18 Operational changes will often lead to new skills being required that may be met by training programmes or additional recruitment and/or redundancies. These issues require the specialist input that the human resource function can bring.

IT and engineering

2.19 Other key functions of the organisation require consideration. The IT department's importance reflects the development stage of the operations role. Modern production operations are highly computer dependent and as such will have an ongoing dialogue with IT services.

2.20 An integrated approach to IT where systems carry information on suppliers, deliveries and stock management are important in regard to the input stage of the transformation process. The availability of real time information aids the operations role particularly when planning and scheduling production.

2.21 Engineering staff bring specialist skills to an organisation. Their ideas will often result in development through to production. The involvement in cross-functional teamwork with engineering is important as operations will take over responsibility for manufacture if the concept is developed.

Purchasing and supply chain

2.22 Purchasing forms an increasingly important role in many organisations as companies look at developing supply chain strategies and supplier management programmes. Modern views of the role of purchasing look for cross-functional teamwork and early purchasing involvement as part of purchasing strategies. This can work well with a progressive operations management approach.

2.23 The ongoing interface between production and purchasing is to ensure that suppliers deliver on time with goods of the right quality. Easily said, but a difficult proposition that needs continual monitoring and refinement.

Logistics

2.24 The logistics role is the storage of materials and their movement in and out of the organisation in the most effective manner. Their role will vary greatly but can involve such areas as storage, stock control and distribution, with the objective of managing these operations in the most effective manner to meet company and customer needs.

2.25   This function interfaces directly with the input process of operations as goods must be delivered, stored and moved to the production line when required. This requires a good relationship to be maintained and sound systems to be in place that interface effectively between the two functions.

Conclusion

2.26   It would be a mistake to consider all these functions as discrete activities. Good operations management requires an interface in terms of cross-functional teams, information flows and good communications to be an ongoing feature of the business or service irrespective of the organisational structure used.

3   *Key performance objectives*

Characteristics of performance objectives

3.1   Individual functional areas will draw up their own strategic plans with due consideration of the interdependence of these areas in combining together to meet the aims and objectives specified by the corporate plan. One of the main corporate objectives is survival. In order to survive organisations must be able to respond to change. The ability to respond to change is essential in today's commercial environment. Plans are drawn up using a set of assumptions such as projected growth, cost of raw materials etc. If these projections are not accurate there must be enough flexibility to adapt, reassess and continue to reach the stated objectives.

3.2   Objectives must be clear and measurable and must have a set time frame. The following areas are among those that will be addressed.

- **Customers**: increasing choice, offering greater value, delighting the customer
- **Finance**: increasing profit and sales, reducing costs and losses
- **Internal results**: increasing the number of products brought to market, speeding up delivery time to customers, introducing and measuring a customer returns policy.
- **Growth**: learning and innovation (enabling growth, increasing access to knowledge sources, developing organisational skills, introducing training and education plans, improving access to information)

3.3   At both corporate and functional levels the same three steps are applicable.

- Define a set of workable objectives.
- Balance financial and non-financial measures.
- Track and measure progress against objectives.

3.4   Within the role of operations management objectives must be workable. Objectives should be prioritised and weighted to ensure that those implementing the objective at an operational level are clear on their goals and their time frame.

3.5 Muhlemann, Oakland and Lockyer offer five guides applicable to objectives in the operations environment.

- Where multiple objectives exist, it is unwise to try to satisfy them all simultaneously.
- The greater the diversity, the greater the difficulty.
- Problems become easier if broken into parts.
- Organisations should be kept as small as the market and technology permit.
- Organisational structures should serve the needs of customers.

Influences from the market

3.6 A common view of the operations function is that its purpose is to meet market needs. This view extends into all spheres of the operations function and across both the private and public sectors. Market influences are varied and require differing perspectives from the operations role when viewing performance objectives.

3.7 Most private and public organisations involve a mix of goods and services. Too little emphasis on the service element may lead to customer dissatisfaction; too much may lead to production inefficiencies.

3.8 An organisation should clearly identify the market it is in and set up the operations function to deliver the right balance. This can be difficult to achieve in reality and requires ongoing monitoring of both the product and the service. The product, being tangible, is easier to measure while the service element, being intangible, can prove more complex. Customer feedback should be sought or encouraged to build up a genuine picture. Customer service measures such as order fill, on-time delivery, returns and the number of complaints should be recorded and monitored, and lessons learned.

3.9 Another market consideration is the width and variety of the product range. At one end of the market are organisations with a single offering, such as the utilities sector (electricity, gas, water etc). The danger is that complacency creeps in because of a monopoly situation. To a degree this has been addressed in the utility sector as competition has been introduced.

3.10 R L Galloway in *Principles of Operations Management* gives a good example of lack of variety and the problems it may cause.

'The Ford motor company standardised on the Model T, and its production process became so specialised that, while it was superbly efficient, it could not be changed. The assumption was that no one could want more from a car than the Model T provided. The competition, unable to compete on cost, successfully introduced variety into the market, a move that Ford barely survived.'

3.11 Markets change and the operations function may need to change with them. As mentioned earlier, the greater the diversity, the greater the difficulty. Wide variety must be managed. For the operations manager it provides more complexity in design, stock control, outsourcing, production, customer service requirements etc. The wider the variety the more responsive and flexible the operations function will need to be.

Setting performance objectives

3.12 Slack, Chambers and Johnston take five performance objectives that can be applied to all operations: speed; quality; dependability; flexibility; cost. These objectives can be achieved in isolation but operations works in an integrated manner. The issue facing operations managers is one of 'trade-offs' where you are attempting to find the optimum blend of the key performance factors to deliver the highest level of service from your resources while also meeting organisational goals.

Speed

3.13 Within an organisation speed is important. Speed can reduce stockholding, particularly when linked to an efficient materials requirements planning (MRP) or just in time (JIT) manufacturing system, reducing risks involved with carrying large quantities of stock that may become obsolete or surplus to requirements.

3.14 Another market requirement is availability. This has two aspects: the speed with which the goods or services are delivered, and the reliability with which this is achieved. The speed objective has benefit to an organisation in that the customers' view of speedy delivery of goods and services is that it enhances the overall offering. The organisation must be aware that if the speed of the customer offering is not matched with the reality of supply then reputation can be quickly tarnished.

Quality

3.15 The quality ethos is now well established across many goods and service providers. However, quality has different perspectives depending on the business or service provision you are in. Quality must be adequate to meet customer expectations, but quality that is higher than actually required may result in increased costs with no return.

3.16 Modern methods of quality management can serve to reduce costs, provide increased product reliability and engender an ethos that places quality at the thinking centre of an organisation.

Dependability

3.17 Dependability (ie delivering goods and services when they were promised or the reliability of products and services) is another important market requirement. Customers judge dependability only after the goods and/or service have been delivered. Dependability relates both to products (meeting their claimed performance) or services (such as trains running on time). Waiting (one of Taichi Ohno's seven wastes) does not add value; it serves only to add cost. Dependability gives predictability that things will occur or happen on time. This increases customer perceptions and, in consequence, their confidence in an organisation.

3.18 Dependability also has implications within an organisation. Manufacturing schedules rely on dependability: that suppliers will deliver on time, that machines will be ready for use, that order systems track the order from receipt through to delivery and payment etc. Dependability is a key performance objective for the operations function.

Flexibility

3.19 Flexibility is an essential requirement of the operations function in today's fast changing business environment. This includes fast introduction of new products, late customisation to meet customer needs, linked with the service offering (faster deliveries, timed deliveries, special packaging). The operations role must appreciate the need to meet customers' demands and this in turn means designing processes that are able to change and adapt to suit differing circumstances.

3.20 Internal flexibility helps keep internal operations flowing. No planning will be totally accurate. Suppliers may deliver late, additional demand may come from customers, a coach may crash causing an increase in workload in a casualty department. Whatever the situation, the operations role must be flexible enough to adapt. Flexibility must be built in to the operational process and supported with considered contingency planning where events outside the anticipated norm may occur.

Cost

3.21 Finally, control of costs is important to any organisation. Staff, facilities, machinery, technology and material costs (among others) need to be well managed and controlled. Cost is affected by all the performance objectives discussed above and the operations role is to strike an acceptable balance and still meet the required customer service levels.

3.22 The balancing of the five key performance indicators underpins the operational success of an organisation. Successful management of these key factors contributes substantially to an organisation's success. With confidence in the operational capability to deliver then sales and marketing programmes can be developed that build on this operational success.

3.23 The operations manager will need to constantly monitor the trade-offs in place. Organisations and customers change constantly and ongoing monitoring and adaptation to meet these needs is essential.

4 Strategic outsourcing

The nature of outsourcing

4.1 Outsourcing is the strategic use of resources to perform activities traditionally handled by internal staff and their resources. It is a management strategy where an organisation devolves responsibility to operate non-core functions to specialised service providers.

4.2 From a strategic perspective an organisation can be involved in the entire (vertical) chain that encompasses:

- Raw material extraction
- Design
- Manufacture
- Assembly
- Distribution

4.3 On the other hand, any of these stages can be contracted out. It is a matter of corporate policy to determine the core business area and the amount of vertical integration required. Vertical integration (control of all the factors listed under the bullet points above) offers two main advantages.

• By having everything under central control the objective is to improve reliability and responsiveness. Systems that cover full vertical integration often prove to be too cumbersome and bureaucratic to be effectively managed and are rarely used. The absence of competition can also lead to deterioration in service and quality.

• As outsource providers require to make a profit it is assumed they will be more expensive. Cost savings can be made but the assumption is that a large general operation can be as efficient and flexible as a small specialised one.

4.4 Modern business practice favours a different structure: specialist outsource providers and subcontractors are used where appropriate but are well managed, and links with suppliers are established to enable the development of 'supply chain' thinking through all tiers of the supply chain to reduce areas of waste and cost and to improve areas such as quality.

4.5 Lysons and Farrington in *Purchasing and Supply Chain Management* explain the difference between outsourcing and subcontrtacting in that outsourcing is a long-tern strategic decision while subcontracting is a tactical short-term approach. They give the following scenario.

If you want a beautiful lawn in the neighbourhood and you hire someone to take responsibility for every aspect of lawn care, including cutting the grass, weed control, watering and fertilising, it's strategic sourcing. But hiring someone to cut your lawn is subcontracting.

4.6 Outsourcing is the ultimate expression of a buyer's attitude to a supplier as an extension of in-house resources. Facilities or functions that were produced in-house are instead performed by external contractors working very closely with the buying organisation.

4.7 Zenz has the following analysis of the steps that managers should take to make a success of outsourcing:

• Managers should establish a strategy for the proper balancing of management, contracting and consulting
• Managers should establish a strategy to deal with possible reductions in staff
• Managers should closely integrate the external suppliers
• Managers should provide appropriate communication channels

4.8 Zenz also identifies the questionable assumptions that sometimes underlie the decision to outsource.

• The assumption that strategy primarily involves competitive position in the market place. (The decision to outsource is often taken so as to concentrate on core areas where a competitive advantage is present. This assumes that no other factors are relevant to shaping strategy.)

• The assumption that brand share is defensible without manufacturing share. (In other words, it is questionable whether producers can continue to reap full value from brands or products if they no longer take the full responsibility in manufacturing.)

- The assumption that design and manufacturing are separable. (The questionable assumption here concerns the feasibility of simply designing a product and handing it over to someone else to manufacture. Operations staff must have an input into the design process.)

- Market knowledge is separable from manufacturing.

4.9 'The problem with outsourcing is that while a series of incremental outsourcing decisions, taken individually, make economic sense, collectively they represent the surrender of the businesses's competitive advantage.' This quotation from Zenz calls into question the decisions of those who outsource in order to improve their competitive advantage by shedding non-core activities. Outsourcing distances organisations from their market and the long-term effects must be fully considered.

Span of control within an organisation

4.10 Management of the outsource provider or subcontractor represents a major operational role. In many organisations this role may be carried out with the purchasing department as they can contribute a range of applicable skills in this business area. Their role is also part of the operations function as it forms part of the input–transformation–output process.

4.11 Outsourced business areas still require to be managed. The role of contract management will usually fall within the remit of the purchasing department or be handled by a contract management team.

4.12 Contract management involves ensuring that the standards or service level agreements established when awarding the contract are maintained. This is accomplished by measuring against agreed standards with products (eg by sampling or inspection) or by measuring against key performance indicators (eg 97% delivery within 30 minutes of the agreed time). The objective is to improve on the agreed standards over time.

Core competencies

4.13 Outsourcing has developed as organisations reacted to the overdiversification strategies of the 1980s. Companies then looked at spreading the risk by diversifying into a number of different business areas. For example, British American Tobacco diversified into paper manufacture, US retailing and insurance as well as remaining in cigarettes. They now only remain in cigarettes and insurance.

4.14 In the majority of cases the diversifying strategies were not successful as the acquiring organisations lacked the skills and knowledge to be effective in new business areas.

4.15 This led to many organisations reviewing their activities and deciding to concentrate on core activities. The strategic view (as discussed by Hamel and Prahalad in *Competing for the Future*) encouraged organisations to identify their core business, the parts of their business that are at the heart of their operation and where they excel, and build on this. Areas outside this should be considered for outsourcing to providers who consider the outsourced area their core competency.

Impact on other functions

4.16 Outsourcing places business with an outside organisation. This means that the outsourcing company must consider its communications with the provider. A common approach is communication via a designated individual or team within the provider for operational activities.

4.17 The need is to ensure that communication and cultural issues do not impact on the on-going operations. Regular meeting and discussions between the parties will help to ensure that the outsourced contract continues to run well as part of the overall contract management strategy.

4.18 Outsourcing tends to engender a more cross-functional approach as the different functions involved need to raise and discuss issues in order to highlight concerns and make improvements.

Chapter summary

- The development of strategic plans involves the operations role in linking with other management roles in an organisation.

- Strategic thinking at corporate level involves developing the future direction of the business.

- The supply chain as understood by logistics and purchasing is often referred to in operations as the supply network.

- The supply chain approach requires a new way of thinking in organisations that moves away from separate departments and functions to a more cross-functional approach that looks at what is best for the supply chain (and, in consequence the customer) overall.

- The supply chain approach differs from the traditional perspective in that, rather than each stage acting independently, the network now acts in an integrated manner that manages the flow from source through to customer.

- Operations strategy involves maximising the capabilities of resources in specific markets in a way that meets the aims and objectives given in strategic plans.

- Ideally the processes that will transform the product or service should be flexible enough that new demands can be integrated into existing systems without major changes to the operation.

- The five performance objectives that can be applied to all operations are speed; quality; dependability; flexibility; cost.

- The organisational structure of many organisations is undergoing a fundamental shift.

- Outsourcing is the strategic use of resources to perform activities traditionally handled by internal staff.

Self-test questions

Numbers in brackets refer to the paragraphs above where your answers can be checked.

1   What three reasons does Russell Syson give as to why a more integrated approach to supply chain management can benefit organisations? (1.7)

2   What is the objective of supply chain management? (1.9)

3   What is the role of operations in the supply chain? (1.10)

4   What is the role of logistics in the supply chain? (1.14)

5   What is meant by a matrix structure? (2.5)

6   What five guides applicable to objectives in the operations environment do Muhlemann, Oakland and Lockyer give? (3.5)

7   What is the difference between outsourcing and subcontracting? (4.5)

8   Explain 'core competency'. (4.13–4.15)

Further reading

*   *Operations Management*, Slack, Chambers and Johnston, Chapter 2.
*   *Principles of Operations Management*, R L Galloway, Chapter 2.

CHAPTER 4

The Design of Products and Services

Learning objectives and indicative content

2.1   Analyse the design process for products and services

- Definition of the term design
- Aspects of customer satisfaction
- Approaches to designing better products
- Understanding the full design business process

2.2   Evaluate the benefits that arise through design evaluation and environmentally sensitive design with respect to the product lifecycle

- The contribution of purchasing to design
- Compare and contrast areas of conflict between purchasing and design
- Trade-offs in designing environmentally acceptable products
- Environmentally preferred materials
- Lifecycle analysis
- End of life issues

2.3   Analyse the contribution that purchasing and supply can make to the design of products and services by the application of certain tools

- Standardisation
- Modularisation
- Value analysis and engineering
- Computer aided design

Chapter headings

1   The design process for products and services

2   Design evaluation and improvement

3   Environmentally sensitive design

4   Design tools

1 The design process for products and services

Defining 'design'

1.1 When you consider design your initial thought is probably conceptual, creative design: something new, something cutting edge, something that takes design into a new era. Unfortunately most design is a little more realistic and risk averse than that.

1.2 The dictionaries give a variety of definitions for design. 'The act of producing a drawing, plan or pattern showing details of something to be constructed', 'the arrangement of elements of a work of art' and 'a decorative pattern', are three. The term is wider than all three. It is a blend of concept, taste, style and practicality from a business perspective.

1.3 The purpose of design, in a business sense, is to satisfy the needs of customers. A product is designed to meet customer requirements. While this is of great concern to both designers and marketing, the view of operations is more pragmatic. The main operational concern is whether the product can be made to specification at an acceptable cost. To put it another way: is it designed for manufacture?

1.4 The traditional product/service development process is constrained by the functional personnel involved.

- Designers are looking for the freedom to design. They realise that the practicalities of manufacture, transformation and customer needs will impact on their design but also realise that their role involves creativity and innovation as one of their major inputs into an organisation.

- Finance staff are responsible for financing the research and development that is involved in new product introduction and for monitoring and approving the spend as the new product progresses.

- Purchasing staff have an increasingly important role in new product development. If purchasing is involved early in the design process they can advise on different materials, potential costs and supply problems. They can also involve potential suppliers early in the process if specialist research, involving the skills of suppliers, is called for.

- Marketing staff have responsibility for bringing the new product successfully to market. This involves an awareness of changing tastes and requirements.

- Operations staff have a central role in the new product development process. Whereas purchasing has a crucial role as the external interface between an organisation and suppliers the role of operations has more of an internal focus through the development stages. The concern of operations is the integration of design into the practicalities of production.

1.5 Cross-functional teamwork brings all relevant concerns into open discussion during the formative phase of development and allows for discussion and clarification. This integrated approach helps ensure that all potential areas are discussed by the team who become increasingly familiar with the project and, in consequence, gain a wider understanding and perspective on the issues raised by other team members.

1.6   Slack *et al* refer to the four Cs of design.

- Creativity – design requires the creation of something that hasn't existed before.
- Complexity – design involves decisions on a large number of parameters and variables.
- Compromise – design requires balancing multiple and sometimes conflicting requirements.
- Choice – design requires making choices between many options.

Phases of the design programme

1.7   Muhlemann, Oakland and Lockyer in *Production and Operations Management* state that every design programme will pass through five phases.

- **Conception**: when a draft specification is drawn up in as much detail as possible to provide a clear indication of the nature of the product or service.
- **Acceptance**: this is where the specification is shown to be achievable or not. This stage requires both cross-functional and specific area team working to resolve any issues.
- **Execution**: where the project has developed to the stage where trial runs or models are prepared for critical evaluation.
- **Translation**: here the role of operations management is critical. Lack of involvement between design and operations can prove costly. The translation of the design into a transformation process is an important phase.
- **Pre-operation**: Before progressing to full manufacture or release it is usual to carry out a pilot run or test marketing. Only after full evaluation of pre-operational testing should the project move to implementation.

1.8   The design activity moves through a number of stages during research and development and progresses from a concept through to a workable specification.

1.9   The development stage takes the initial research and moves the concept into something more workable. Development is involved with the improvement of concepts, ideas, existing products, services, techniques or systems into something that is better suited to meet the end objective of customer satisfaction.

1.10   The design stage has two phases.

- The first involves conceptualising the product or service and gradually refining until a specification can be drawn up. The design activity is a transformation process in itself. It takes inputs in the shape of ideas and concepts and through teamwork transforms them into a workable specification.
- The second phase is the process design. It is here that operations have an overarching role. Products and services should be designed in such a way that they can be manufactured or prepared effectively. Ideally the processes that will transform the product or service should be flexible enough that new demands can be integrated into existing systems without major changes to the operation.

Design for manufacture and assembly (DFMA)

1.11 One systematic approach to analysing a proposed design and establishing methods of saving manufacturing and assembly costs is known as **design for manufacture and assembly**. The title is largely self-explanatory. The method forces the designer and development team to consider the cost and practical implications involved in taking the design through to manufacture.

1.12 This technique has been said to achieve significant cost reductions.

- Component part reductions of 30 per cent
- Assembly cost reductions of 40 per cent
- Overall product cost reductions of up to 35 per cent

1.13 Many DFMA methods employ charting techniques where various identified measures of performance and potential manufacturing targets are established and measured against criteria such as the following.

- Design efficiency (functional analysis of each part)
- Handling analysis (relative handling cost of each part)
- Fitting analysis (assembly costs for each part)

1.14 Sequence flowcharts before and after analysis demonstrate the improvements and savings made. The process generally demonstrates a very significant change in the processes and ways in which products can be put together.

Aspects of customer satisfaction

1.15 Organisations will introduce new products/services periodically to add to the range and keep ahead of the competition or to replace unfashionable/obsolete products and services.

1.16 A product is anything that satisfies a customer need or want. We often consider products as tangible objects that a customer buys, but we need to remember that the customer is buying something to satisfy a need or want. This satisfaction might be achieved through the purchase of a service.

1.17 Muhlemann, Oakland and Lockyer (in *Production and Operations Management*) provide a number of guidelines for achieving reliability in product design. These are summarised in Table 4.1.

1.18 So what is a new product? The answer is not as obvious as it first appears. Is it something totally new, designed using cross-functional teams, tested on focus groups and designed giving the optimum performance from the operations team? Or is it something new to a particular organisation, a close copy of something else or something where the rights have been acquired from another company?

Table 4.1 *Designing reliability into products*

Use proven designs, and proven processes and operations	This is obvious – a design that is tried and tested is that much less likely to fail, and the same can be said for a manufacturing process
Use the simplest possible design	Simple components, few in number, are less likely to fail than a large number of complex components
Use components known to have high reliability	Tackling reliability at the component level is easier than at the total product level
Consider the use of redundant parts	If two identical parts are placed in parallel the second can kick in if the first fails
Design to 'fail-safe'	As noted already, nothing is completely fail-safe, but setting an ideal target is a means of achieving high standards.

1.19   A new product should be perceived in terms of customers' needs and wants. A new product can be an innovation, a major invention, an updated replacement or an imitative product. Each of these alternatives offers challenges to the operations team in terms of designing the appropriate transformation process. Totally new products will require a totally new approach whereas with replacement or imitative products lessons can be learned from what has happened before or from how other organisations organise their transformation processes. The latter two are therefore the fastest to market in the majority of cases.

1.20   The stages in the NPD process are shown in Figure 4.1.

Figure 4.1 *The NPD process*

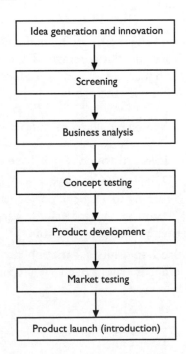

1.21 The NPD process is lengthy and thorough. Despite this, many products fail once they reach the market. Kotler (*Marketing Management*) says that new products fail for many reasons.

- Shortage of important new product ideas in certain areas
- Fragmented markets
- Cost of the NPD process
- Capital shortages
- Faster development time for competitors
- Shorter product lifecycles

1.22 Achieving customer satisfaction requires a blend of good and appropriate design, an anticipation of customers' needs and high levels of customer service. Without the first of these being achieved it is difficult to see how the other two will redeem the situation.

1.23 The design process will be ongoing. As time, technology and customer preferences evolve there is a need to monitor changes and consider adapting the product if necessary. Adaptation will only be viable if the anticipated profits from future sales exceed the cost of making the proposed design, manufacturing and marketing changes.

1.24 The technique of value analysis examines this from a manufacturing and purchasing perspective, looking at cost reductions, excess product features and manufacture over time where production costs may have gone down or product features are no longer appropriate.

Understanding the full design business process

1.25 An integral part of product design and development is the role of quality in the processes and materials employed. Quality issues will be discussed later in the text but it is worthwhile at this stage to consider the perspective given on design by the Japanese quality guru Genichi Taguchi.

1.26 The Taguchi approach (often referred to as 'Taguchi methodology') requires quality to be built in to the product from the design stage. To build in quality offers considerable benefits over the life of a product; waste can be reduced, reworking will be unnecessary and customers will be satisfied with the product.

1.27 Taguchi methodology has three elements to its control of quality at the design stage.

- Systems design: achieved through careful selection and evaluation of parts, materials and equipment.
- Parameter design: according to Taguchi, performance deteriorates when the design parameters deviate from their target values. Targets must be set within specified parameters and met with minimum variation.
- Tolerance design: used to reduce variation around the target value further by tightening those tolerances that have a large impact on variation.

1.28   It is the concept of building quality in from the start, and getting it right first time, that is important. To go back and redesign products, systems and the transformation process after the product or service launch is highly expensive and should be avoidable if good management processes are used.

1.29   Another key tool used within the design process is quality function deployment (QFD). QFD aims to ensure that the final design actually satisfies the customer's needs. Market research is instituted both in respect of eventual customers, and also with regard to 'internal customers'. Their requirements are recorded and must be satisfied before the design can be regarded as complete. This ensures that the design is specified correctly and can be obtained in production.

1.30   The entire QFD process has been said to lead to the following benefits.

- Improved quality
- Increased customer satisfaction
- Improved company performance
- Improved time to market
- Lower cost in design and manufacture
- Reduction in design changes/problems
- Improved product reliability

1.31   In reality it is not possible to exert the same tight control over design as is possible with operations. Designs should be appropriate for their time of manufacture but as time moves on, technology advances and customer tastes change, redesign and revisiting products and services will be necessary.

1.32   Service design involves much the same considerations as product design. The role of operations in service development is through positive involvement during the development and design phases through to delivery and in designing those processes that allow for delivery to be made. Much of service design focuses on the consistent delivery of the service: the need to make the service clear and understandable, the need to ensure staff are adequately trained and knowledgeable and the design of processes to support effective delivery. Although product manufacture focuses on customers through methodology such as quality function deployment the increased interface with customers, which is a feature of most aspects of service delivery, ensures that customer needs are considered from the concept stage.

2   *Design evaluation and improvement*

The contribution of purchasing and supply

2.1   The role of cross-functional teams in new product development has already been discussed. One of the main players in the team approach will be the purchasing department. Purchasing can bring a range of skills and knowledge to the process that enables a considered and realistic approach to be evaluated.

2.2   Purchasing have a crucial role in that they can form the link between the internal development team and suppliers. This link role enables purchasing to investigate materials and sources of supply and advise the team of suitability. This interface role will grow in importance as the project develops.

2.3   Following the initial design and concept stage greater emphasis is placed on the practicality of design, the materials to be used and the suitability for manufacture. Purchasing can investigate materials and components which can then be appraised for suitability.

2.4   New product development also gives purchasing the opportunity to design the supply chain from the start. This is an unusual opportunity as many supply chains are established over time and improved by reducing areas of waste and cost over time. With new materials and components there is an opportunity to fully consider and plan the supply chain from an early stage. Involvement in the team approach also gives purchasing the opportunity to get the views of other team members on supply chain issues in order that the design meets their needs from the earliest stage.

2.5   Purchasing will often take a lead role in the design and development process as their link role between the organisation and suppliers is crucial in an organisation's ability to take the design through to production.

2.6   As the design project progresses the objective is to finalise the design specification. When working with suppliers who need to carry out development work it would be necessary to issue performance specifications. These indicate what is wanted from the material or component and allow suppliers to develop or adapt their products to meet requirements. When these are finalised they will be formalised into a conformance specification that is, in essence, the final specification that enables the product to advance to manufacture.

Product specifications

2.7   A key area for purchasing in the NPD process is the development of product specifications. Once designs have been signed off an important step is to finalise the requirements to be ordered from suppliers. Often this is accomplished by means of a formal specification although ordering by brand name may be appropriate in certain circumstances.

2.8   There are two main types of specifications: conformance specifications and performance specifications.

2.9   **Conformance (functional) specifications**: here the buyer details exactly what he expects the part or material to consist of. Conformance specifications can be difficult to draft unless the product is clearly understood and developed. If the specification is poorly drafted and the product supplied does not perform to its intended function the buyer bears the risk.

2.10   It may be that once a specification is tightly defined, there is only a small number of suppliers available. This will restrict opportunities and may endanger continuity of supply.

2.11 **Performance (design) specifications**: here the buyer aims to describe what is expected from the part or material in terms of the functions it will perform and the level of performance expected. It is then the supplier's responsibility to furnish a product that will satisfy these requirements. A performance specification may underpin a simultaneous (value) engineering project.

2.12 Performance specifications offer a number of advantages over conformance specifications, particularly at the design phase.

- They are easier to draft. This can be particularly important where the buyer has little technical knowledge of the product.

- They place more responsibility with the supplier. If the part supplied does not perform its function the buyer is entitled to redress.

- They widen the potential supplier base. If the task is to supply something that will perform a particular function, the ingenuity and expertise of a wide range of suppliers could potentially provide a wide range of possible solutions.

2.13 Sound specifications are a vital step in assuring the quality of the eventual product. Basic requirements of such a specification are that it should be up to date (reflecting the latest design decisions, and also the latest developments in the supplier's products) and that it should contain a detailed technical description, accompanied by a copy of the design as appropriate.

2.14 In the NPD process, the lead role in the process of preparing specifications is often taken by designers or engineers. If additional features are required there may be input from the marketing team. The role of purchasing is to collate the requirements into a formal specification that meets the needs of both internal and external users.

Areas of conflict between purchasing and design

2.15 As we have seen, designers are often looking to make a statement with their proposed product. The cross-functional team approach is highly effective at moderating design by considering aspects such as practicality of manufacture, an appraisal of costs, establishing the costs of supply among other areas. The team working agenda permits detailed discussion and evaluation of the design from the practical aspects that other business functions can bring.

2.16 Purchasing are looking to secure supply on a regular basis, to minimise costs, to ensure quality and, where appropriate to form a long-term or partnership relationship with suppliers. This practical aspect will often conflict with the excesses of design.

2.17 The conflict is between the ideal of the design and the practicalities of delivering it. An example is the design of a new car where the original concept may be quite bold but is moderated when it comes to manufacture. Issues such as building on an existing floor plan, customer acceptability, costs of materials, sources of supply etc, all serve to moderate the design into a more practical product to manufacture.

2.18 Dowlatshahi, quoted by Lysons and Farrington, draws attention to the differences that may occur between purchasing and design: see Table 4.2.

Table 4.2 *Purchasing orientation vs design orientation*

Purchasing orientation	Design orientation
• Minimum acceptable margin of quality, safety and performance	• Wide margins of quality, safety and performance
• Use of adequate materials	• Use of ideal materials
• Lowest ultimate cost	• Limited concern for cost
• High regard for availability	• Limited regard for availability
• Practical and economic parameters, specification, features and tolerances	• Close or near perfect parameters, specifications, features and tolerances
• General view of the product	• Conceptual abstraction of product quality
• Cost elimination of materials	• Selection of materials
• Concern for JIT delivery and supplier relationship	• Concern for overall product design

2.19 The conflict purchasing have with design is similar to the conflict areas such as operations or finance will have. Operations are looking for the design to be manufactured in a cost effective and efficient way, finance are looking to cost the ramifications of the design. The need is to obtain a balance between conflicting needs while ensuring the design retains the practical features required to meet customer needs.

Specifications online and the use of e-procurement

2.20 In many organisations purchasing is taking a more proactive role than has been the case in the past. The increased spend on component items as opposed to making in-house, the recognition of supply chain management and the move to outsourcing selected functional areas of the business are just three examples of why this is occurring.

2.21 The role of e-commerce is having a considerable impact on procurement. E-commerce encompasses e-sourcing (an upstream activity that uses the internet to make decisions and form strategies regarding how and where services or products are obtained) and e-procurement (a downstream activity using the internet to operate the transactional aspects of purchasing, authorising, ordering, receipting and payment processes for the required services or products). E-commerce goes further in procurement as it also covers the use of the internet to build more collaborative ways of working between the customer and supplier, and within organisations themselves.

2.22 E-commerce enables purchasing to:

- Find and qualify suppliers
- Issue invitations to tender
- Check real time inventory
- Receive invoices
- Access catalogued data
- Run reverse auctions

- Issue call off orders
- Monitor performance
- Make payment
- Issue specifications online

2.23   In consequence procurement has more tools and faster methods available that can be used to increase the efficiency and the effectiveness of the purchasing operation.

2.24   Issuing specifications online is part of an integrated approach that enables faster, more accurate communication between purchaser and supplier. In today's business world where closer collaboration is a strategic aim the use of e-commerce tools and methods is helping to drive business forward.

2.25   One of the most effective ways that purchasing can contribute to reducing the environmental impact of products and services is to ensure that specifications are drafted in such a way as to incorporate environmental issues. Key areas such as an increase in recyclable material, reduction of packaging and reduced requirement for the inclusion of hazardous material should all become part of the specification process.

3   *Environmentally sensitive design*

Trade-offs in designing environmentally acceptable products

3.1   The design of products in such a way as to minimise their impact on the environment is becoming increasingly important. Environmental issues have traditionally focused on production processes and environmental regulation has concentrated on pollution from industry. It is recognised that people cause pollution.

3.2   Packaging is designed to be thrown away thereby adding to landfill sites. Noxious fumes can be the result of poorly designed factories or manufacturing facilities that do not use energy efficiently. Plastics require processing before their end journey to the landfill site. Pollution is a result of the throwaway society but is also a consequence of poor planning and design.

3.3   Design issues have traditionally concerned themselves with aesthetics, function and profitability. However, decisions made during the design phase have a direct impact on the materials and energy used during manufacture and the energy consumed and pollution produced during the product's lifetime.

3.4   Environmentally sensitive design has three aspects: design for environmental manufacturing, design for environmental packaging and design for disassembly.

3.5   **Design for environmental manufacturing**: this aspect of manufacture offers an attraction for many manufacturing organisations as implementation will serve to reduce cost. However, this gain will not be made without investment.

3.6   Manufacturing must be designed to minimise energy consumption, emissions and waste. For the operations manager this means a new set of considerations relating to process design (reducing energy consumption and minimising waste) and material design (to minimise waste and pollution during product manufacture and disposal).

3.7   Three drivers – increasing costs, increasing consumer awareness on environmental issues and increasing legislation – look set to make environmental manufacturing a subject of higher level debate in the future.

3.8   **Design for environmental packaging**: environmental packaging has been subject to European legislation for some years and centres around four main areas.

- Minimising the use of packaging materials. This is increasingly being enforced by making the manufacturer liable for disposal costs.

- Encouraging the use of reusable pallets, totes and packaging. This is made possible by adopting unitised sizes throughout an industry, coupled with a returns capability.

- The use of biodegradable packaging materials is growing in consumer acceptance and provides companies with an additional selling point.

- The use of recyclable packaging materials involves a number of design considerations. Initially the right material should be used to last the intended lifetime. Filler materials should be carefully selected for disposability and the packaging should be designed for disassembly.

3.9   **Design for disassembly**: the 1991 BMW Z1 Roadster was conceived and designed for disassembly and recycling. The side and other panels are designed to come apart. The use of glues was limited and replaced with fasteners to enable areas such as the bumpers and the dashboard to be removed and disassembled more easily. At design, the portion of the car to be recycled was 80 per cent. BMW now aims for 95 per cent.

3.10   Beitz ('Designing for ease of recycling', *Journal of Engineering Design*, 1993) identifies the following considerations.

- Designing for ease of disassembly, to enable removal of parts without damage

- Designing for ease of purifying, to ensure that the purifying process does not damage the environment

- Design for ease of testing and classifying, to make it clear as to the condition of parts which can be reused and to enable easy classification of parts through proper marking

- Designing for ease of reconditioning – this supports the reprocessing of parts by providing additional material as well as gripping and adjusting features

- Designing for ease of re-assembly, to provide easy assembly for reconditioned and new parts.

3.11   Beitz goes on to argue that when a product reaches the end of its life it should be able to be dealt with in such a way that it has future use.

3.12   Design for the environment (DFE) is becoming increasingly important. J Fiskel defines DFE as 'a systematic consideration of design issues related to environmental and human health over the lifecycle of a product'. This definition highlights the key areas of a systematic approach that reflects the whole life of the product, not just the design and development stages.

3.13 Increasing environmental awareness will mean that design will change. Slack et al highlight the following reasons for this.

- Source of materials used in a product
- Quantities and sources of energy consumed in a process
- The amount and type of waste material created during the manufacturing process
- The life of the product itself
- The end of life of the product – can the product be disposed of safely? Can it be recycled?

3.14 In many ways the above list causes issues for the operations manager. To balance the factors relevant for making the right decision, in a given set of circumstances, involves compromise. One approach is to apply a lifecycle analysis to the product. This will involve balancing the above environmental issues over the whole life of the product in order to arrive at an environmentally aware decision.

3.15 This decision will then require justification in a business situation.

Lifecycle analysis

3.16 Buyers must consider a wide range of factors relating to their purchasing activities. Environmental impact is one of them but areas such as cost, quality and delivery are always important too.

3.17 CIPS consider whole life costing (lifecycle costing) as a best practice tool for evaluating options for any substantial procurement. Whole life costing (WLC) is a technique used to establish the total cost of ownership over the entire life of the product. The WLC approach addresses all the elements of cost and can be developed to produce a spend profile over the product's anticipated lifespan. WLC can be developed further to consider disposal costs, therefore establishing the WLC over the entire life of the product.

3.18 CIPS explain the technique as follows.

In whole life costing, all costs over the life of goods and services are taken into account. This enables savings in running costs to offset any increase in capital costs. The savings are calculated for each year of the equipment or service contract life. It shows either a simple payback time or the payback during the life of the equipment or service contract. It can be applied to most situations to justify extra expenditure.

3.19 Whole life costing requires an evaluation of the costs of ownership. These can be categorised under six main headings.

- **Pre-acquisition costs**: such as research, sourcing, preparation of tenders and structural changes to allow for the product.
- **Acquisition costs**: including the purchase price, delivery, installation and commissioning etc.
- **Operating costs**: embracing labour, materials, consumables, electricity usage, environmental costs etc.

- **Maintenance costs**: such as spares and replacement parts, servicing, reducing output with age etc.

- **Downtime costs**: lost profit, extra labour costs, costs resulting from non-performance and claims resulting from non-performance.

- **End of life costs**: disposal, ongoing liabilities, decommissioning, sale for scrap, resale etc.

End of life issues

3.20 Whole life costing involves considering the entire life of a product from the design stage through to disposal. As we have seen this approach is becoming increasingly embedded in business processes from the design stage.

3.21 One area that is difficult to quantify at the time of purchase is the end of life costs. Legislation in this area is likely to be far tougher at the time of decommissioning than it is now and this should be factored into any calculations. The uncertainty about legal regulation should be balanced against an organisation's stance on corporate social responsibility issues where good practice may enable a company to be ahead of merely fulfilling its legal obligations.

3.22 European legislation is placing considerable emphasis on environmental issues surrounding the product lifecycle and this is being enacted into English law. The EC Directive on Waste Electrical and Electronic Equipment (WEEE Directive) places responsibilities on both manufacturers and users in relation to design, recycling and disposal. The UK Waste Electrical and Electronic Equipment (WEEE) Regulations 2006, which implement the Producer Responsibility aspects of the WEEE Directive, came into force on 2 January 2007. Other aspects of the Regulations have since been rolled out: the requirement to mark EEE products with a producer identifier and crossed-out wheelie bin 'do not recycle' symbol) came into force in April 2007; and the VCA (Vehicle Certification Agency) became the enforcing body, to make sure that retailers and distributors of electrical equipment play their part in helping household users, in July 2007.

3.23 Other environmental legislation concerns packaging and waste (EC Packaging and Waste Directive 94/62/EC). This concerns identification of the 'waste stream' and covers all aspects of waste, recycling and disposal. A further example is the proposed legislation on end of life vehicles (ELVs) in relation to the composition of vehicles going on to the market and the levels to which they should be recycled. The legislation aims to reduce, or prevent, the amount of waste produced from ELVs and increase recovery of usable materials and recycling

3.24 In 2003 the European Commission published the Integrated Product Policy (IPP) outlining its strategy for reducing the environmental impact caused by products throughout their life cycle. The IPP is based on five key principles.

- **Lifecycle thinking**: aims to reduce a product's environmental impact from the cradle to the grave. In doing so it also aims to prevent individual parts of the lifecycle from being addressed in a way that results in the environmental burden being shifted to another part.

- **Working with the market**: establishing incentives in order that the market moves in a more sustainable direction and rewarding companies that are innovative, forward-thinking and committed to sustainable development

- **Stakeholder involvement**: aims to encourage all those who come into contact with the product (industry, consumers and the government) to act across their sphere of influence and encourage the purchase of more environmentally aware products and how they can better use and dispose of them

- **Continuous improvement**: the IPP seeks to encourage improvements that can be made to decrease a product's environmental impacts across its lifecycle.

- **Policy instruments**: the IPP approach requires a number of different initiatives and regulations to be enacted. The initial emphasis will be placed on voluntary initiatives although mandatory measures may be required.

3.25 The Eco-Management and Audit Scheme (EMAS) will be made more product focused and organisations will be encouraged to adopt the systemised and recognised approach embedded within it.

3.26 End of life issues are increasingly becoming an integrated aspect of product management. Organisations need to balance directives and legislation, stakeholder views and corporate social responsibility issues in a proactive and positive manner to ensure good practice is followed.

Environmentally preferred materials

3.27 The environmental impact of a material can occur at all stages of the material's lifecycle, from extraction and processing through its useful operating cycle to disposal or recycling. These impacts are not always apparent and require an environmental risk appraisal approach in order to ascertain the issues involved.

3.28 The use of environmentally preferred materials is being adopted by many purchasing departments who are increasingly developing strategies and policies with regard to environmental purchasing. The purchasing department has a key role to play: as the interface between the organisation and suppliers it can apply environmental supply chain issues that can be filtered down the supply chain.

3.29 Environmental purchasing focuses on the ideal of waste reduction. Environmentally preferred products or services are those that have a lesser or reduced effect on human health and the environment when compared with competing products or services that fulfil the same function. Preferred products or services may include, but are not limited to, those that contain recycled content, minimise waste, conserve energy or water and reduce the amount of toxic material disposed of or consumed.

Guidance by ISO

3.30 Environmental standards under ISO 14000 are a series of international standards on environmental management. These standards provide a framework for the development of the system and the supporting audit programme.

3.31 ISO 14001 was first published in 1996 and specifies the actual requirements for an environmental management system. It specifies a framework of control against which an organisation can be audited by a third party. It applies to those environmental aspects that the organisation can control and over which it can be expected to have influence.

3.32 ISO 14001 is an international standard that specifies a process for controlling and improving an organisation's environmental performance. Detailing the specification of an environmental management system, it is also the standard against which an organisation can be audited and certified.

3.33 ISO 14001 enables companies to identify elements of their business that impact on the environment and produce objectives for improvement supported by regular review for continual improvement.

3.34 Other standards in the ISO 14000 series are guidelines. These include the following:

- ISO 14004 provides guidance on the development and implementation of environmental management systems
- ISO 14011 provides guidance on the audit of an environmental management system (now superseded by ISO 19011)
- ISO 14020 provides guidance on labelling issues
- ISO 14040 provides guidance on lifecycle issues

3.35 Auditing can be carried out against generic ISO 14000 criteria. However different approaches are permitted to meet local, national or industry specific requirements.

- **Type 1 (ISO 14024)**. Environmental claims are based on criteria set by a third party being based on the product's lifecycle impacts. The awarding body can be governmental or private. Examples include the EU Eco-label, the German Blue Angel and the Nordic Swan.
- **Type 2 (ISO 14021)**. Environmental claims are self-declared by suppliers, eg 'made of x% recycled material'.
- **Type 3 (ISO 14025)**. These environmental claims give quantified product information based on a full lifecycle analysis. Car companies such as BMW and Volvo are currently leading the way.

4 Design tools

Standardisation

4.1 The British Standards Institution (BSI) describes a standard as 'a published specification that establishes a common language, and contains a technical specification or other precise criteria, and is designed to be used, consistently, as a rule, a guideline, or a definition'.

4.2 Standards define many commonly accepted products, services and safety levels etc. Standards may be internal or external.

Internal standards

4.3   Internal standards may be developed by an organisation for inventory management purposes. Management of the stock range is often coupled with the need to standardise components or assembly items particularly if the items are frequent purchases. The need to manage stock effectively has been identified as a key business issue. The waste from obsolete or redundant stock can be severely detrimental to profitability and the need to buy effectively requires a committed approach to stock management. Aided by effective coding and IT systems organisations will seek to manage stock in such a way as to reduce stock holding where possible and to ensure that sound policies are pursued in relation to stock management.

4.4   Standardisation involves reaching agreement in areas such as size, shape, colour, properties, performance etc. Organisations frequently purchase a greater variety of products or services than is necessary. Here are some reasons why this may occur.

- Specifiers prefer to design their own items.
- Specifiers do not check whether similar items already exist.
- The organisation does not have an inventory control system that vets new products.
- The organisation's information systems make it difficult to establish what items are already in use.

Management of the stock range

4.5   The introduction of new products coupled with the new components or parts required for assembly can increase the overall number of parts on the order book of an organisation. Management of the stock range requires organisations to monitor the introduction of new components and parts by asking questions about how necessary the part is and whether the requirement can be met with an existing component and part.

4.6   Proliferation of stock items can be a common occurrence if the introduction of new stock is not managed well or if the product coding system is deficient. New items should require authorisation before being entered onto the system, with responsibility given to one individual or department.

4.7   Variety reduction programmes are an integral part of good inventory management. Holding inventory is expensive; holding duplicated or unnecessary stock is an area that deserves regular review. Variety reduction will cause an organisation to ask a number of questions. The first is a move to standardisation on areas such as product sizes, suitability of new products to use existing registered components and reduced offerings on colours and finishes. Variety reduction programmes will often involve cross-functional team working with the purchasing department who will often have similar standardisation objectives.

4.8   Approval for new items requires a formal approach from those involved. This will involve an examination of why new stock items are being entered on to the system and ensure the relevant questions are asked.

- Why is the item required?
- What is the potential future demand?
- Can the need be met by a current stock item?
- Can the new item replace any item currently held on the existing inventory?
- Is it essential to stock this item? Can the supplier deliver on a just-in-time basis?

4.9 Variety reduction or adoption of standardised parts serves to ensure that purchasing can be better managed and controlled and instils a discipline on an organisation in relation to the introduction of new parts and components. Unnecessary duplication will often lead to redundant or obsolete stocks that contribute greatly to waste within organisations. In today's trading environment this should not be acceptable.

External standards

4.10 External standards are defined by outside organisations. There are a number of different sources of standards.

- Industry standards, often developed by trade associations in specific industry or service sectors, eg car manufacture, local government and banking
- National standards, which are those established and agreed within a country such as the British Standards Institution (BSI) standards or DIN standards in Germany. BSI is the oldest standards body in the world. Formed in 1901 it publishes over 20,000 standards and operates in over 100 countries.
- International standards such as those of the International Standards Organisation (ISO). ISO is a federation of national standards bodies from over 150 countries and promotes the development of standardisation with the objective of facilitating international trade.
- European standards, the most familiar being the CE marking which defines certain requirements for a wide variety of products.

4.11 Purchasers should be familiar with the standards that exist for the products and/or services within their remit. Each standards body will publish indexes of these standards by hard copy, CD-ROM or on the internet. IT enables rapid searching for particular standards. Purchasers of a new item should identify whether any appropriate standards exist before spending time and money developing an in-house specification.

4.12 Many standards can be complex and buyers must establish the suppliers' depth of knowledge in relation to them. If their experience is not considered sufficient the purchaser can, if applicable, work with the supplier to ensure that the product or service to be provided meets the required specification standard.

4.13 The principal advantages and disadvantages of standards are summarised in Table 4.3.

Table 4.3 *Advantages and disadvantages of standards*

Advantages of standards
• They simplify suppliers' quotes, because if all suppliers are quoting to the same standards then other decision criteria can be applied.
• They promote competition as suppliers have a common benchmark to quote against.
• They are increasingly important in international trade as they form a basis for a common understanding between trading partners.
• They help remove uncertainty as to what is required.
• The purchaser does not have to write a specification for items covered by standards.
• They promote standardisation, and, in consequence, reduction of inventory.
• They can reassure customers, who often see conformance with a standards as an indication of quality and safety.
Disadvantages of standards
• Any standard represents a compromise agreed by the various parties that prepared it. Meeting it may not necessarily satisfy all the purchaser's requirements.
• The standard will reflect the point in time when it was produced. Standards may not reflect the latest technology or practices.

Modularisation

4.14 A modular approach to assembly has become increasingly common over recent years. Common in the construction industry for many years the approach allows for multi-functional assembly items to be integrated into product design and delivery. Examples can be seen in areas such as car assembly where the modular unit is integrated with the car's IT system. This enables diagnostic fault finding and replacement of the module in a fast and convenient manner. The same technique is seen in computer manufacture where a number of multi-functional modules are combined together to form the end product.

Value analysis

4.15 Value analysis presents a role for purchasing following the product launch. As time passes customers' tastes change and technology advances. As a consequence a product may fail to meet customers' current expectations and may not be making the best use of new materials and design. As R&D and initial production costs have been recouped there is a chance to consider price reductions.

4.16 Value analysis has been defined as 'the organised, systematic study of the function of a material, part, component or system to identify areas of unnecessary cost. It begins with the question "What is it worth?" and proceeds to an analysis of value in terms of the function the item performs'. (Gary J Zenz, *Purchasing and the Management of Materials*)

4.17 The origin of the technique lies in the Second World War when it was developed by Larry Miles of General Electric in the USA as a response to wartime shortages of materials. His idea was that careful attention to the make-up of products would lead to changes that would save money. At the same time, he believed that quality would not suffer; indeed a more critical investigation of what was included in a product, and why, would lead to improvements in quality.

4.18 These days the concept has been adopted in a large number of manufacturing firms. Alongside it there is a technique referred to as value engineering (closely linked with simultaneous engineering), which considers design from the conceptual stage. Value analysis involves looking afresh at a product already in existence.

4.19 This is the distinction adopted in this text, but you should be aware that other authors distinguish the terms differently. For example, in some accounts you will find that the distinction lies in who initiates and manages the process. If it is the engineering department, then the term used is **value engineering**; on the other hand, it tends to be purchasing personnel in charge of **value analysis** exercises. Clearly, this method of distinguishing the terms overlaps with the previous one. Unless it is important to distinguish the two in a particular context, we will usually refer simply to value analysis and leave the reader to infer that the same applies to value engineering.

4.20 A possible problem with value analysis in the sense used above is that the changes in the configuration of a part or assembly may make it difficult to use in other products of which it forms one element. Another shortcoming is that each value analysis exercise, to the extent that it leads to change, is in effect shortening the lifecycle of the product that is being changed. The effect may be to cancel out the benefit that was supposed to arise.

4.21 For these reasons, among others, there is merit in the value engineering approach because, in effect, it gets things right from the beginning and minimises the need for later change. Many organisations now place considerable emphasis on value engineering all new products to the extent that this is feasible. However where the process was not used at the design and engineering stage, there may be increased scope for the application of value analysis at a future date.

4.22 Whichever term is used, the process is the same. The idea is to establish what function a particular part is fulfilling; then to consider the various design options for achieving this function to the desired standard; and finally, to analyse the cost of alternatives.

4.23 This approach is summarised in the five 'tests for value' that were developed in General Electric's pioneering use of the technique.

- Does use of the material, part or process contribute value?
- Is the cost of the material, part or process proportionate to its usefulness?
- Are all the product features actually needed?
- Can a lower-cost method be used while retaining the features and functions that add value?
- Is anyone paying less for this part?

4.24   A more detailed checklist is quoted by Dobler and Burt (*Purchasing and Supply Chain Management*).

- Can the item be eliminated?
- If the item is not standard, can a standard item be used?
- If it is a standard item, does it completely fit the application or is it a misfit?
- Does the item have greater capacity than required?
- Can the weight be reduced?
- Is there a similar item in inventory that could be substituted?
- Are closer tolerances specified than are necessary?
- Is unnecessary machining performed on this item?
- Are unnecessarily fine finishes specified?
- Is 'commercial quality' (ie the most economical quality) specified?
- Can the item be made more cheaply? Can it be bought more cheaply?
- Is the item properly classified for customs and shipping purposes to obtain the lowest transportation costs?
- Can the cost of packing be reduced?
- Are suppliers being asked for suggestions to reduce cost?

4.25   The specific outcomes of a value analysis exercise may be reduced costs and/or improved quality, but this is not the only benefit to the organisation. Individuals involved in this kind of exercise find that they look at their work in a different way, no longer regarding previous decisions and engineering as binding, but taking a fresh approach. The whole process of value analysis therefore fosters a positive approach towards innovation and overcomes the entrenched resistance to change that may otherwise be encountered.

Value engineering

4.26   Value engineering is the application of value analysis from the development stage onwards. A simultaneous engineering approach can be instigated where suppliers can be involved and offer research and development using their specialist skills in their supply area.

4.27   An example is the simultaneous approach used by Ford and Pilkington Glass where the Ford car design and Pilkington car windscreen and windows are developed collaboratively. If the car design does not work in concert with the thickness and structural integrity required of the windscreen and windows then both organisations can work together to make design improvements and modifications until a suitable product is engineered.

4.28   Value engineering attempts to organise the design and development of new products by deploying cross-functional teams, including specialists from all the functions that can contribute to overall objectives, as well as external suppliers. The aims of this approach are as follows.

- To ensure quality is built in from inception, not merely 'inspected in' later. (Estimates suggest that from 60 per cent to 80 per cent of costs are committed at the design stage.)
- To reduce the need for engineering changes at a later stage.

- To reduce time to market – the lead time between inception and launch.
- To reduce development and production costs.
- To improve sensitivity to customer needs.

4.29 Value analysis, value engineering and the other methodologies discussed demonstrate the thought and commitment that organisations put into bringing products from the design stage into production in a way that meets customer needs cost effectively.

Computer aided design (CAD)

4.30 As discussed in Chapter 2 the use of technology in both the design and manufacturing process has led to rapid improvements in recent years. Organisations can link their CAD/CAM systems directly with the communications and manufacturing systems. This assists both in speeding up the approval time for design and in designing tooling and operations processes.

4.31 CAD was a system originally developed by IBM in 1960 for use in the motor industry. It is a computerised design process for creating new products or components or altering or amending existing ones. An example of the modern application can be seen in Formula One racing where, because of the competitive need to bring new parts or designs online quickly, a high degree of testing is carried out using stress or windflow simulations to enable parts to be used quickly with minimum testing and a high degree of safety.

4.32 The CAD designer uses a desktop computer, supported by specialist software. The ability to share the designs with other users, often in different locations and countries, can allow for specialist input if required. Lysons and Farrington in *Purchasing and Supply Chain Management* list the following features.

- A three-dimensional projection of any part of the screen
- Calculations of area, volume, weight and stress
- A databank of existing products or part designs as what is required may only be a variation on what is available
- Simulation of strength and stress tests without the need for a prototype
- Analysis of manufacturing considerations relating to the production of an item
- Several alternative design solutions for consideration by the designer
- The translation of the approved design into two-dimensional drawings for use in manufacturing
- Bills of materials, the parts list for the items required to make the product

4.33 Computer-aided manufacture (CAM) is linked to CAD as the CAD design provides the design and instruction to take through to manufacture. The CAD/CAM system may form part of a more integrated computer integrated manufacturing (CIM) system where design, planning and manufacturing are linked via computer systems.

4.34 The end objective of CIM is the integrated computerisation of all aspects of the supply chain from supply to end delivery.

Chapter summary

- Design is described by Arjan J Van Weele as 'the cradle of costs'.

- Operations management has a duty to be involved in the design process at the earliest possible stage in order to ensure the product or service design is one that can progress through design onto production and through to the customer in a cost-effective and timely manner.

- Selling a concept or delivering a service provides a different set of challenges to operations management.

- The integrated approach of cross-functional teams helps ensure that all potential areas are discussed by the team who become increasingly familiar with the project and, in consequence, gain a wider understanding and perspective on the issues raised by other team members.

- Organisations will introduce new products/services periodically to add to the range and keep ahead of the competition or to replace unfashionable/obsolete products and services.

- Purchasing has a key role in the new product development process. Purchasing can bring a range of skills and expertise to the cross-functional development team from the earliest stage.

- The design of products in such a way as to minimise their impact on the environment is becoming increasingly important.

- One of the most effective ways that purchasing can contribute to reducing the environmental impact of products and services is to ensure that specifications are drafted in such a way as to incorporate environmental issues.

- Environmentally sensitive design has three aspects: design for environmental manufacturing, design for environmental packaging and design for disassembly.

- A CAD/CAM system may form part of a more integrated computer integrated manufacturing (CIM) system where design, planning and manufacturing are linked via computer systems.

Self-test questions

Numbers in brackets refer to the paragraphs above where your answers can be checked.

1   What is the purpose of design, in a business sense? (1.3)

2   What are the 'four Cs of design'? (1.6)

3   What are the five phases that every design programme will pass through according to Muhlemann, Oakland and Lockyer? (1.7)

4   What three resultant savings are claimed for design for manufacture and assembly (DFMA)? (1.12)

5   What are the stages of the new product development process? (1.20)

6   What is the difference between e-sourcing and e-procurement? (2.21)

7   What are the three aspects of environmentally sensitive design? (3.4)

8   List the six categories of costs in whole life costing. (3.19)

9   What are the advantages and disadvantages of using standards? (4.13)

10   Define 'value analysis'. (4.16)

Further reading

•   *Operations Management*, Slack, Chambers and Johnston, Chapter 1.

•   *Production and Operations Management*, Muhlemann, Oakland and Lockyer, Chapter 2.

Try visiting the following websites:

•   www.defra.gov.uk

•   www.europa.eu.int

CHAPTER 5

The Design and Management of the Operations Network

Learning objectives and indicative context

3.1   Analyse the critical features of an operations network and explain how they contribute to the management of supply and demand.

- Network design and investment
- Strategic decisions in developing a network
- Feasibility factors
- Benefit factors
- Financial factors
- Organisational structure
- Integration
- Outsourcing: make versus buy

3.2   Distinguish between the different process types in manufacturing and service industries.

- Process types in terms of variety and volume
- Processing technologies
- Process layouts and workflow

Chapter headings

1   Network design and investment

2   Product and process design

3   Process layouts

1 Network design and investment

1.1 Integrated management of the supply chain (the 'network' that links suppliers, your organisation and customers) is increasingly recognised as a core competitive strategy. Organisations can no longer operate alone but need to operate on a cooperative basis with the best organisations in their supply chain in order to succeed. Supply chain management is the integration of these activities through improved supply chain relationships, to achieve sustainable competitive advantage.

1.2 The supply chain includes the management of information, procurement activities, inventory management, order processing, production scheduling, logistics, and customer service through to disposal of packaging and materials. With modern developments the reach can be extended to include product recycling and disposal.

1.3 The supplier network encompasses all organisations that provide inputs, either directly or indirectly, to the focal company. Each 'first tier' supplier (the supplier to the focal company) has its own suppliers (second tier suppliers) who, in turn have their third tier suppliers etc. Supply chains are essentially a linked network of suppliers and customers with every customer a supplier to the next downstream organisation.

1.4 Internal functions within an organisation drive the network. The operations function includes control of the different processes used in transforming the inputs provided by the supplier network. The coordination and planning of these work flows can be particularly challenging, particularly in diverse manufacturing environments, and need effective management in order to minimise waste and maximise productivity.

Strategic decisions in developing a network

1.5 The strategic plan forms the basis for the direction of the organisation and, in consequence, the investment decisions that will need to be made in order to meet the planned aims. In the vast majority of situations organisations are looking to adapt existing processes and facilities in the most appropriate way to meet any changes in direction rather than invest in new ones.

1.6 Ideally the processes that will transform the product or service should be flexible enough that new demands can be integrated into existing systems without major changes to the operation. Network design is not only about the most efficient and effective system, it is also about flexibility: flexibility to meet strategic changes, flexibility to adapt to future needs, as well as flexibility to respond to changes in the business environment.

1.7 To assess the design of the operations network the organisation must visualise the entire network. The organisation can then take a strategic view as to how best to use the operations network to compete effectively in the long term. This viewpoint also enables operations management to take a step back from their normal working environment and identify any links in the network that are particularly significant.

1.8 The operations role has the transformation process at its core but the entire network encompasses both the inputs and the outputs of the organisation. The inputs are the supply side of the operation: the materials, components, people, ideas, data and information that flow into the transformation process. The outputs interface with the demand side of the organisation (the customers).

1.9 The supply side of the operation consists of a number of suppliers who directly supply the organisation. These 'first-tier' suppliers are so-called as they deliver directly to the organisation. It is with these suppliers that we have the most contact and may look to form longer-term business relationships. The 'second tier' represents the suppliers who supply to our suppliers. These are of interest to us (although not often directly), as our demands on areas such as quality, price and delivery need to be met by these suppliers in order that the 'supply chain' functions effectively. These second-tier suppliers are the first-tier suppliers to our own first-tier suppliers.

1.10 On the demand side of the operation there may be a number of intermediaries between the ultimate customer and ourselves. To our organisation our customer may be a warehouse or distributor. These are our direct customers and form the 'first tier' on the demand side. The warehouse or distributor may feed into a retail network. The retailer is a 'second-tier' customer. The eventual consumer is a 'first tier' customer to the retailer but a 'third-tier' customer to us. That is not to say we disregard their views. It is after all these final consumers who we are trying to 'delight'.

1.11 From an organisation standpoint the immediate concern is the first tier that you are dealing with. Organisational emphasis is on ensuring supplies of the right quality delivered to the right place at the right time and on transforming these supplies to meet the demands of the first-tier customers.

1.12 Quality issues, environmental concerns, ethical sourcing and competitive considerations can all be made clear in discussions and agreements with suppliers. To enforce these demands they will be passed along the supply chain to the suppliers' suppliers. Suppliers will be required to meet and/or evidence agreed criteria in areas such as service quality (evidenced by ISO standards such as the ISO 9001 group of standards) or environmental standards (evidenced by the ISO 14001 group of standards) and so on. Our suppliers then make similar demands on their suppliers.

1.13 The link with suppliers is often referred to as 'upstream' operations. Equally the link with customers is known as 'downstream'. This is all illustrated in Figure 5.1.

Figure 5.1 *Tiering*

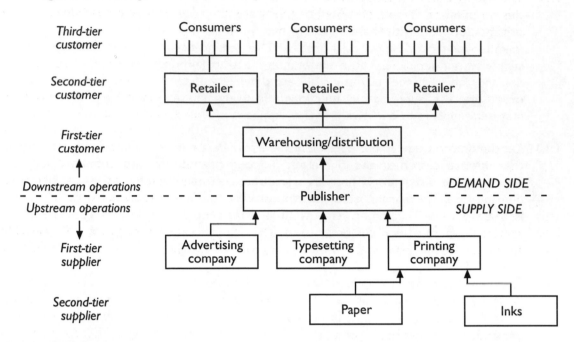

The supply network

1.14 The supply network is a number of supply chains that together describe the flow of goods and services from their original sources to their end users. Interdependent networks such as these have been described by Martin Christopher as 'a confederation of mutually complementary competencies and capabilities which compete as an integrated supply chain against other supply chains'.

1.15 Network design and management requires a modern view of business relationships to be considered and developed. Supply chain thinking emphasises 'win-win' scenarios, rather than the more conventional adversarial approach. Identified gains and improvements must be shared so that all members of the supply chain benefit. Improvements identified by the use or implementation of shared information technology, analysis of storage and distribution requirements and reductions possible through identified areas of 'waste' are all examples of how a 'partnering' approach can bring cost savings and efficiency improvements to the supply chain.

1.16 Marshall Fisher distinguishes between 'innovative' and 'functional' products.

- 'Functional' products include items such as stationery or basic foodstuffs with long product lifecycles and stable, predictable demand. Profit margins are low; therefore the emphasis of the network is on cost minimisation by long production runs, efficient distribution and storage, and low inventories.

- 'Innovative' products have unpredictable demand and shorter product lifecycles. Profitability will be higher than with 'functional' products over a shorter time frame. The supply network will need to be quick from design to market and also flexible and responsive to market demand.

1.17 The network for 'functional' products will focus on cost and being lean (taking areas of waste out of the supply chain) while the 'innovative' network requires speed, flexibility and the ability to adapt to market changes.

Downstream networks

1.18 Downstream management equally requires careful consideration. Different customers may have different needs, all of which must be satisfied. As an example, the warehouse or distributor may require regular deliveries in 40-foot containers with seasonal variations. Retailers may want smaller quantities from the warehouse but placing emphasis on regular supplies. The eventual consumer wants the goods to be readily available on demand. The needs of the demand tiers must be fully understood and also regularly updated when designing the transformation-output link of operations.

1.19 The objective of downstream management is to meet not only the needs of first-tier or second-tier customers (if appropriate) but also to meet the needs of the end customer or user.

Design decisions

1.20 Slack *et al* highlight the overall network perspective as important because it helps to highlight three important design decisions.

- How should the network be configured? How can the organisation shape the network to best meet its own needs? Can better control be achieved by supplier reduction, removing tiers (eg by encouraging merging of suppliers), by moving responsibility or by an innovative approach? Should the organisation own more of the supply chain (ie take over a first-tier supplier – known as vertical integration) or will this detract from concentration on core activities?

- Where should each part of the network owned by the organisation be located? Near suppliers, overseas, near motorway links, near a readily available labour force?

- What physical capability should each part of the network owned by the company have? Decisions in this area require considerable foresight and planning. Long-term capacity management decisions form a crucial aspect of operations management and will be considered further as this text progresses.

Financial factors

1.21 All the above and other questions involve investment decisions. These decisions relate to the allocation or reallocation of spend or resources to identified areas that have been strategically considered. These areas may be premises, projects, machinery, products or service centres amongst others.

1.22 Investment decisions are influenced by a number of changing situations that organisations will constantly face.

- **Expansion**: the decision facing an organisation when considering expansion is that investment in building, plant and machinery is both capital intensive and long-term in nature. Decisions must be well thought through and thoroughly costed. Alternatives such as make-or-buy decisions, outsourcing and leasing may be appropriate.

- **Diversification**: where decisions are made to invest in new products or services. This strategy causes operations to re-evaluate their current resources as new networks and transformation processes may become appropriate.

- **Changing technology**: this is one of the most fast-moving areas of business and one of the most difficult to visualise into the future. Technology investments are crucial to design and development and play a key role in both stock management and customer service. Investment decisions must be carefully evaluated and appropriate to meet current and future needs.

- **Replacement**: of existing plant, machinery etc. Options such as leasing, outsourcing, hiring may be appropriate and should be evaluated.

- **Changes in the business environment**: increasing emphasis is being placed in areas such as corporate social responsibility (CSR), environmental and ethical issues and supply chain management. These and other issues require an organisation to consider both external and internal issues when evaluating investment decisions.

Feasibility factors

1.23   The feasibility of network design centres around the ability to find suitable supply chain partners and the location or locations of the operation. Supply chain partnerships involve a closer degree of integration between organisations with the purchasing emphasis moving to developing a more strategic relationship.

1.24   Organisations will increasingly evaluate a supply chain partner's willingness to develop longer-term or strategic relationships. One major flaw in the supply chain scenario is that all organisations will want to develop closer relationships. This is not always the case. A number of questions for organisations wishing to establish long-term business relationships were given by Robert Spekman in *Strategic Supplier Selection: Understanding Long-Term Business Relationships*.

- Has the organisation signalled a willingness or commitment to a partnership-type arrangement?

- Is the organisation willing to commit resources that it cannot use in other relationships?

- How early in the product design stage is the organisation willing or able to participate?

- What does the organisation bring to the relationship that is unique?

- Will the organisation have a genuine interest in joint problem solving and a win-win agreement?

- Is the organisation's senior management committed to the process inherent in strategic partnerships?

- Will there be free and open exchange of information across functional areas between companies?

- Does the organisation have the infrastructure to support such cross-functional interdependence?
- How much future planning is the organisation willing to share with us?
- Is the need for confidential treatment taken seriously?
- What is the general level of comfort between companies?
- How well does the organisation know our business?
- Will the organisation share cost data?
- What will be the organisation's commitment to understanding our problems and concerns?
- Will we be special to the organisation or just another customer/supplier?

Benefit factors

1.25 The benefit from closer relationships comes from gaining satisfactory answers to the above questions. The closer integration leads to an improved understanding of a mutual business situation where partners can combine to contribute above their individual weight.

1.26 The topic of organisational structure is mentioned at this point in your syllabus. You should refer back to Chapter 3 for detailed coverage of the topic.

1.27 Internal supply chains are that part of a supply chain that occurs within an individual organisation. With the multi-divisional and global organisational structures found in many large businesses it is likely that these internal links will be quite involved and complex. An understanding of the internal supply chain is important in understanding the overall impact and contribution that the supply chain concept can bring. The development of supply chain maps (flowcharts) for major supply chains is a useful discipline. Process map development is usually accomplished through the use of cross-functional teams as part of a supply chain review. Operations must have a central role in this process and in understanding the supply chain as the flow from the supply chain evidences itself as the inputs coming into the organisation.

1.28 Once an understanding of the internal supply chain is gained the logical extension is to analyse the external aspect of the supply chain, again using process mapping and cross-functional teams. Once the key supply chains have been identified then the main supply chain members can be weighted as the most critical to the organisation's supply chain management goals. Strategies can then be developed to maximise the benefits of the supply chain approach with these providers.

Outsourcing versus make-or-buy decisions

1.29 Organisations must be fully aware of the optimum capacity level of their operations. The need is to maximise the use of your manufacturing facilities in order to gain economies of scale in production and maximum profitability.

1.30 To operate at the optimum capacity level requires planning and foresight from operations management. Make-or-buy decisions are fundamental to any business, either manufacturing or service. Do we make in-house? Do we invest in machinery and/or technology? Do we staff the operation? Do we provide for the overhead costs of the operation? Do we need to control the operation internally as core to our business? Have we the skills to manufacture in-house? Or do we buy in from outside?

1.31 Make-or-buy decisions face all organisations. From the concept stage organisations can look to make everything (ie only buy raw materials) or to minimise everything (ie buy everything from external suppliers). The decisions are based on a number of factors.

- Strategic planning
- Manufacturing capacity
- Suitable external suppliers
- Relationships with suppliers
- Effects on the manufacturing workforce
- Labour market conditions
- Sales forecasts

1.32 Managing the make-or-buy decision while ensuring optimum capacity utilisation is a difficult balance for the operations manager to achieve. It requires excellent business knowledge of all strategic, tactical and operational levels of the organisation to implement effectively.

1.33 Outsourcing is a strategic use of outside resources to perform activities traditionally handled by internal staff. Organisations began outsourcing the physical activities of a business such as facilities management, logistics and production to a large degree from the 1980s onwards. In addition the outsourcing of IT is increasingly common. However, all 'non-core' businesses can be seen as possible candidates for outsourcing.

1.34 Outsourcing is addressed at a strategic level in operations as investment decisions can be substantial in terms of cost and commitment and, in consequence carry a high degree of risk if proved unsustainable. The role of the finance function during the design and capital equipment purchase processes is to question all potential investment decisions. One question that will be asked will be: 'do we need to make this ourselves (with the investment that entails) or can we outsource the work to a supplier or business partner?' It is only when that argument has been fully discussed and evaluated that any go ahead will be given.

Core competencies

1.35 Competencies are 'the activities or processes through which the organisation deploys its resources effectively' (*Johnson & Scholes*).

- **Threshold competencies** are the basic capabilities necessary to support a particular strategy or to enable the organisation to compete in a given market. (The effective use of IT systems, or fast idea-to-market innovation cycles would now be considered a threshold competence in most markets.)
- **Core competencies** are distinctive value-creating skills, capabilities and resources which (according to Hamel and Prahalad) add value in the eyes of the customer; are scarce and difficult for competitors to imitate; and are flexible for future needs. They offer sustainable competitive advantage: for example, by enabling differentiation or cost leadership, or putting up barriers to competitor entry into an industry. Hamel and Prahalad argue that 'senior managers must conceive of their companies as a portfolio of core competencies, rather than just a portfolio of businesses and products'.

1.36 The concept of core competencies is used in make/do or buy (or strategic outsourcing) decisions. Strategic outsourcing should only be applied to:

(a) **Non-core** competencies, which if outsourced will benefit from the expertise, technology or cost efficiency of a specialist supplier **without** disadvantaging the organisation with loss of in-house capability or vulnerability to market risks; and

(b) Activities for which external contractors have the required competence, capability and capacity.

1.37 The make/do or buy options can thus be depicted as follows: Figure 5.2.

Figure 5.2 *Competencies and contractor competence*

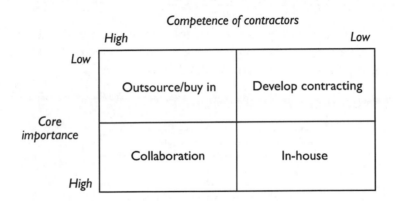

Repositioning strategies

1.38 The concept of repositioning an organisation within the supply or value chain implies the extension of its operations or control to a wider range of upstream or downstream activities – and a greater share of responsibility for creating and adding value.

1.39 Repositioning strategies include: organic or internal development and diversification into activities one step up or down the chain; acquisition of, or merger with, organisations one step up or down the chain; and/or strategic collaboration and integration with organisations one step up or down the chain. These are growth strategies. Repositioning may also, however, include withdrawal or contraction: outsourcing or subcontracting activities, say, or divesting from activities, in order to narrow the organisation's focus to its core competencies.

1.40 **Vertical integration** refers to strategies by which an enterprise gains control over the processes involved in supply or distribution.

• **Backward** integration occurs when an organisation becomes its own supplier of raw materials, components or services: in other words, it controls the inputs to its business. For example, a bakery might set up its own flour mill – or acquire an existing flour-milling business. This has the key advantage of providing secure supply and greater control over input quality and cost – as well as claiming a share of the profits obtainable in the supply market.

- **Forward** integration occurs when an organisation enters areas concerned with the outputs of its business. A manufacturer, for example, might open or acquire a chain of retail outlets, franchise dealerships or a direct marketing business. This has the key advantage of strengthening relationships and contacts with end-users – as well as claiming a share of the profits obtainable in the distribution market.

1.41 Repositioning in either direction may help an organisation to extend its core competencies and capacity, and commentators identify a major trend towards the increasing 'verticalisation' of supply chain management activities. At the same time, the concept of core competence suggests that any given organisation will also want to 'stick to the knitting' to some extent: in other words, to leverage its resources by doing what it is best at – and outsourcing to others what they are best at and can perform more efficiently on its behalf.

2 Product and process design

2.1 Process design involves the sequence of operations together with the appropriate use of technology involved in transforming products from the design stage into actual goods or services. An example would be a visit to the dentist: Figure 5.3.

Figure 5.3 *Process design: visiting the dentist*

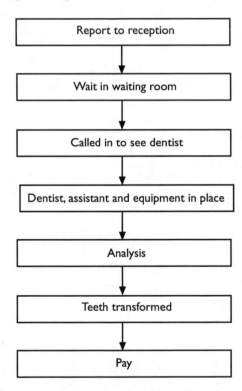

2.2 This is a sequence of events or operations (inputs) leading to the transformation process: teeth transformed and payment secured.

2.3 The more complex aspect of the visit to the dentist involves the time spent with the dentist. General equipment will be required for all patients (dental lighting, reclining chair, and mouthwash). Specialist equipment will be required to account for a number of different permutations (eg X-rays, extractions, descaling). To add to this the specialist skills of the dentist are required at the agreed time.

Timetabling

2.4   The timetabling of activities is a feature of repetitive service functions. Examples include bus, train and air services, dentists, cinemas, teaching, etc. These are all 'customer push' systems where customers need to take advantage of the timetabled operation at the required time.

2.5   We are all aware of the issues surrounding timetabling as a function. Buses run late, appointments are subject to delays and staff delivering a specialist service are late or are taken ill. Communication is a key customer service aspect here. Many London bus stops now have travel information on the current situation regarding the arrival of a bus route at a given stop. Customers or clients who fail to arrive without notification also cause problems as service specialists (such as doctors or dentists) may not have a client at the given time, leading to waste.

2.6   Timetables are arrived at by weighing a number of factors such as past experience, potential bottleneck or pinch points, preferred order or sequence and customer feedback. They are ideally designed to suit the needs of both the service provider and the customer but often fall somewhere in the middle.

2.7   Process design has two aspects.

*   The technical aspect that involves the sequencing of operations, the application of technology and the methods used for the transformation process. Sequencing involves determining priorities. In the case of the dentist advance booking and the use of timetables achieve this. In manufacturing, sequencing may be influenced by the physical nature of the transformation equipment being used or the timing of work arriving where the complementary mix of work may determine the priority given to particular jobs.

*   The economic aspect caused by commercial and competitive factors, leading to process improvements over time. Hayes and Wheelwright argue that operations managers are not only involved with the economic aspects but also need to consider limitations and constraints placed on the organisation such as skills requirements, legal implications and existing facilities.

Jobbing, batch, mass and flow production

2.8   Manufacturing operations are concerned with a process of transformation or conversion. The way in which this transformation process takes place differs from one industry to another and sometimes from one firm to another within the same industry.

2.9   A classification employed within operations management is based on the type of process employed. This concept is based on the size, length and range of the production run from a lot size of one unit (of variable size) to a continuous flow of manufacture. The main possibilities are jobbing production, batch production, flow production and mass production.

2.10 **Jobbing production** (or job shop) refers to situations where the output is a finished product produced to the specification of a particular customer. Owing to the nature of the operation which could be highly specialised (eg making bespoke furniture) there may be a high level of skill required by operatives with emphasis on quality output. The job shop concept extends to integrating a number of dependent processes, an example of which could be in producing a print run. Here the printing press may be set up to run one particular job; when that is completed the press is then reconfigured to run another job. The first job is then routed to other areas that add value to the process such as folding, trimming, stapling and binding. Each stage in the jobbing production run performs its function on the job as the work arrives.

2.11 A major issue in the job shop process concerns scheduling. When jobs arrive from other areas a waiting line can develop. In a job shop environment operations managers are much concerned with issues of scheduling the work in the proper amount and sequencing the flow of work in order to balance the costs of idle time against the costs of having jobs waiting.

2.12 Project production is similar in process to the job shop approach, with work completed in series of interdependent stages. This is a familiar process in industries such as construction or engineering; the finished product is an office building, a bridge, a highway etc, ordered by a particular customer. Each job is a separate entity, and its production is distinct from the production of any other job. This type of jobbing is also referred to as project management.

2.13 In **batch production**, as the name suggests, the unit of output is a batch of like products. The process is appropriate when the producer manufactures many standard products but none in sufficient quantity for them to justify the setting up of an assembly line devoted to continuous production. Batch production is a very common method – perhaps the most common method – of work organisation found in the manufacturing environment.

2.14 Typically, the work involved will be divided into stages with dedicated workers and machines at each stage. All products in the batch will first pass through Stage 1 and will be worked on by the workers and machines dedicated to this stage. Once complete they will move to Stage 2, and so on until all stages of production are complete. Batch runs allow for optimum batch sizes that move along the production process in such a way that scheduling and sequencing can be planned in advance, lessening idle time or bottlenecks in the process. The size and number of batches depends on the demand (either orders received and/or forecasts) and the technology involved in the production process. The role of the operations manager is to meet the need by scheduling production within the constraints of the technological limitations of the production process.

2.15 **Flow production** is usually taken to mean a system in which products flow from one stage of production to the next without interruption. An example would be the petroleum industry which does not produce discrete units but transforms crude oil through a multistage process in a series of individual stages to produce the final required output. Contrast this with batch production in which a product is not passed from one stage to the next until all products in the batch have completed the earlier stage. The aim of flow production is that any particular product will be undergoing a transformation process for every minute of its time in the production cycle. To achieve this, it is important that all stages of production are of equal length; otherwise, bottlenecks will arise at stages with longer duration. Another implication is that production is broken down into a large number of very small steps, enabling a high degree of specialisation of labour.

2.16 **Mass production** simply means production on a large scale. In correct usage, the term does not refer to any particular type of production – it may be organised on job, batch or flow lines – but only to the scale of production.

Approaches to provisioning

2.17 The type of production method has an impact on provisioning – the process of ensuring that materials are on hand when required. The types of materials involved will also influence the approach. This can be demonstrated by comparing jobbing and flow production.

2.18 In a jobbing environment, all equipment and materials must be ready at all times, so that the jobbing worker can move on to a new stage of production whenever it is convenient. In a flow environment, the exact time when a particular material or particular item of equipment is needed is determined by the interaction of different production stages. Just in time (JIT) systems are appropriate for flow production but not for jobbing production.

2.19 In a jobbing environment, there is little standardisation of materials and processes. Each will vary considerably in line with customer requirements. In a flow environment, some measure of standardisation is essential.

2.20 A jobbing system can cope with variations in incoming materials. A flow system is much less flexible: incoming materials must be exactly to specification and delivered on time.

Professional, service organisations and mass services

2.21 Service processing systems are influenced by volume and variety considerations and the need to provide processes that meet customer service expectations. Customers are not generally interested in your systems, procedures and processes – what they are interested in is that the service is delivered.

2.22 Professionals such as dentists, accountants and solicitors will usually offer the timetable approach to service provision with set appointments related to hourly rate charges. Additional charges for preparation, material used, travel time, etc, will usually be charged in addition.

2.23 The rate will reflect the 'back office' provision, the receptionists, the researchers, the clerical function, the IT support, etc. At the start of this section we looked at a trip to the dentist. The time with the dentist is just part of a series of processes that enable the visit to take place and the service to be performed. The integration of 'back office' and 'front of office' allows the operation to work effectively and is a common operational theme in the operations management of services.

2.24 Service organisations such as the Royal Automobile Club (RAC), local authorities and banks whose primary (though not exclusive) function is one of providing a service are not well adapted to the timetabling approach.

- The RAC will need good forecasting in order to effectively service breakdowns. A pattern of call-outs can be established to set a 'norm' for the average day. However, other factors such as bad weather, bank holidays and sporting events need to be factored in, in order that both local and national demand can be met. The service provision is supported by a central call centre just outside Birmingham. It is geographically central and linked to the motorway network.

- Local authorities face a different set of service criteria. Many specialist services are provided, usually as a back-office function. Contact with local authority staff will be by telephone, e-mail or appointment. The front office is via a reception area that serves to direct people in the right direction rather than answer queries.

- Banks have utilised the increasing effectiveness of IT both to cut costs and to make the operation more effective. The use of debit and credit cards, telephone calls handled via call-centres and computer generated statements are all familiar examples. Banks have been criticised for their lack of personal interaction with customers. However, they could be said to be proponents of modern operations management in their use of effective and efficient systems and processes that make full use of IT support.

2.25 Mass services such as airlines, railways and mainstream hotels face another differing set of criteria. As with the RAC scenario they face peaks and troughs in demand for their services. Whereas the RAC can vary the number of mechanics on call the three examples above are not in that position. They need to utilise the aircraft, trains and rooms throughout the day or year.

2.26 Mass services increasingly rely on IT systems to support their operation (eg e-ticketing, Travelcards and shared networks, both air and rail). The back-office function tends to dominate the operation, as it is the effective delivery of the processes that underpins the operation.

Hayes and Wheelwright

2.27 Hayes and Wheelwright list a number of considerations when evaluating process technologies and the roles of technical specialists and operations managers: Table 5.1.

2.28 The Hayes and Wheelwright list relates to the design of manufacturing processes but how can it be applied to the service sector? In essence few changes need to be made. Time-spans may need to be linked with IT processes rather than set-up times and reliability measured in terms of customer service levels but everything else applies.

2.29 The operations processes are highly important in delivering the service provision. Although operations management is frequently criticised for its production origins and its alleged lack of application to service industries there is an increasing correlation in the thinking behind both sectors.

Table 5.1 *Analysis of processes*

Mechanics	How does the process work? What physically happens and how does it happen?
Economics	How much does it cost in the short and long term?
Time-span	What is the set-up time? How long does it take per unit once set up?
Constraints	What can't be done? What is very difficult to do in an acceptable time/cost frame?
Uncertainties	What can go wrong? What do people worry about? What is predictable and what isn't?
Skills	What isn't done automatically? How long will it take to learn the processes?
Flexibility	How does the process react to changes? Which changes are easy and which are not?
Reliability	What tolerances does the process meet? How repeatable are those tolerances?

3 Process layouts

The importance of layout

3.1 The layout of an operation refers to the physical location and positioning of the transforming resources. The layout includes the physical appearance and characteristics of the operation and will affect the organisation of the facilities, the technology used to support the operation and the flow of work through the unit.

3.2 Layout is important as it defines the 'shape' of the operation and the flow of work through the unit. The speed and even flow of work through the unit is fundamental to achieving success. Decisions relating to workflow, methods to be used and the organisation of the unit should be made prior to the facilities being laid out. Relatively small changes can cause disruption to the intended plan and may cause disproportionate problems.

3.3 The objectives of good facilities layout include the following.

- Maximising the return on the fixed investment by enabling optimum production levels to be achieved and by minimising the amount of floor space required.
- Minimising materials handling and transportation requirements
- Ensuring that labour is utilised effectively and efficiently
- Reducing the hazards in the production operation that may affect production workers and products
- Allowing for flexibility for changes that may come from new products, processes or growth in demand
- Enabling a smooth, logical flow of product or customers through the processes

3.4 The techniques employed in designing a layout are based on many years of experience and, in recent years, supported by IT design systems such as PLANET (planned layout analysis and evaluation technique), CORELAP (computerised relationship layout planning) and COFAD (computerised facility design).

3.5 Muhlemann, Oakland and Lockyer detail the following considerations.

Table 5.2 *Criteria for good layout*

Maximum flexibility	Can be rapidly modified to changing circumstances. Particular attention to ease of access for services (more easily addressed at design stage than later on)
Maximum coordination	Entry and exit should be designed in a manner that suits both issuing and receiving departments. The layout as a whole needs to consider other areas of the organisation's business and customers.
Maximum use of volume	Facilities should utilise the full available volume of premises. Cables, conveyors, racking, storage of tools etc can all be planned in such a way as to minimise the use of floor space.
Maximum visibility	All people and materials should be observable at all times.
Maximum accessibility	All servicing and maintenance points should be readily accessible. Legislative requirements such as the Health and Safety at Work Act and the Disability Discrimination Act also place the onus of clear and unfettered access on employers.
Minimum distance	All movements should be necessary and direct. Unnecessary movement adds cost not value (Taichi Ohno).
Minimum handling	Ideally no handling but where it is required it should be reduced to a minimum by the use of appropriate devices such as forklifts, conveyor trucks etc.
Minimum discomfort	Adequate heating and lighting. Noise pollution, smells and excessive sunlight can cause problems.
Inherent safety	All layouts should be inherently safe, and no person should be exposed to danger.
Maximum security	Safeguards against fire, moisture, theft etc, should be considered in the original layout rather than by the addition of doors and cages at a later point.
Efficient process flow	Work and transport flow should not cross. The flow of work should be even, with no bottlenecks that may cause excess stocks to be stored on a temporary basis. The flow of paperwork should complement the physical transformation of the product.
Identification	Wherever possible, working groups should be provided with their own 'working space'. This helps in team building and aids productivity.

The four basic layouts

3.6 There are four basic types of layout. These are not mutually exclusive and often overlap each other.

3.7 **Fixed position layout**. The transforming, rather than the transformed, resources move. In other words, the product remains in one position and the workers, materials and tools move to it. The reason is that the transformed resources may:

- Object to being moved
- Be too delicate to be moved
- Be too big to be moved

3.8 An example would be shipbuilding. As the ship is too big to move, the transforming resources come to it. Other examples are construction sites (too big to be moved), surgery (too delicate to be moved) and high-class restaurants (would object to being moved).

3.9 The main issue with the fixed position layout is one of accessibility to the location, storage and control of the movement surrounding the fixed position. This leaves the fixed position vulnerable to disruptions in planning and control as different contractors may require access to the same point at the same time. A common adaptation of the fixed position layout is an assembly line where the product remains in a fixed position but is moved to the workers and materials by conveyor belt or overhead cranes.

3.10 **Process layout**. Here the layout is designed to suit the needs of the transforming resources. Related processes are grouped together. Products, information and customers flow from process to process according to their needs. The problem is that different products, information and customers have differing needs.

3.11 An example would be a supermarket where some processes are grouped together both for marketing and convenience reasons: tea, coffee, hot chocolate drinks; tinned fruits, pet food. The grouping together also makes stock replenishment easier. More specialist areas such as freezer cabinets require technology; fresh fruit and vegetables require more frequent stock replenishment. A manufacturing example would be machine components that need to undergo different processes during manufacture (eg machining, heat treatment and finishing). The item moves from one process to the next.

3.12 The process layout is often used where volume is low, several products are made and flexibility is required (eg one product may require drilling, milling, trimming and painting while another may require sawing, milling, trimming and polishing). Often general purpose low-cost machines are used, enabling work to be shifted to another machine in case of breakdown. As equipment used in a process layout does not require to be in a particular sequence machines that produce excessive noise, fumes or vibration etc, can be situated in isolated areas.

3.13 To the operations manager the process layout involves complexity in planning and control as routing and scheduling can be involved. The process layout will lead to costlier materials handling, larger work in progress inventory, increased storage and floor area requirements, increased costs for skilled labour, more frequent inspection and greater supervision.

3.14 **Product (or line) layout.** Transforming resources are located entirely for the benefit of transformed resources. Product layout is frequently used in a repetitive production system where the number of end products is small, and the parts or components used are highly standardised or interchangeable (eg the manufacture of computers). Layout by product is appropriate for the production of a small range of products in large quantities. This leads to a simple flow that is easy to control, but requires standardised products. Each product, customer or item of information follows a prearranged route in which the sequence matches the sequence in which the processes have been set.

3.15   The product layout arranges the equipment according to the progressive steps involved in the manufacturing process. This layout enables the use of specialised and/or high volume equipment supported by materials handling by conveyors or automated guided vehicles. For the operations manager quality is more consistent, production and job control are easier and smaller aisles are required making the floor area more productive. Disadvantages may include the high initial investment cost, increased vulnerability to work stoppage, the repetitive nature of the work and a lessening in flexibility.

3.16   A service example would be a customer being served along a counter at a self-service restaurant. Start with the menu, move to the starter server, move to the main course server, move to the dessert server, move to the drink server, and finally pay.

3.17   **Cell (group) layout.** This layout is indicated when a product is manufactured by means of group technology, ie equipment and operations have a common sequence that can be effectively grouped together. This enables economic production of small lots, minimising work in progress, space requirements and production leadtimes. The layout is arranged so that similar groups of resources to be transformed are processed in a single area. After being processed in one area, the transformed resources move to another area for further processing. The cell layout tries to bring an ordered state to the complexity of flow that is often a feature of process layouts.

3.18   Cell layouts differ from layouts by product as they are used for the manufacture of similar (but not the same) items required for the batch manufacture of the final product. Cell work will often involve groups of workers, working as a team. This approach fits in well with modern quality orientated production organisations where team working and a team approach have proven invaluable.

3.19   The choice of the appropriate layout type will be influenced by the nature of the product and/or service to be provided together with the volume and variety characteristics of the operation. The objectives of the operation will also influence the decision. Is it to minimise cost or is it to be flexible or to attract the most customers? Whatever decision is arrived at, we must consider a range of operational factors relating to minimising movement, adhering to health and safety legislation and ensuring a suitable flow of work or customers through the process without bottlenecks or queues.

3.20   The advantages and disadvantages of each layout are summarised in Table 5.3.

Table 5.3 *Advantages and disadvantages of layout types*

Type of layout	Advantages	Disadvantages
Fixed position	Very high mix and product flexibility Product or customers not moved or disturbed Wide variety of tasks for staff	High unit costs Scheduling of activities and space can be difficult May mean considerable movement of plant and staff
Process layout	High mix and product flexibility Robust system in the case of disruptions Reasonably easy supervision of plant or equipment	Low facilities utilisation Can have very high level of work in progress or customer queuing Complex flow can be difficult to manage
Product layout	Low unit costs for high volume Allows for specialisation of equipment Materials or customer movement is convenient	Can have a low mix and limited flexibility Not very robust if disrupted Work can be very repetitive
Cell layout	Can offer a good compromise between cost and flexibility Fast throughput Group work can result in good motivation	Can be expensive to rearrange the existing layout May require more plant and equipment Can give lower plant utilisation

Chapter summary

- The network design is led by the strategic objectives of the organisation.

- Integrated supply chain management (the 'network' that links suppliers, your organisation and customers) is increasingly recognised as a core competitive strategy.

- The supply side of the operation consists of a number of suppliers who directly supply the organisation.

- On the demand side of the operation there may be a number of intermediaries between the ultimate customer and ourselves.

- The link with suppliers is often referred to as 'upstream' operations. Equally the link with customers is known as 'downstream'.

- Process design involves the sequence of operations together with the appropriate use of technology involved in transforming products from the design stage into actual goods or services.

- The main methods of production are jobbing, batch, flow and mass production.

- Layout is important as it defines the 'shape' of the operation and the flow of work through the unit.

- The layout of an operation is to do with the physical location and positioning of the transforming resources.

Self-test questions

Numbers in brackets refer to the paragraphs above where your answers can be checked.

1   Define a supply network. (1.14)

2   What are the objectives of downstream management? (1.19)

3   Detail six of the relationship questions asked by Robert Spekman in *Strategic Supplier Selection: Understanding Long-Term Business Relationships*. (1.24)

4   Define 'process design'. (2.1)

5   What factors are considered when developing timetables? (2.6)

6   How does jobbing production differ from batch production? (2.10, 2.13)

7   What criteria must be satisfied by a layout? (3.5)

8   How does a process layout differ from a product layout? (3.10, 3.14)

9   What are the advantages and disadvantages of a fixed position layout? (3.18)

Further reading

- *Operations Management*, Slack, Chambers and Johnston, Chapter 6.

- *Production and Operations Management*, Muhlemann, Oakland and Lockyer, Chapters 11, 12.

Job Design and Work Organisation

Learning objectives and indicative content

3.3   Compare and contrast different approaches to job design.

- Definition of the word job
- The use and techniques of work study and work measurement
- Advantages and disadvantages of the different approaches to job design
- FW Taylor/Gilbreth's work
- Scientific management approach
- Motivational approaches
- Socio-technical systems approach
- Human factors approach
- Empowerment and self-managed systems

Chapter headings

1   Jobs and job design

2   The scientific management approach

3   Motivational approaches

4   The socio-technical systems approach

5   Empowerment and self-managed systems

1 *Jobs and job design*

The importance of job design

1.1 The definition of a job at its simplest level is given by GA Cole in *Personnel Management* as 'a collection of tasks assigned to a position in an organisational structure'.

1.2 The allocation of tasks should be balanced to enable a reasonable workload with a variety of tasks that stimulate the worker. The blending of a natural grouping of tasks into a job may be the result of a rational exercise or as a matter of convenience. If a job is designed as the result of a rational exercise then consideration can be given to the role and content and the job can be designed to suit the needs of the individual and the organisation. If the job is formulated as a matter of convenience then it is likely to be poorly constructed, possibly repetitive and lacking in variety and challenge.

1.3 Davis and Canter, often seen as the developers of the concept of job design, defined the role as follows: 'the organisation (or structuring) of a job to satisfy the technical-organisational requirements of the work and the human requirements of the person performing the work'. Davies's later work identified a number of design issues in structuring jobs.

- Identifying job boundaries
- Identifying the factors at work in jobs
- Determining methods of estimating and controlling these factors
- Developing systematic design methods
- Developing criteria for evaluating designs

1.4 Davis went on to conclude that, in order to achieve more effective performance and greater job satisfaction on the part of the employee, it was necessary for jobs to be 'meaningful' to the individual concerned. This idea has become a dominant feature of modern approaches to job design as the concept of the 'quality of working life'.

1.5 Job design and work organisation can be defined as: 'The specification of the contents, methods and relationships of jobs to satisfy technological and organisational requirements as well as the personal needs of jobholders'. We can look in more detail at the elements of this definition.

- **The specification of the contents**. What is involved in the job? What level of skill or knowledge is required?
- **Methods**. How and where is the work to be organised and carried out?
- **Relationships of jobs**. Where does the job fit into the organisational structure? How much autonomy will the job have?
- **To satisfy technological requirements**. Technology and the use of technology is a prime consideration of organisations. Job design should reflect this.
- **To satisfy organisational requirements**. Organisational requirements will include the type of person, their suitability and how well they meet the expectations of the organisation.
- **The personal needs of jobholders**. This involves consideration of what employees want from a job, what motivates them and what will encourage them to stay.

1.6   Huczynski and Buchanan point out that 'the design of an individual's job determines both the kind of rewards that are available and what the individual has to do to get those rewards'.

1.7   Hackman *et al* have focused on certain core job dimensions that contribute to satisfaction.

- **Skill variety**: the opportunity to exercise different skills and perform different operations, as opposed to micro-specialisation and repetition
- **Task identity**: the integration of operations into a 'whole' task (or meaningful segment of the task), as opposed to task fragmentation
- **Task significance**: the task has a role, purpose, meaning and worth within the organisational and individual value system
- **Autonomy**: the opportunity to exercise discretion or self-management in areas such as target-setting and work methods
- **Feedback**: the availability of information by which the individual can assess his progress and performance in relation to expectations and targets and the opportunity to give feedback and have a voice in performance improvement

1.8   A job which has these core dimensions will lead to the jobholder experiencing the psychological states of experienced meaningfulness and responsibility and will produce work of high quality, will be highly satisfied with work, and will stay in his job and maintain a good attendance record.

1.9   Research by Paul Hill similarly suggests that the psychological requirements of a 'full job' for the individual are as follows.

- The content of the work should be reasonably demanding of the individual (in terms other than sheer endurance) and should have some variety.
- An individual should know what his job is, what are the standards of success and how he is performing in relation to them.
- There should be an opportunity to learn on the job and to continue learning.
- There should be some social support and recognition within the organisation.
- An individual should be able to relate their work and output to the objectives of the company and to their place in the community.
- There should be perceived potential for the job to lead to some sort of desirable future (though this does not necessarily imply promotion).

Division of labour

1.10   Division of labour becomes relevant to job design as soon as the volume of work is enough to employ more than one person. It involves dividing the task into smaller parts that can each be accomplished by a single person.

1.11 This division of work allows for each person to specialise in a certain area. Specialisation brings with it an increase in skills and improvements in efficiency and effectiveness. If the task is relatively straightforward it will be easier to learn. The repetitive nature of the task may allow for technology to be improved to meet the needs. For example, the process can become automated, as on a car production line where each operative traditionally carried out a single repetitive task with the product coming to them on an assembly line.

1.12 Division of labour does have certain disadvantages. It leads to monotony, giving rise to boredom and carelessness in workers. Absenteeism can be high as workers find their role too stifling. The repetition of the work can lead to injury. There is no interaction between the defined roles; this limits the identification of problem areas and does not encourage improvement in processes.

2   The scientific management approach

F W Taylor

2.1 One of the most influential rationales for job design has been the need to achieve optimum output. This is the rationale of 'scientific management' where human work and effort is seen in terms of its relationship to machines and the systems created for them.

2.2 Frederick Winslow Taylor, writing in 1911, expounded principles of **scientific management**. He attempted to impose machine-like disciplines on the work carried out by factory operatives.

2.3 The movement he started, the 'scientific management' movement that reached its peak in America during 1900–1930, has had lasting effects. He was a perfectionist, always looking for the 'one best way'.

2.4 He hated the term 'soldiering', which was the term in those days for workers just doing what the informal workgroup had established as a fair day's work. He was employed as a chief superintendent or consultant in various steel factories, his most successful experience being at Bethlehem Steel, where after two years he achieved a 200% increase in productivity with only a 50% increase in wages. His techniques were as follows.

- To initiate a time study rate system. Taylor would begin by finding the fastest worker in the organisation. He then examined that person's movements on the job, suggested the elimination of unnecessary movements, and took the speediest rate at which this 'first class person' could work and make other workers accountable to it (with minor adjustments for newness at the job, rest periods, and unavoidable delays).

- To create functional foremen. Taylor fought against using the military model in organisations. No manager was to have disciplinary powers. The notion of 'functional' means supervision over some aspect of work, not supervision over people. This notion essentially meant the creation of specialised clerks with oversight over some aspect of the production.

- To establish cost accounting (also known as task management). This approach involves the use of instruction and routing cards and a timekeeping system where workers punched a clock when they finished a job. Labour variance could then be analysed, and management had the reporting tools they needed to identify bottlenecks. Rewards and punishments would be calculated by how the numbers looked on paper.

- To devise a system of pay for the person and not the position. Taylor instituted a system of 'piece rates' where workers or gangs were paid according to output. There were no attempts under Taylorism at job rotation; each worker was expected to specialise in a particular task they did well.

2.5 Taylor's basic principles of job design were as follows.

- All aspects of work should be investigated on a scientific basis to establish the laws, rules and formulae governing the best methods of working.

- An investigative approach to the study of work is necessary to establish what constitutes a 'fair day's work'.

- Managers should act as the planners of work.

- Co-operation between management and workers is based on the 'maximum prosperity' of both.

2.6 His technique was basically as follows.

- Decide on the optimum degree of task fragmentation, breaking down a complex task into its most basic component parts, which would represent the whole 'job' of a worker or group of workers.

- Decide the most efficient way of performing each operation, using work study techniques and time and motion study to determine the simplest way to perform a task, eliminate wasteful motions (physical movements) and set standard times for all operations.

- Train employees to carry out their single task fragment in the most efficient way.

2.7 Jobs were therefore 'micro-designed': reduced to single, repetitive motions. The micro-division of labour was based on a production line organisation of work and offers some efficiencies for this type of work. Each task is so simple and straightforward that it can be learned with very little training. Since skill requirements are low, the effects of absenteeism and labour turnover are minimised, and workers can easily be replaced and redeployed. Tasks are closely defined, standardised and timed so that output quantity and quality are more easily predicted and controlled.

2.8 Taylor suggested that such a system was beneficial to workers as well as management.

'The man who is fit to work at any particular trade is unable to understand the science of that trade without the kindly help and cooperation of men of a totally different type of education… It is one of the principles of scientific management to ask men to do things in the right way, to learn something new, to change their ways in accordance with the science and in return to receive an increase of from 30% to 100% in pay.'

2.9 Two distinct but related fields of study developed from this thinking and will be examined in greater depth later in this chapter. Together these areas are referred to as work study.

- **Method study** focuses on determining the methods and activities that should be involved in jobs.

- **Work measurement** examines the time taken in performing a job or a series of jobs.

Frank and Lillian Gilbreth

2.10 Frank and Lillian Gilbreth analysed 17 basic movements of the hand (all based on the ability to search, grasp, load, select, hold, and transport). They also experimented with different types of factory whistle blasts, suggestion boxes, and intramural programs among employees.

2.11 In their writings from about 1915 through 1920, the Gilbreths begin to talk about 15 to 16 'motion cycles', but rarely named them all and didn't allude to any comprehensive system. Indeed, it was not until the late summer of 1924, following Frank Gilbreth's death, that the 'therblig system' was presented in two articles in *Management and Administration*.

2.12 'Therbligs' are a system for analysing the motions involved in performing a task. The identification of individual motions, as well as moments of delay in the process, was designed to find unnecessary or inefficient motions and to utilise or eliminate even split seconds of wasted time. Frank and Lillian Gilbreth invented and refined this system, roughly between 1908 and 1924. (Therblig is an anagram of Gilbreth.)

2.13 The production systems employing scientific management approaches such as those of Taylor and the Gilbreths led to many improvements in efficiency and productivity at work. However, over time, it became apparent that the repetitive nature of this approach led to factors such as high absenteeism, lateness, poor attention to quality and restrictions in the flexibility of labour.

The use and techniques of work study

2.14 Work study comprises both method study and work measurement.

- Method study is concerned with establishing optimum working methods.
- Work measurement is concerned with establishing time standards for the working methods.

2.15 Method study will usually be carried out first unless there is a need to compare old and new work methods.

2.16 Work study is mainly concerned with human manual work, in particular the efficient design and execution of work and also the development of standards of performance. The principles were laid down by F W Taylor and have been applied, but not without some criticism and updating, over the subsequent years.

2.17 Work study is defined by the British Standards Institution as: 'A generic term for those techniques, particularly method study and work measurement, which are used in the examination of human work in all its contexts, and which lead systematically to the investigation of all the factors which affect the efficiency and economy of the situations being reviewed, in order to effect improvements.'

2.18 The essential aims of work study are as follows.

- To establish the most economical method of doing the work.
- To standardise this method, together with the materials and equipment involved.
- To establish the time required by a qualified or adequately trained worker, while working at a defined level of performance.
- To install this work method as standard practice.

2.19 Work study can be viewed as a comparatively low-cost way of designing work to attain high productivity or improving productivity in existing work by improving existing methods and reducing ineffective or wasted time. Improvements are sought utilising existing equipment and resources. Therefore improvement is not dependent on redesign or restructuring of products, processes or operations.

2.20 The technique is applied in circumstances where a maximum return is anticipated. The evaluation of results, whether they are increases in throughput, better utilisation of equipment or labour, reduction in waste, improvements in safety or a reduction in training time, should outweigh the cost of the investigation.

2.21 Considerations that might be applied include the following.

- The anticipated life of the job
- The contribution manual work makes to the job
- The wage rate for the job
- Utilisation of equipment, machines, tools; the costs involved, and whether the utilisation is dependent on the work method
- The importance of the job to the organisation

2.22 Does the work study exercise relate to existing jobs or to proposed or anticipated jobs? As new products and services are designed or new equipment used, jobs must be designed or re-designed. The question is to what extent work study should be used. One tool that can be applied to assess the factors involved is cost/benefit analysis.

2.23 New products will require operations managers to design and develop effective and efficient processes and procedures from the outset. Existing jobs may be re-evaluated for a number of reasons such as a change in the product or service, new equipment being utilised or changes in the wage structure. Other reasons may come from operational feedback reports or staff that may show poor utilisation, excessive overtime, poor quality or high scrap wastage rates.

Method study

2.24 Method study is 'concerned with the systematic recording and critical examination of existing and proposed ways of doing work, as a means of developing and applying easier and more effective methods and reducing cost' (BSI). Method study, when applied to an existing job, involves seven steps, which can be memorised by the mnemonic SREDDIM: select, record, examine, develop, define, install and implement, maintain. This provides a formal approach to identify and develop solutions in a structured series of steps.

- **Selection of the work to be studied**. The first stage in method study is to select jobs that are appropriate. There are numerous jobs going through an operation at any one time, so the one/s selected must have economic reasons for their selection. Factors that would be considered include return on investment and areas that are causing delays or bottlenecks in an operation where the problems add cost in related areas.

- **Recording the work method**. The objective is to obtain a record of the work method for subsequent evaluation. This is discussed in more detail later.

- **Examine the method**: The purpose of the recording stage is to examine the existing method thoroughly and meticulously with the objective of identifying areas for improvement. The aim is to evaluate the effectiveness of the operation as a whole and to identify where changes (work flow, material, design of the product or service) would be beneficial. This stage is also discussed in more detail below.

- **Develop an improved method**. By this stage there is usually a sound understanding of potential improvement areas. A process improvement formula is applied to each activity of the job. This essentially consists of four steps: eliminate, combine, sequence and simplify. Aspects such as health and safety, ergonomics and the smooth flow of work need to be incorporated to ensure that when the new method is defined and implemented it will operate successfully.

  Often outside consultants are involved at this stage; they can be more objective. The use of a quality circle improvement team can involve the organisation in the process with the eventual aim of taking ownership of the new methods. Workers should be involved in changes through teamworking, suggestion schemes and discussion on change areas.

  New methods should be thought through, planned and tested prior to implementation to ensure that the changes are workable as part of the production system.

- **Define the new method**. It will be necessary to describe the new method in detail for others to install or operate it. The definition is a statement of the new work method and can be referred to in case of any disputes or misunderstandings.

- **Install the new method**. Installation is a 'project management' exercise with initial training followed by a 'learning curve' period, then reappraisal if necessary with a target date for full implementation. New methods, after agreement and costing, must be installed. The installation and implementation will require good change management practices such as openness, discussion and information sharing, as support from all levels within the company is essential. Following successful testing, installation can be made on a phased or a one-off basis. The phased approach enables lessons to be learned but is slower. The one-off approach requires that full testing has been carried out beforehand as complete certainty is required when commencing production.

- **Maintain the new method**. Once the new method is installed a period of maintenance is required. Unnecessary changes should not be permitted but periodic checks should be carried out to see if the method is satisfactory and if anticipated performance objectives are being met. Any introduction of a new system requires different work methods and practices to be employed with every member of the team familiar and conversant with the new approach. New processes must be monitored and measured both by hard data (eg figures such as control charts or measurements for statistical process control) and soft data (eg feedback from operatives).

2.25   When recording the work method (the second of the seven steps in SREDDIM) we must consider both the procedures for obtaining data and the type of record required.

2.26   The procedure by which the information is to be obtained may be direct observation, electronic data capture, video recording or recollection (in the case of the diary being used).

2.27   Whatever method or methods are chosen they are designed either to record the sequence of activities of a job, or to record the path of movement of a job or to record the time interrelationship of the activities involved in the job.

2.28   With regard to the type of record required, a number of different tools can be applied.

- **Diary record**: a record of work method, normally constructed by the worker in the form of a diary or list of activities (BS 3138).

- **Flow diagram**: a diagram or model substantially to scale which shows the location of specific activities carried out and the routes followed by workers, materials or equipment in their execution (BS 3138); also linked to string diagrams and travel charts.

- **Multiple activity chart**: a chart on which the activities of one or more subjects (worker, machine or equipment) are recorded on a common timescale to show their interrelationship (BS 3138).

- **Flow process chart**: a process chart setting out the sequence of the flow of a product or customer, or a procedure, by recording all events under review using the appropriate process chart symbols (BS 3138). Flow process charts are used for material; for worker and material; and for equipment.

2.29   With regard to examination of the data (the third step in SREDDIM) the mnemonic PPSPM is useful during interviews. This stands for purpose, place, sequence, person, means.

- **Purpose**. What is being done? Why is it being done? What else could be done? What should be done?

- **Place**. Where is it being done? Why there? Where else could it be done? Where should it be done?

- **Sequence**. When is it being done? Why then? When else could it be done? When should it be done?

- **Person**. Who does it? Why them? Who else could do it? Who should do it?

- **Means**. How is it done? Why that way? How else can it be done? How should it be done?

2.30   The structuring of questions in this accepted way makes it easier to identify possible alternative or more effective methods particularly when combined with supporting data.

Work measurement

2.31   Work measurement is defined as: 'The application of techniques designed to establish the time for a qualified worker to carry out a specified job at a defined level of performance.' (BS 3138). Work times are of importance to the operations manager as they are invaluable in scheduling and capacity planning where timing is an important planning tool.

2.32   Work cannot be allocated to an individual or a team without an estimate of the time involved. Standard times, once established, can be used to set labour rates, for performance measurement, to determine the effectiveness of equipment and/or to determine standard operating costs. Machine times are relatively easy to measure, but physical human work is more difficult as it will have both a physical and a mental input. The mental input is difficult to measure but good practices can be of benefit.

Time study

2.33   Time study is: 'A work measurement technique for recording the times and rates of working for the elements of a specified job carried out under specified conditions, and for analysing the data, so as to obtain the time necessary for carrying out the job at a defined level of performance.' (BS 3138).

2.34   The aim for work measurement is to determine the time required for a job to be carried out under specified conditions. The recording will require information relating to the worker or workers, machine/s, materials, layout, method, etc. Jobs will consist of a variety of repetitive tasks, occasional elements, interaction with machines, etc. For time study to be applied effectively it is necessary to divide the job being measured into elements.

- To gain a better understanding of the job
- To segment the exercise into manageable chunks
- To permit a more accurate study
- To distinguish between different types of work
- To differentiate 'machine' and 'worker' elements
- To enable time standards to be evaluated
- To enable times for certain common or important elements to be extracted and compared

2.35   A job is observed through a number of cycles. Each element (above) is timed and a subjective rating of the performance of the worker is given. Times are averaged to give the result with consideration being given to the performance of the worker.

2.36   One important aspect of work study is the use and application of the principles of motion economy.

- Effort should not be wasted.
- Tools and materials should be placed as close as possible to the operator.
- Movements should be automatic, if possible.
- People should be supported by machines for holding and lifting tasks.
- Materials handling should be minimised.
- If possible, the operation should be done in multiples.
- Permit position changes.

- Sit, rather than stand.
- Keep movement symmetrical – make work flow.
- Ensure working areas are at the correct height for the operative.
- Where possible use both hands.
- Ensure ease of location of parts and equipment.

2.37 Work measurement has attracted many criticisms. Slack *et al* make the following observations.

- The ideas on which the concept of a standard time is based are impossible to define precisely. How can one possibly give clarity to the definition of qualified workers, or specified jobs, or (especially) a defined level of performance?

- Even if one attempts to follow these definitions, all that results is an excessively rigid job definition. Most modern jobs require some element of flexibility, which is difficult to achieve within rigidly defined jobs.

- Using stopwatches to time human beings is both degrading and usually counterproductive. At best it is intrusive; at worst it makes people into 'objects for study'.

- The rating procedure implicit in time study is subjective and usually arbitrary. It has no basis other than the opinion of the person carrying out the study.

- Time study, especially, is very easy to manipulate. It is possible for employers to 'work back' from a time which is 'required' to achieve a particular cost. Also, experienced staff can 'put on an act' to fool the person recording the times.

3 Motivational approaches

The Hawthorne effect

3.1 The Hawthorne Studies were conducted from 1927 to 1932 at the Western Electric Hawthorne Works in Cicero, Illinois where Harvard Business School professor Elton Mayo set up a series of experiments to examine productivity and work conditions. These experiments started by examining the physical and environmental influences of the workplace (brightness of the lighting, humidity, etc), and later moved into psychological aspects (eg group pressure, working hours, breaks, leadership, etc).

3.2 Preliminary experiments looked at the effect of lighting on productivity. These experiments showed no clear connection between productivity and the amount of illumination but they did cause researchers to question what changes would influence output. Mayo wanted to find out what effect fatigue and monotony had on job productivity and how to control them through such variables as rest beaks, work hours, temperature and humidity. Various experiments were designed incorporating the above factors to differing degrees. In addition, workers were divided into teams for comparison but the significance of team working was also realised when the end results were evaluated.

3.3   Mayo found what he called the **Hawthorne effect**: the response of the workers appeared to be affected by their sense of being a group and of being singled out for attention. 'Management, by consultation with the female workers, by clear explanation of the proposed experiments and the reasons for them, by accepting the workers' verdicts in several instances, unwittingly scored a success in two most important human matters – the women became a self-governing team, and a team that cooperated wholeheartedly with management.'

3.4   The groups, comprising six women in each, were singled out from the rest of the factory workers. This in itself raised their self-esteem. When consulted they felt empowered. The Hawthorne effect has been described as the reward you get when you show attention to people. The mere act of showing people that you are concerned usually spurs them on to better job performance.

3.5   Mayo came to the following conclusions.

- The aptitude of individuals is an imperfect predictor of job performance. Although individual ability is important the output produced is strongly influenced by social factors.

- Informal organisation affects productivity. The researchers found a group life among workers.

- Workgroup norms affect productivity. The group themselves recognised what is 'a fair day's work for a fair day's pay'.

- The workplace is a social system made up of interdependent parts. The worker is a person whose attitudes and effectiveness are conditioned by social demands from both inside and outside the work plant.

- The need for recognition, security and a sense of belonging is more important in determining a worker's morale and productivity than the physical conditions under which they operate.

3.6   According to Huczynski and Buchanan (*Organisational Behaviour*): 'The Hawthorne studies signalled the birth of the human relations school of management'. This was an approach consciously geared to positive human relations at work, and its impact can be seen in many aspects of human resource management today such as empowered teamworking, job design and motivational programmes aimed at offering greater job satisfaction, employee involvement schemes and 'people-friendly' policies employed by some organisations.

Motivation hygiene theory

3.7   Following the Second World War emphasis was placed on the relationship between job and organisation design and productivity. As early as 1950 job rotation and job enlargement were being put forward as a means of overcoming boredom at work with its associated problems.

3.8   During the 1950s and 1960s Frederick Herzberg developed a 'two factor' theory of motivation. He interviewed Pittsburg engineers and accountants to find out what 'critical incidents' had made them feel good or bad about their work.

3.9   In his theory he distinguished between 'motivators' and 'hygiene' factors. The hygiene factors included salary, supervision, company policy and administration. These could cause dissatisfaction if workers were unhappy with them, but could never lead to positive motivation even if perfectly satisfactory. The 'motivators' included achievement, recognition, responsibility, advancement, growth and the work itself. Herzberg highlighted two basic needs of individuals.

- The need to avoid unpleasantness, satisfied by hygiene factors
- The need for personal growth, satisfied at work by motivator factors only

3.10   'When people are dissatisfied with their work it is usually because of discontent with environmental hygiene factors.' These include company policy and administration, salary, style of supervision, interpersonal relations, working conditions and job security. An individual is much more likely to be dissatisfied with his pay, for example, than satisfied with it: he may be temporarily satisfied with a pay rise, but only until he begins to take it for granted or compare it to others.

3.11   Herzberg's two factors highlighted the two types of reward that can be offered to individuals at work.

- **Intrinsic rewards** arise from the work itself, and (in a sense) from within the worker: challenge, interest, team identity, pride in the organisation, the satisfaction of achievement and so on.
- **Extrinsic rewards** do not arise from the work itself, but are within the power of others (typically management) to award or withhold: wages or salary, bonuses, prizes, promotion, improved working conditions and so on.

3.12   From his theory Herzberg developed a set of principles for the enrichment of jobs.

- Removing some controls while retaining accountability
- Increasing personal accountability for work
- Assigning each worker a complete unit of work with a clear start and end date
- Granting additional authority and freedom to workers
- Making periodic reports directly available to workers rather than to supervisors only
- The introduction of new and more difficult tasks into the job
- Encouraging the development of expertise by assigning individuals to specialised tasks

3.13   Job enrichment aims to create greater opportunities for individual achievement and recognition by expanding the task to increase not only variety but also the responsibility and accountability of the individual.

Vroom's expectancy theory

3.14   Expectancy theory basically states that the strength of an individual's motivation to do something will depend on the extent to which he expects the results of his efforts to contribute to his personal needs or goals. Victor Vroom worked out a formula by which human motivation could be assessed and measured, based on expectancy theory.

He suggested that the strength of an individual's motivation is the product of two factors.

- The strength of his preference for a certain outcome. Vroom called this 'valence': it can be represented as a positive or negative number or zero – since outcomes may be desired, avoided or regarded with indifference.

- His expectation that the outcome will in fact result from a certain behaviour. Vroom called this 'subjective probability'. As a probability, it may be represented by any number between 0 (no chance) and 1 (certainty).

3.15 In its simplest form, the expectancy equation may be stated as follows.

$$F = V \times E$$

Where:

F = the force or strength of the individual's motivation to behave in a particular way
V = valence: the strength of the individual's preference for a given outcome or reward
E = expectancy: the individual's perception that the behaviour will result in the outcome/reward

3.16 In this equation, the lower the values of valence or expectation, the less the individual's motivation. An employee may have a high expectation that increased productivity will result in promotion but if he is indifferent or negative towards the idea of promotion he will not be motivated to increase productivity. The same would be true if promotion was of high importance to him but he did not believe higher productivity would get him promoted.

3.17 Expectancy theory can be used to measure the likely strength of a worker's motivation to act in a desired way in response to a range of different rewards, so as to find the most effective motivational strategy.

The Porter and Lawler model

3.18 Porter and Lawler developed a more comprehensive model of motivation which they applied primarily to managers. The model suggests that the amount of effort exerted depends on the value of a reward to the individual plus the amount of energy the individual believes is required to earn the reward, and the perceived likelihood of his receiving it. The last two factors are, in turn, influenced by a number of factors, such as actual rewards received for past performance.

Figure 6.1 *The Porter-Lawler model of motivation*

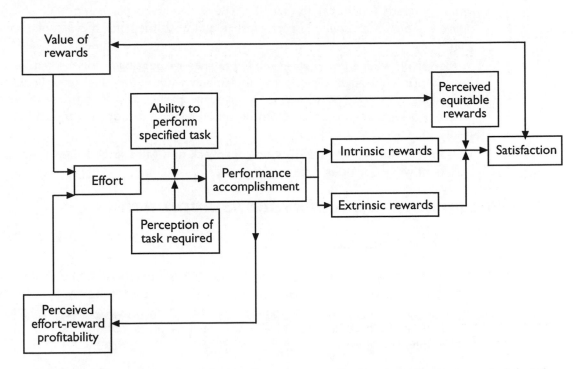

3.19   Actual performance in the job is affected not only by the effort expended by the individual, but also by his understanding of the task and the extent of his ability to perform it. The individual's perception of whether or not the extrinsic rewards for performance levels (such as pay) are equitable will affect satisfaction in the job. At the same time, the intrinsic reward of satisfaction in the job will affect perception of whether the extrinsic rewards are equitable. This model uses a contingency approach to motivation. Managers should develop a balanced offering of intrinsic and extrinsic rewards for performance, with recognition that:

- Motivation is not the sole influence on performance: team members need to be trained to perform the task and must be given a clear understanding of what is expected.

- Motivation depends on the subjective perceptions of team members as to the value of rewards, the perceived effort-reward link and the equity of the rewards offered.

The job characteristics theory

3.20   The job characteristics theory considers the motivational aspect of job design and in some ways builds on motivation hygiene theory. The core job is regarded as critical because it leads to personal and work motivation. Under the theory, job design should encompass five main job dimensions.

- **Skill variety**: to the extent that the worker needs to utilise a manageable variety of skills to effectively perform the job.

- **Task identity**: where the worker is involved as early as possible in the process through to as late as possible. This gives more 'ownership' of the process to the worker, making the role more meaningful.

- **Task significance**: where the worker's role is regarded as critical as a contributor to the success of other jobs in the function (eg when involved in group work or cross-functional teamwork). The worker will place more emphasis on delivering personal quality in performance and both they and the organisation will gain.

- **Autonomy**: where the worker will experience responsibility for the outcomes of their work. Although difficult to implement when operating to schedules or timetables, the area of autonomy is growing, particularly in high-tech areas or where workers are operating from home or remote locations, although it is not restricted to just those areas.

- **Feedback**: the worker receives task feedback and gains knowledge of the actual results of work activities.

4 The socio-technical systems approach

Evolution of the new approach

4.1 The 1960s saw a move away from the idea of jobs as basic organisational units in a work system towards a wider view that saw jobs as part of a socio-technical system. Within a socio-technical systems approach management chose the most appropriate configuration of social resources (people) and technical resources (machines, computers, etc) to meet sets of conditions at a given time.

4.2 Socio-technical systems theory, according to Davis and Trist, has two major assumptions.

- That in any work system output is achieved through the joint operation of social as well as technical systems

- That every socio-technical system is affected by the culture and values of its environment

4.3 The 'social system' (people, teams, relationships and roles) embraces both formal and informal groups such as official teams and unofficial groups based on friendship, interests etc. The 'technical system' encompasses tasks, processes, production and computer equipment.

4.4 The socio-technical approach differs from the scientific management approach in that the latter was built around machines that people have to design their work around The socio-technical approach offers the perspective that we do not have to build jobs around machines or computers. We have the alternative of assuming that machine or computer-based systems can be adapted to meet the needs of human beings.

4.5 The approaches to job design have largely been focused on the individual job. In reaction to this the socio-technical systems approach slowly evolved. The approach concentrates on the 'working group' and the objective is to develop a match between the needs of the group and the organisation in relation to technology.

4.6 The approach is based on the concept of the organisation as an open system with the workgroup as a subsystem of the total organisation. This view is of particular relevance to operations management because much of the thinking around this business area relates to how to optimise operations management potential in the current environment.

4.7 The approach views organisations as similar to living systems such as biological cells in that they are engaged in active transactions with the environment. Raw materials or customers form the inputs into the organisation and finished goods and services form the output. The environment will exert pressure in different ways (through competition, the influence of suppliers and customers and legislation etc). Changing economic situations, changing values in society, new products or services and numerous other factors require the organisation to adapt if it is to survive.

4.8 As these factors impact on the internal design and functioning of an organisation it is important that the organisation is aware of environmental changes when seeking to design its social and technical systems.

4.9 The socio-technical approach to designing organisations is built around the following set of guiding propositions.

- The design of the system must fit its goals.

- Employees must be actively involved in designing the structure of the organisation.

- Control of variances in production or service must be undertaken as close to their source as possible.

- Subsystems must be designed around relatively self-contained and recognisable units of work.

- Support systems must match the design requirements of the organisation.

- The design should allow for a high quality of working life.

- Changes should be made as required to meet changing environmental pressures.

4.10 Individual jobs are redesigned following consultation with those involved with the objective of combining the needs of the worker with both the technical and group working needs of the organisation. This redesign may need to be a continuous process.

4.11 It has been suggested that within this environment four categories of job characteristic are significant in terms of motivation and performance.

- Responsible autonomy, including the group's acceptance of responsibility, self-regulation, self-evaluation and self-adjustment to cope with changes

- Adaptability to a number of changes and unforeseen events. The group (perhaps a cross-functional team) requires a mix of skills with a certain amount of fluidity between members in order to meet changing situations

- Variety of tasks in order to build a wider skills base

- Participation in team/group working as a business fundamental

4.12 The socio-technical systems approach does have its limitations. The concept of autonomous work groups and/or cross-functional teamwork has not gained widespread acceptance as yet. Focusing on the group and not the individual may not meet individual needs appropriately enough.

4.13 Other areas have also been highlighted.

- The roles of both supervisory staff and specialist advisors may be affected or eliminated.

- Movement of personnel between work groups with high levels of autonomy may be difficult, reducing management flexibility.

- Difficulties can be experienced in implementing socio-technical systems in existing work situations.

- The concept of a participative design process may not be acceptable or may prove too time consuming for the organisation.

- Management may be unprepared to take the risk of radically different approaches to organising work. Cross-functional teamwork is fast growing in acceptance. Structuring the entire organisation into formalised group working will take longer.

Activation theory

4.14 This theory is based on the idea that to maintain productivity work must offer challenge and variety. In essence, it requires the jobholder to be 'active'.

4.15 The activation theory puts forward three principal proposals to enhance the job.

- **Job enrichment**: increasing the workers' roles and responsibilities but not necessarily their volume of work.

- **Job enlargement**: increasing the number of tasks in a given role. There is however an onus on management to ensure this enlargement is manageable by the individual.

- **Job rotation**: where applicable, moving workers between jobs to provide better variety and to develop a wider range of skills.

4.16 Results of the activation theory have been mixed. While some workers embrace and are motivated by this approach others prefer a more predictable regime and tasks.

5   *Empowerment and self-managed systems*

The nature of empowerment

5.1   Considering the points we have discussed to date, what attributes of jobs contribute to the motivation of employees and can be further developed into principles for the design of jobs? Some of the following factors appear particularly relevant.

- An optimum level of variety
- An appropriate degree of repetitiveness
- An optimum level of responsibility for decisions where a degree of discretion is present
- Employee's control over their own job
- The presence of goals and regular feedback
- A perceived contribution to a socially useful product or service
- Opportunities for developing social aspects
- Opportunities for team-working

- Perceived skills
- Empowerment is one way that can be used to help achieve many of these factors.

5.2 The following are definitions of the term 'empowerment' given by a number of leading human resource practitioners.

- 'What (companies) mean by empowerment varies dramatically ... Many of them are really talking about firing middle management. But companies which are really serious are talking about an orderly distribution of power and authority.'
- 'It means people using their own judgement in the interests of the organisation and the customer within a disciplined context.'
- 'The purpose of empowerment is to free someone from rigorous control by instructions and orders and give them freedom to take responsibility for their ideas and actions, to release hidden resources which would otherwise remain inaccessible.'

5.3 Empowerment has two key aspects. It involves giving workers discretion to make decisions about how to organise work in order to achieve task goals and making workers responsible for achieving production and quality targets.

5.4 Empowerment is essentially a process of decentralising control over business units, or devolving/delegating responsibility, or removing levels in the organisation to increase flexibility and initiative.

Benefits of empowerment

5.5 The argument is that empowerment (like job enrichment) is satisfying to the worker. It offers opportunities for employees to satisfy their 'higher order' needs through the work itself, by giving greater scope, challenge, interest and significance to the job.

5.6 Empowerment is also intended to enhance organisational effectiveness. It increases employee commitment and harnesses their creativity and initiative. It shortens the lines of communication and decision-making at the interface of the organisation with customers and suppliers, facilitating responsiveness.

5.7 Empowerment also takes advantage of front-line experience and expertise. 'The people lower down the organisation possess the knowledge of what is going wrong with a process but lack the authority to make changes. Those further up the structure have the authority to make changes, but lack the profound knowledge required to identify the right solutions. The only solution is to change the culture of the organisation so that everyone can become involved in the process of improvement and work together to make the changes' (Max Hand, *Management Accounting*).

5.8 Arguments against empowerment include the following.

- Empowering staff implies a loss of control. Discretion is being given to individuals who are unaccustomed to taking business decisions.
- Centralised control offers advantages of whole-organisation perspective and consistency of performance between subunits. Empowerment may lead to disintegration and inconsistent quality, as units focus on their own objectives.
- Not all employees want empowerment. They may view extra responsibility with suspicion, or may simply feel insecure about the erosion of traditional methods of working.

- Empowerment can be perceived as an attempt to manipulate employees into giving commitment – without giving them general control.

- If people feel they are being asked to take on more responsibility, they will expect to be paid more. Empowerment may be an expensive approach to motivation, rather than a 'substitute' for monetary reward.

Group working

5.9   It may be advisable to focus on work groups and activities rather than on the needs of individuals. Group working can clearly bring benefits to the individual but these go beyond the social aspects and into a wider range of skills requirements that some individuals may relate to more than others.

5.10   A specification of objectives for the group is essential with the group leader and/or task performer often setting goals. This should allow for greater commitment and flexibility within the work system and allow for the personal development of team members. Guidelines for effective teams include the following.

- Groups should number no fewer than four and no more than twenty.
- The group should have a designated leader who has responsibility for performance.
- The group should be assigned tasks that make up a complete unit of work.
- Group members should as much as possible plan their own work.
- Group members should then be involved in evaluation of both their work and the group's work overall.

5.11   Job design is of particular importance to operations managers as operations will usually contain most of the organisation's human resources. It has a particular importance as job design defines how people go about their working lives, shapes their expectations and influences their contribution. It is a major contributory factor in developing the organisation's culture – the shared values and beliefs that underpin an organisation.

Chapter summary

- The role of the operations manager will involve interaction with all levels of employees within the organisation.

- The division of work allows for one person to specialise in a certain area and that specialisation brings with it an increase in skills and improvements in efficiency and effectiveness.

- Scientific management is often categorised as 'the worker as a machine' as it applies strict work management principles that imposed a machine-like aspect on the role of workers.

- The Hawthorne effect has been described as the reward you get when you show attention to people

- Job enrichment aims to create greater opportunities for individual achievement and recognition by expanding the task to increase not only variety but also the responsibility and accountability of the individual.

- As with the activation theory, the job characteristics approach is not universally successful. It appears to suit certain individuals more than others and may be more suited to certain organisations than to others.

- Job design is of particular importance to operations managers as operations will usually contain most of the organisation's human resources.

- Work study is mainly concerned with human manual work, in particular the efficient design and execution of work and also the development of standards of performance.

- Work study consists of two aspects: method study (concerned with establishing optimum working methods), and work measurement (concerned with establishing time standards for the methods).

Self-test questions

Numbers in brackets refer to the paragraphs above where your answers can be checked.

1   Define a job. (1.1)

2   Define job design and work organisation. (1.5)

3   What were Taylor's basic principles of job design? (2.5)

4   What are the essential aims of work study? (2.21)

5   What are the principles of motion economy? (2.36)

6   What conclusions did Mayo come to following the Hawthorne Studies? (3.5)

7   In job characteristics theory, job design should encompass which five main job dimensions? (3.20)

8   According to Davis and Trist socio-technical systems theory has two major assumptions. What are they? (4.2)

9   What are the two key aspects of empowerment? (5.3)

Further reading

- *Operations Management*, Slack, Chambers and Johnston, Chapter 8.

- *Production and Operations Management*, Muhlemann, Oakland and Lockyer, Chapter 17.

- *Production and Operations Management*, Ray Wild, Chapters 7 and 8.

CHAPTER 7

The Planning and Control of Resources

Learning objectives and indicative content

1.3   Compare the different characteristics of products and service operations and analyse how they impact on operations management practice.

- Capacity management

4.1   Explain the objectives for operations planning and control (OPC) and the actions necessary to control operations.

- Definitions of OPC
- The different stages of OPC
- Definition of capacity
- Strategic capacity planning
- Measuring capacity
- Smoothing capacity
- Capacity calculations

Chapter headings

1   Operations planning and control

2   The planning and management of capacity

3   Loading, scheduling and sequencing

1   Operations planning and control

Defining planning and control

1.1   The central role of operations management is the transformation process. Enabling the transformation process to operate to its most effective level requires a high degree of planning and control of an organisation's activities. The role of planning and control in operations is to manage the continuing operational activities while still satisfying customer demand.

1.2   Planning can be defined as 'the setting of the intention for what is supposed to happen' while control is 'the process of coping with changes in variables' (Slack *et al*). Control is the practical actions that can be taken to bring the plan back on track. To accomplish this requires that options are available such as additional shift work, outsourced manufacture or temporary staff etc. Without practical options control cannot be exercised.

1.3   The plan is a mechanism enabling management to visualise the future and to evaluate whether it has sufficient critical resources (resources that could limit the organisation's ability to accept orders now or in the future). All organisations face cost constraints and no organisation has infinite resources. Planning and control decisions must be made about the effective deployment of those resources.

1.4   A plan is a description of what is intended to happen. Clearly drawing up this plan can be a difficult and complex process and it is an area of business that occupies a considerable amount of management time. A plan is a set of expectations based on the aims of corporate strategy and placed into an operational context in order to deliver those expectations.

SMART objectives

1.5   An operational plan will involve setting a number of objectives to ensure that the plan has been met. An objective is something you want to achieve and will often be outlined using the SMART framework.

- **Specific**. Objectives should be succinct, precise and understandable.

- **Measurable**. Objectives should clearly state tangible targets that can be measured in the future. The targets should be compatible with both internal and external constraint factors and be flexible enough to react to a change situation.

- **Achievable**. Objectives should be challenging but also achievable. They should act as a motivational spur.

- **Realistic**. Objectives should be based on sound market research and analysis. The plan should be agreed, understood and accepted by all those concerned as a practical and workable way forward.

- **Timebound**. A timescale should be established against the achievement of each objective in order that project or cross-functional teams are aware of the need for completion by a certain date.

1.6   The strength of SMART objectives is that they are simple to understand, quantifiable and in consequence easier to measure, monitor and control.

The time frames of OPC

1.7   Planning and control within operations will exist over three (often overlapping) time frames.

- Long-term planning and control will often have a primarily financial perspective. Long-term planning is by necessity based on forecasts about future developments and events and as such will be based on many assumptions that may or may not occur as predicted. The longer the forecasting timeframe the more difficult it is to attain accuracy.

- Medium-term planning and control will involve addressing issues in order to bring long-term planning back on track or modifying it to meet a changed or changing situation. It involves setting targets and objectives that form the basis for many aspects of operations management. Planning at this level also requires taking a future perspective and, as a result, contingency planning (a 'what if?' scenario) can be considered ahead of time if it is felt that a planning assumption or situation change may impact on the plans in place. Contingency plans offer the organisation a considered and prompt response in case of planning changes.

- Short-term planning and control is usually at the weekly or daily operational planning and control level and is often about responding quickly to operational or unforeseen problems and rectifying and remedying them in order to meet both medium-term and long-term plans and controls.

1.8 Ray Wild defines operations planning as 'concerned with the determination, acquisition and arrangement of all the facilities necessary for future operations'. Planning involves matching the supply of an operation's products and services with the expected demand for them and putting in place the infrastructure to enable delivery.

- **Determination**: involves effective forecasting and/or demand management techniques to accurately predict future requirements, the planning of capacity availability, and scheduling of that capacity to meet and effectively deliver those requirements.

- **Acquisition**: resources will need to be available to meet the planned requirements. Acquisition may refer not only to owned, leased or hired machinery but also (by extension) to outsourced areas of an organisation's operational requirement (storage, maintenance, security etc), where the skills or availability of services are acquired in order to deliver the objective.

- **Arrangement**: the design of the operation determines the capability. Planning serves to determine what the operation actually does and how it does it.

- **Future operations**: the definition also considers the ability to be flexible and have adequate facilities to meet the future operational needs either in-house or by effectively outsourcing the requirement.

Aggregate sales and operations planning

1.9 Strategic plans are established in advance of operations. In the case of production these plans form the basis for deciding operational requirements in terms of machinery, capacity, layout etc that will be needed to meet the strategic objectives. Aggregate plans and operations planning seek to bring those advance strategic decisions in line with the actual requirements for manufacture.

1.10 Aggregate planning will include the forecast demand and the capacity. Aggregate planning looks at the long- to medium-term production need and how this need is to be met. Aggregate planning will examine areas that allow the more short-term materials and capacity requirements planning to be implemented more effectively. Questions considered at this level include the following.

- Should areas of manufacturing be outsourced or subcontracted?
- Should production levels be kept constant or respond to demand?
- Should stock be used to alleviate fluctuations in demand (ie produce excess stock in periods of low demand and use stock in periods of high demand)?
- How can work patterns be changed to respond to changing demand?
- Can the size and skills of the workforce be changed with demand?
- Can demand be smoothed?
- What level of customer service, in terms of orders correctly fulfilled at the projected time, is the target?

Actions necessary to control operations

1.11 Wild goes on to define operations control as 'concerned with the implementation of a predetermined operations plan or policy and the control of all aspects of operations according to such a plan or policy'.

1.12 Control means ensuring that the plan is on track and coping with unforeseen circumstances as they arise; remedying them and bringing the plan back on track. Control is the process where plans are modified or adapted so that they can still meet their objectives, even though the initial assumptions made when drawing up the plan may no longer be valid.

1.13 Tocher (as quoted in Muhlemann, Oakland and Lockyer) gives four conditions that are necessary for the existence of a control function.

- There must be a specified set of times at which a choice of action is possible.
- At each time there must be a specified set of actions from which to choose.
- A model must exist which can predict the future of the system under every possible choice.
- There must be a criterion or objective on which a choice of action is based by a comparison of predicted behaviour of the system with the objective.

1.14 An evaluation of possible actions should be made and their outcomes assessed. Control can only be applied if a choice can be made.

1.15 Operations control systems are highly dependent on information. The flow of goods into, through and out of the organisation can all be monitored by the use of IT. Where the physical movement of goods is controlled through linking ordering, delivery, storage, internal transport, transformation, end storage, despatch and delivery to the customer, the control is exerted by the recording, measuring and monitoring of the effectiveness of this movement.

1.16 The flow is predominantly monitored through the inventory management system and the activity scheduling system. These should interface effectively to give a smooth 'information flow' of operations information.

1.17 Control systems require definition of the requirement or objectives, the adequate level of detail and information, the ability to choose options and a system that can identify and react to issues. The majority of operational control systems are 'closed systems' (in that outputs feed back into the system) where outputs are monitored in order that control may be exercised. The system must be able to record output, compare actuals with intended results and highlight to operations managers any areas of discrepancy that require action to be taken.

1.18 Operations planning and operations control are closely linked and highly dependent on each other. Planning can be seen as a course of action undertaken prior to the commencement of operations while control occurs during and immediately after production.

Stages in operations planning and control

1.19 Wild details the main stages in operations planning and control and identifies the area of responsibility of capacity management that will be examined further in the following section.

- **Demand estimation or measurement.** An essential requirement of planning is a statement of the demand to be met. This will require accurate forecasting and/or demand management to ensure a high degree of correlation between estimates and actuals.

- **Aggregate capacity planning.** The objective of aggregate capacity planning is to develop a medium- to long-term plan examining the facilities and resources needed in order to satisfy anticipated demand. The term aggregate in capacity terms is concerned with the total demand.

- **Master operations schedule.** The master operations schedule develops in response to the aggregate capacity plan and is a breakdown of the main operations required for each expected item of demand. The master operations schedule translates the aggregate capacity plan into a workable operations format.

- **Rough-cut capacity planning:** involves the analysis of the master operations schedule in order to identify time-phased capacity requirements. Rough-cut capacity planning concentrates on the abilities of operations and resources to meet anticipated capacity requirements. It serves as a method of testing the master operations schedule and its ability to meet the demands expected of it.

- **Detailed operations schedule.** If the master operations schedule proves robust following the application of rough-cut capacity planning the next requirement is the development of a detailed, time-phased operational schedule that can be translated into actual production.

- **Short-term rescheduling and prioritising and control.** An essential feature of any operations schedule is the ability to be flexible as capacity demands change. The operations control system will monitor the changes and update the detailed operations schedule as appropriate.

1.20 For OPC to be effective the plan must lie within reach of the operation (ie it must be workable). The role of the control aspect is to ensure that the requirements of the plan are met.

2 *The planning and management of capacity*

Forecasting demand

2.1 Capacity management involves matching the operating system with the demand placed on the system. Capacity management is a key requirement of operations management as all other operations plans and actions are dependent on the availability of capacity. Capacity is the ability to produce work in a given time.

2.2 Effective system capacity and system efficiency are measures of an organisation's ability to meet customer requirements.

2.3   Capacity management requires medium- and long-term forecasts in order to plan ahead. Resources must be in place to meet anticipated demand. However, forecasts may be unreliable. Concentrated effort must be invested to ensure that forecasts are based on sound business projections and are as accurate as circumstances permit. Investment and related decisions will be made on the basis of these forecasts so they will need to be updated as appropriate.

2.4   The design of operations networks is highly dependent on the accuracy of long-term forecasts. Strategic decisions are made about the long-term direction of the organisation and it is the role of the operations function to enable the strategic goals to be met.

2.5   Accurate long-term forecasts are essential to operations management as they dictate the manufacturing or service provision requirement that needs to be met. The development of long-term operational plans is based on the organisation's strategic plan. Operations managers must then make decisions relating to resources, system design and capacity management strategies in order to deliver the projected requirement in the most effective and efficient manner.

2.6   Demand is difficult to predict, particularly over the longer term. However, decisions made at this stage (including capacity decisions) will have a major impact on an organisation's ability to meet the demands placed on it in the future.

2.7   Capacity to meet that demand establishes a limit on possible productivity. The organisation will evaluate possible strategic options (at this stage, as well as at the later operational stage) such as outsourcing, subcontracting, partnering, co-destiny business relationships, joint ventures, increased horizontal and/or vertical integration. These options may limit the investment required or introduce gains in cost sharing, technological input or wider market spread that may enhance the organisation's strategic and operational capability.

2.8   Forecasting has an important role to play at all levels of operations management. Accurate strategic forecasting allows for investment and related decisions to be taken with a degree of certainty. For the operations manager this confidence in strategic forecasts can translate into a more effective and efficient system as considered long-term decisions have been made and are implemented within an appropriate timeframe.

2.9   Unfortunately this is not often the case. Strategic forecasting involves a number of assumptions relating to competitors, prices, availability of supplies, the economic environment and a host of other related factors, all of which are subject to change. Forecasting is a continuous process where changes are common. The key is that updates are passed to those concerned in order that remedial action can be considered and taken as appropriate.

Measuring capacity

2.10   Muhlemann, Oakland and Lockyer distinguish between three different capacity levels.

- **Potential capacity**: is the capacity that can be made available within the time frame detailed in the strategic plan. This aspect requires accurate forecasting linked to a resource analysis that will allow for plans to be developed in order that anticipated demand will be met.

- **Immediate capacity**: is the capacity available within the current budget period. Immediate capacity is constrained by a number of factors such as the availability of cash, manpower, skills and equipment; the ability to outsource or subcontract; and the technical complexity of the task and the number of tasks. Muhlemann, Oakland and Lockyer give a simple example: the capacity of a restaurant is limited by the size of the eating area, or the number of tables.

- **Effective capacity**: is the capacity used during the existing budget period. Effective capacity measures the effectiveness of the ongoing operation and can be influenced by a range of factors such as technical abilities in the planning stages, implementation of activities, flexibility and skills of the workforce, and purchasing, outsourcing and subcontracting skills.

2.11   Capacity planning and control decisions require operations managers to take a sequential approach to assessing their ability to meet demand. As forecasts will largely prove inaccurate to differing degrees the role of the operations manager is to work within the existing operational framework to deliver the organisation's requirement.

2.12   The stages in capacity planning and control are as follows.

- Measure aggregate or overall demand and capacity over a specific timeframe (units produced, revenue received or tonnes produced).

- Identify alternatives or changes that can be made to capacity plans.

- Choose the most appropriate capacity plan.

2.13   The decisions taken by operations managers when developing capacity plans will affect different aspects of performance. Slack *et al* list the following considerations.

- **Costs**: will be affected by the trade-off between capacity and demand. Under-utilisation of capacity will be reflected in higher unit costs.

- **Revenues**: require the trade-off to be considered in the opposite way. High capacity should result in a commensurate revenue yield.

- **Working capital**: will be affected by the approach to inventory control. If the organisation effectively implements systems such as MRP, MRP II, JIT etc then capital held in stock can be kept to a workable minimum.

- **Quality**: of both goods and services may be affected by peaks and troughs in demand. As an example concentration could be placed on quantity manufactured at the cost of quality.

- **Speed of response**: can be aided by holding additional inventory or finished goods but at the cost of working capital tied up.

- **Dependability**: will be affected by an organisation operating to maximum capacity as it may be more prone to suffer from the effects of disruptions to the production schedule.

- **Flexibility**: is enhanced by surplus capacity. If demand and capacity are balanced or demand is exceeding capacity then it is more difficult to have a level of flexibility.

2.14 Time may be a constraint on capacity management where a customer has a specific delivery date. In this situation operations managers may 'plan backwards', ie they allocate the final stage of the production operation to the period where delivery is required, and this is then passed down the production process stages in reverse of normal practice. This process identifies whether there is adequate time to meet the production demands or whether capacity needs to be increased on a temporary basis if available.

System efficiency

2.15 Capacity, being the ability to produce work in a given time, is measured in the **unit of work**. For example, a factory that has a capacity of 10,000 'machine hours' in each 40-hour week should be capable of producing 10,000 'standard hours of work' during a 40-hour week. Whether the factory can actually produce this will depend on several factors.

- The amount of work involved in the production (does it require 1, 3, 9 standard hours?)

- What time is required in production (including set-up time and maintenance)?

- The design and productivity of the factory and its effectiveness at delivering operational requirements.

2.16 The nature and mix of most operations makes measuring capacity difficult. It is only where the product or service repeats that it is relatively easy to measure. Mass production (where items repeat in a similar manufacturing format) allows for accurate measurement; however, when a variety of items are manufactured then the task becomes more complex.

2.17 The variety of products means that machines have to be changed or reconfigured, maintenance may need to be carried out during any changeover and the machines may not be totally compatible with each other (for example, the output quantity in a given hour may be different). Quantities produced may be smaller, losing the gains that could be made from lengthy production runs. Measurement is consequently more involved with a greater number of variables.

2.18 Goldratt and Fox put forward the argument that the capacity of the system is governed by its weakest link, ie the bottleneck. If Machine 1 produces 500 units an hour while Machine 2 (that refines the output from Machine 1) works at 400 units per hour, the true capacity is 400 units per hour despite the higher efficiency of Machine 1.

2.19 A high level of control must be exercised by operations managers in order that bottlenecks do not occur. Differing production rates cause additional problems such as temporary storage, reduction in the effectiveness of capital employed and an overall reduction in the efficiency of the transformation operation.

2.20   The capacity of an operation that was envisaged at the design stage may not be evident in practice. Capacity planning may look at the theoretical design capacity but the practical capacity may be different. Different products than anticipated, machine breakdowns, maintenance and bottlenecks all reduce the capacity of the operation. The term **effective capacity** is often used to give a true picture of the production capability of an operation.

2.21   The late 1970s and early 1980s saw a rapid period of growth in capacity planning tools. The use of computers allowed the integration of purchasing, inventory management and production/operations to a degree that had not been possible before. Systems such as materials requirements planning (MRP) allow for this integrated approach to go ahead and also incorporate forecasts as well as actual orders on hand.

2.22   Such systems allow for production scheduling and capacity management to be linked with the operations that supply to it in such a way as to minimise inventory and have stock on hand when required for the transformation process – in essence, matching inputs with outputs. The benefit for capacity management is an increased degree of predictability that allows operations managers to plan ahead and by doing that to maximise capacity.

Adjusting capacity

2.23   Adjusting capacity is usually a consideration when the operation cannot meet the demands being placed on it. These issues are often considered at a strategic level when the need for a production operation is being justified and are built in to the strategic and operational plans. Often though, this is not the case. Some of the methods open to operations managers are as follows.

- **Increasing operating times**: change from a two-shift to a three-shift system (eg instead of operating two eight-hour shifts increase to three eight-hour shifts). This is easier said than done. In practice the workforce may object, residents nearby may object and trade unions may object. If, however, this approach can be implemented it will often increase the effectiveness of the operation by maximising existing resources.

- **Overtime**: this is often the most responsive method of increasing capacity. The extension of the working day allows labour to be available when required to meet increased capacity requirements.

- **Use of part-time staff**: by hiring temporary staff at peak times. Operational issues such as insufficient training, security clearance and third-party costs (using an agency) may arise. This approach is coming under increased scrutiny as organisations consider their stance on corporate social responsibility issues and evaluate whether this 'hire and fire' approach is ethically correct in today's business environment.

- **Subcontracting**: if considered during the strategic stage the organisation may have established long-term links with subcontractors. The subcontracting issue is often an operational concern. There are often issues regarding the profit margin of the subcontractor, quality standards and ethical and environmental concerns that must all be fully considered before entering into any contractual business relationship of this type.

Measurement

2.24 Measurement must be in an accepted and meaningful format to the operation. In the example above there is the input measure of capacity (machine hours available) and the output measure of capacity (the number of units manufactured in a given time period).

2.25 Complexity with **inputs** and **outputs** will often mean that operations will choose to use one only as a main measure. In the above example, colleges can categorise inputs as the number of students who enrolled compared to the number who successfully passed.

2.26 With hospitals it is more complex. **Inputs** could be the number of patients requiring treatment, but consideration should be given to the **level** of treatment required. Outputs depend on the variety of services offered by the hospital. If the hospital specialises in a certain area then more meaningful measurements can be obtained, while if it offers a general mixed service output figures may mean little.

2.27 With colleges there is the problem of the academic level of students, the past academic record and the commitment of each student. Social considerations are relevant (eg would you expect a higher retention rate in an inner city college or a small-town college?) When benchmarking performance measures against other colleges are you comparing like with like?

Capacity management strategies

2.28 Capacity management is concerned with ensuring that the capacity of the operation matches the evolving demands of the business in the most effective and time efficient manner. The aim of capacity management is to balance various factors.

- **Cost and capacity**: to ensure that any processing capacity purchased is justifiable in terms of both business need and the efficient use of resources.
- **Supply against demand**: making sure that the availability of goods or services matches the demands made on the business.

2.29 Capacity management deals with the identification of present and future business requirements in order to ensure that demand needs are met cost effectively.

2.30 There are two main strategies for capacity management.

- **Capacity leading demand**: here capacity is designed to be able to produce more goods or services than the forecast demand. The operation should then have enough capacity to meet anticipated demand. This ensures that revenue is maximised and that customer satisfaction standards are high. This approach also means that the operation will operate with a certain amount of 'slack' built in to meet increases in demand and as a result the utilisation of the operational capability may be low.
- **Capacity lagging demand**: here capacity will not meet the demand anticipated of it. This ensures that resources will have a high degree of utilisation but may still be insufficient to meet anticipated demand, causing customer dissatisfaction.

Smoothing capacity

2.31 Where possible organisations will endeavour to have demand fluctuations smoothed out or eliminated altogether. There are various techniques to achieve this.

2.32 Offering inducements to customers (such as price reductions, additional quantities etc) may advance demand. Although profit margins may be affected, the exercise may be cost effective as the operation keeps running and the product being manufactured may offer the least reduction in profit margin.

2.33 Encouraging customers to wait for completion of their orders will clearly affect customer service levels and the reputation of the organisation and requires careful handling and management.

2.34 Subcontracted manufacture may be utilised to meet peaks in demand. However, the process is time-intensive for operations management, as contractual agreements will be entered into, specifications agreed and quality standards established and monitored among a range of other related issues.

2.35 Spare capacity may be used to build up stock that can be used or sold at a later date. Finished stock bears not only the delivery price of the component parts but also the cost of the transformation process that goes into the finished item. Holding finished inventory ties up capital and also a major risk is that the stock may deteriorate or become obsolete.

2.36 Reducing downtime of machines by preventive maintenance can minimise problems caused by demand peaks. The same idea lies behind more effective work practices, enhanced mechanisation or automation, offering inducements to employees or increasing work shift patterns (eg increasing from two eight-hour shifts to a 24-hour operation incorporating three eight-hour shifts).

2.37 Re-evaluating and improving product design may attain customer service and productivity gains.

2.38 Re-examining the flow of work through the transformation process, particularly if bottlenecks are apparent, may also help to smooth production.

2.39 Smoothing of the capacity system is considered at all levels of the organisation. Smoothing is the matching of orders to capacity over an identifiable timeframe and brings considerable benefits in terms of planning and structure to the operations manager.

2.40 Production scheduling attempts to smooth demand in order to produce a stable manufacturing plan. This may involve increasing production runs beyond immediate requirements in anticipation of future orders. This will, of course, mean that excess finished stock will be held for a period of time. This goes against the idea of producing what the customer wants when they want it; however, the need for effective and efficient use of capacity will in certain situations take precedence. The efficient use of the production set-up, perceived future production demands and customer forecast projections would all be used to justify why seemingly excess stock will be made. The argument is about capacity but also needs to justify itself financially.

2.41 A feature of many organisations is how they cope with seasonal fluctuations to their business. Seasonality of demand is very common for a wide variety of reasons such as climate, social, festive, religious and political factors.

2.42 Customer service is a major contributor to an organisation's view of demand and capacity management strategies. If customer satisfaction is high on the agenda then a strategy on capacity leading may be adopted; and by contrast, if cost constraints dominate, a capacity lag approach may be employed.

2.43 Decisions relating to demand and capacity strategies are made at all levels of the organisation as it is accepted that strategic decisions based on forecasts will, to differing degrees, prove inaccurate calling for remedial action to be taken at lower levels of the management hierarchy.

3 Loading, scheduling and sequencing

The nature of scheduling

3.1 A schedule is a representation of the time necessary to carry out a particular task. Scheduling is one of the more complex tasks facing operations managers, as they need to balance a range of resources to achieve the best overall result.

3.2 Machines have varied capacities and capabilities and staff will have a wide range of skills and degrees of specialisation. Scheduling requires operations managers to develop a 'timetable' approach to production or service delivery (with commencement dates, progression dates and completion dates) to ensure that the required resources are available at each stage of the operation.

3.3 A job schedule shows the plan for the manufacture of a particular job or the sequence of service operations. It is created through 'work/study' reviews that determine the method and times required or (often in the case of service delivery) through experience and refining what has been done before.

3.4 The job schedule is a small 'project' that requires tasks to be completed in a certain order in order to effectively deliver the desired outcome.

3.5 Most operations will carry out a range of production tasks simultaneously. This will entail amalgamating several job schedules into a workable and productive plan of action. This process is known as 'scheduling' and the result is known as the production schedule or the factory schedule for the operation as a whole.

3.6 There are two key issues with production scheduling.

- The measurement of performance. This is often a battle between financial performance requirements (minimise stockholding) and marketing performance requirements (produce enough to meet customer demand).
- The large number and complexity of production schedules. Most operations are running a large number of production processes and runs simultaneously.

3.7　There are a number of variables that must be taken into account in order to deliver an effective production schedule.

- Delivery dates
- Job schedules for each relevant production task
- Capacities of the production sections
- The efficiency of these production sections
- Planned holidays
- Anticipated sickness
- Projected absenteeism
- Projected training
- Availability of required materials

Loading

3.8　Loading describes the amount of work allocated to a machine or work centre. For example a unit operates two eight-hour shifts for six days a week. It is apparently available for 96 hours a week. However, a number of factors must be considered as they can impact on the availability of the work unit.

- Statutory holidays
- Weekends
- Maintenance
- Machine reliability
- Absenteeism

3.9　**Finite loading** allocates work to a machine, unit, person or group of people up to a set limit. This limit is based on an estimate of the capacity available and is not exceeded. Finite loading can prove suitable in a number of situations.

- Where it is possible to place a limit on the load (eg by using an appointment or timetabling system)
- Where it is a requirement to limit the load (eg for safety reasons)
- Where the cost of limiting the load is not considered too expensive (where for marketing reasons in particular limiting production offers exclusivity to customers)

3.10　Finite capacity scheduling systems have developed considerably in recent years. There are now few manufacturing and services areas where finite loading cannot be used practically. It has been used in jobbing manufacture for many years but is now equally practical in more complex batch manufacture operations. The use of finite loading will often be seen in continuous production, as even this method will have some batch production aspects within it.

3.11　**Infinite loading** does not limit the amount of work accepted. It is a system that will try to cope with the loading placed upon it. This can happen in the following situations.

- Where it is not possible or practical to limit the load (eg the Accident & Emergency operation of a hospital). To address the possible fluctuation in loading, doctors and nurses are 'on-call' should the need arise.

- Where it is not necessary to limit the load. At times the 'loading' in a restaurant will be low and at other 'peak' times high. Initially people will queue and eventually some may go elsewhere. If a finite system approach were used there would be a need to book and a possible limit at the time you can spend at a table.

- Where the costs or issues involved in limiting the load are prohibitive (eg customers turned away from a January sale as the store is considered full).

Sequencing

3.12 Sequencing determines the best order for progressing demands through an operation. Whether the demand sequence is finite or infinite, decisions must be taken with regard to the order in which the work will be undertaken.

3.13 This can present the operations manager with many complex and interrelated decisions. Later in the text we will examine critical path analysis. In essence, certain things must be achieved before progression can be made to the next step. There is a 'critical path' or sequence that is essential to progress from one stage to another. That does not stop preparation in advance but it will mean that the operations manager must be fully aware of the critical stages in the operation.

3.14 For example, a car being resprayed must be rubbed down, prepared and primed to accept the paint, then sprayed and dried. Materials can be readied in advance and staff can be readied but the sequence is set by the nature of the job.

3.15 Sequencing is often governed by priority rules, which take the elements of a particular scheduling problem and, using an applicable procedure, aid in working out the plan. The plan can be further influenced by the organisation's own priorities such as customer preferencing or the interdependence of machines or people in the process.

3.16 The rules include the following.

- FCFS: **First come, first served** where jobs are sequenced as they arrive (eg buying a railway ticket). This is also referred to as FIFO: first in, first out.

- LIFO: **Last in, first out** which is not often used in operations. An example would be people getting in and out of a lift. However, the method will often have an adverse effect on service particularly where customers are involved.

- LPT: **Longest processing time** goes first which can be particularly relevant when set-up times are long or where gains can be made from economies of scale in production.

- SPT: **Shortest processing time** goes first where jobs are allocated according to the shortest time they will have at a workstation. This enables a greater number of customers' needs to be satisfied.

- EDD: **Earliest due date** where jobs are allocated on the basis of their completion date with the earliest one first.

Gantt charts

3.17 Developed by Henry L Gantt, Gantt charts are a visual tool that has widespread acceptance in scheduling. The Gantt chart represents time as a bar on a chart.

Figure 7.1 *Gantt chart*

	STOCK CHECK ITEMS SIGNED OFF				
	Monday	Tuesday	Wednesday	Thursday	Friday
TARGET *ACTUAL*	150 / 100	100 / 125	150 / 150	150 / 150	75 / 100
NOTES:	Working with trainee	One hour overtime			Dvlpmt mtg cancelled

3.18 Charts are now usually constructed and amended on computers but this can restrict their visual impact. Where a number of operatives are involved in the manufacturing process it is still common to display on a whiteboard chart. If Gantt charts are computer-based then different levels of entry are required for those who are authorised to amend details and for those who merely need to view the chart.

3.19 Gantt charts can be used to plan alternative schedules in advance. Computer programmes will assess various options presented and gauge the operational outcome which can then assist in choosing the optimum scheduling route for a given operation or set of operations.

3.20 Variations on the Gantt chart theme include the following.

- Load charts that show the loading and idle time for machines or operators
- Flow charts that display orders or jobs in progress in order to show how work is progressing against a schedule

3.21 These variations are often incorporated into one chart.

Line balancing

3.22 Line balancing is a technique to ensure that resources are deployed effectively among the workstations. Each stage of the production line should be designed to operate at the same rate (ie the capacity of each of the sequenced workstations should be the same). This requires not only planning of the capacity loading but also consideration of both idle and maintenance time.

3.23 The objective is to maximise productivity by using the machines or people to their total practical capability. To achieve this requires planning, particularly relating to the timing of operations and the problems that can be caused by bottlenecks within the process. Line balancing, despite the best advance planning, can be very difficult. It is estimated that it will take over three months of operation in car manufacture to balance the line effectively.

3.24 It is usually not possible to operate at 100 per cent efficiency. The production/operations manager needs to consider the following questions.

- What is the maximum output of the production line?
- What labour is required?
- What will be the efficiency of labour with this proposed layout?

3.25 To assist with these considerations a precedence diagram can be developed which seeks to maximise the operation. As with Gantt charts much of the calculation work and analysis is now handled by IT systems but the operations manager is still required to bring practical experience to bear on the resultant computer output.

Figure 7.2 *Precedence diagram*

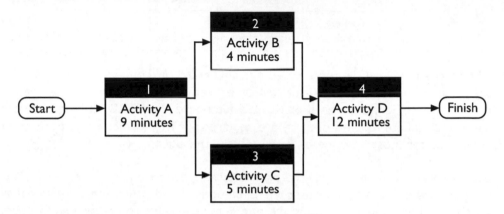

3.26 The precedence diagram gives a visual display of the tasks to be performed together with the sequence they will be performed in.

3.27 The balancing of assembly or manufacturing lines is clearly a complex and involved task with many considerations and variables to be evaluated and possibly re-evaluated. Precedence diagrams are one tool that can be used and they will normally be integrated within a computer-based system. The most accepted is known as COMSOAL (Computer Method of Sequencing Operations for Assembly Lines) which generates various solutions in response to the parameters set but will still require the operations manager to make the final operating sequence decision.

3.28 Work cycle times establish the rate of output for the production or assembly line. Calculation of cycle times is important as it serves to establish the maximum time required to perform the given operation, usually on one machine or for a defined operation.

$$\text{Output capacity} = \frac{\text{Daily working (operating) time}}{\text{Cycle time}}$$

Scheduling in low-volume systems

3.29   In Chapter 5 we looked at process types in manufacturing and service industries. This chapter introduced process, product and cell layout operations and their applicability for different types of operation.   The type of operation or mix of these methods of operations has a high impact on the ability and flexibility of any operation and its ability to deliver effective and efficient product or service.

3.30   Scheduling in low-volume or 'job shop' systems is often more complex and involved than more predictable mid- or high-volume systems. Job shops such as garages, bespoke furniture manufacture or even hospitals or any manufacture or service operation where production or service is carried out to customers' order requirements or needs, each differing in their wants, requires an increased degree of planning and monitoring for the needs to be satisfied effectively.

3.31   As a result each order must be planned to maximise resources and availability, often at short notice, and monitored as it progresses through an organisation's operational structure.

3.32   As an example, take the operation of a garage. Customers are encouraged to book ahead (ie this permits a 'timetabling' approach). Each element of the work cycle (such as 20 minutes to change oil, 60 minutes to change brakes etc) has already been calculated, based on industry norms and past experience.

3.33   This allows the operations manager to plan and schedule work after consideration of staff and available resources. Some jobs will take longer than anticipated and some may be quicker.

3.34   New demands will be made as customers suffer breakdowns or faults with their cars that must be scheduled in or delayed until a suitable 'slot' can be found. Delays may result in lost business. Diagnosis may take an unpredictable amount of time. Customers may need to be contacted before repair work can be started. Spares may need to be delivered. Resources required may already have been allocated so there may be a delay in commencement of the remedial work.

3.35   Planning by means of Gantt charts offers a visible and flexible approach for the low-volume operation where not only the scheduler but also the operatives require to view the plan for the day. The Gantt chart provides a visible representation of the plan and workload and so enables discussion and revision in a flexible and responsive manner. This may prove a suitable and effective planning and scheduling tool in these particular circumstances.

3.36   More complex operations (whether in manufacturing, assembly or service) may be more reliant on computer based assessment and scheduling. However, the principle and approach remain fundamentally the same.

3.37   The garage operation often requires that cars pass from one 'work station' to another (eg diagnosis of the problem, holding area, maintenance bay, tuning operation before completion). Work stations must be scheduled, staff available when required to carry out their particular role at the work station, timings planned and communicated to avoid bottlenecks and possible alternatives considered in case of delays and 'slack' in another area (eg valeting the car).

3.38 Job shops or similar operations with many work centres provide a high degree of complexity particularly with regard to scheduling. To effectively accomplish their workload a number of factors must be considered and monitored on an ongoing basis.

- Rough planning and sequencing at the front-line or office
- Rough prioritisation that refines over time
- Flexible staff
- Decentralisation of certain detailed sequencing decisions to operatives
- Progress chasing in real time
- Regular review of operational activities with a view to the continual improvement of the operation.

3.39 The job shop operation is one where planning can only be proactive to a certain degree. Much of the planning is reactive in the sense that it responds to fast moving and changing circumstances. Often the size and complexity of the job means that investment in more sophisticated capacity and scheduling tools and methods would not be cost effective and may prove too complex in operation.

Scheduling in intermediate-volume systems

3.40 Intermediate or batch systems are designed to take advantage of the relative size of each order and the repetition of the manufacturing or assembly process. Batch systems could operate in the same way as job shop operations, but this would not maximise the economies of scale that can be gained in manufacture or assembly or the reduction in variety offered that permits an increased degree of specialisation.

3.41 Batch systems (eg a production run of 10,000 units of product A followed by a production run of 20,000 units of product B) enable a **master production schedule** (MPS) to be developed. This MPS enables machines to be allocated in the most effective manner.

3.42 The development of the MPS is dependent on a number of associated factors.

- **Aggregate sales and operations plan**. This covers medium-term projections, without detailing individual orders, and identifies the range of products that are expected to be manufactured. The plan will be broken down to detail batch sizes, estimated delivery dates and estimated production dates and times.

- **Materials requirements planning** (MRP). The MPS can be broken down into requirements for each batch production run under a materials requirements plan. The material requirements plan enables ordering of the right net quantity of items at the right time to enable the manufacturing process to go ahead in the anticipated manner while minimising stockholding to a practical level.

- **Capacity requirements planning** (CRP). This examines (over a planning period – often a day or a few days) the availability and capacity of machines to meet projected manufacturing demands. The aggregate sales and operations plan enables 'rough cut' planning; the capacity requirements plan refines this into operational practicality.

3.43 Aggregate planning tries to find ways of meeting demand while maintaining production at a stable level and satisfying any other specific constraints and/or objectives. It enables operations managers to fully consider issues in advance so that they can plan accordingly when implementing the MPS for work to be carried out over a short timeframe and will be considered and evaluated in greater depth in the following chapter.

Scheduling in high-volume systems

3.44 High-volume systems should be easier to manage than job shop or batch systems owing to the repetitive manufacture involved. The organisations involved in high-volume production are usually large multinationals that gain from economies of scale in production. The concentration of effort is focused around the elimination of waste, improved throughput times and maximisation of resources.

3.45 The assembly line is one of the most visual representations of a high-volume system. The idea when first introduced was an adaptation of the system used in meat processing and grain mills, where conveyor belts moved goods and overhead cranes to the workers.

3.46 Owing to the predictable nature of mass manufacturing, scheduling becomes less of an issue. Greater issues arise in relation to line balancing in order to maximise the benefits to be gained.

3.47 Modern views of the assembly line are focused around the application of JIT systems and continuous flow manufacturing (CFM). Continuous flow focuses on producing one item at a time (or a small and consistent batch of items) through a series of processing steps as continuously as possible, with each step making just what is requested by the next step.

3.48 Parts are built as they are needed while maintaining efficient use of operators and machines. Flexibility is used as a substitute for work in progress inventory. A 'product focus' is established in all areas of the operation and all non-value added activities of the operation are eliminated.

3.49 Continuous flow can be achieved in a number of ways, ranging from moving assembly lines to integrated manual cells. The continuous flow approach is also known as **one-piece flow**, **single-piece flow**, and **make one, move one**.

3.50 CFM focuses on lowering the work in progress inventory and replacing it with flexibility and increased labour productivity. CFM can bring the following benefits.

- Simplify the manufacturing operation into product or process flows.
- Organise manufacturing operations so that one day resembles the next.
- Establish flow or cycle times that are consistent with total man hours.
- Use activity based costing methods to analyse in detail potential areas of cost savings.

Chapter summary

- The central role of operations management is the transformation process

- Planning and control within operations will exist over three (often overlapping) time frames.

- Control is the practical actions that can be taken to bring the plan back on track.

- Capacity management involves matching the operating system with the demand placed on the system

- Scheduling is the effective timing of the use of resources to meet organisational requirements and is a common feature of all organisations.

- Scheduling requires a route or sequence to be followed in order to complete the task at hand.

- Loading describes the amount of work allocated to a machine or work centre.

- Finite loading allocates work to a machine, unit, person or group of people up to a set limit.

- Infinite loading does not limit the amount of work accepted on a machine or work centre.

- Line balancing ensures that resources are deployed effectively among the work stations.

- Scheduling in low-volume or 'job shop' systems is often more complex and involved than more predictable mid- or high-volume systems.

- Planning by means of Gantt charts offers a visible and flexible approach for the low-volume operation where not only the scheduler but also the operatives require to view the plan for the day.

- Intermediate or batch systems are designed to take advantage of the relative size of each order and the repetition of the manufacturing or assembly process.

- CFM focuses on lowering the work-in-progress inventory and replacing it with flexibility and increased labour productivity.

Self-test questions

Numbers in brackets refer to the paragraphs above where your answers can be checked.

1   Define planning. (1.2, 1.4)

2   Explain SMART objectives. (1.5)

3   How does Ray Wild define operations planning? (1.8)

4   What do control systems require? (1.17)

5   Muhlemann, Oakland and Lockyer distinguish between what three different capacity levels? (2.10)

6   What methods are open to operations managers when adjusting capacity? (2.23)

7   What are the two main strategies for capacity management? (2.30)

8   Define and explain a 'schedule'. (3.1)

9   What is the purpose of 'sequencing'? (3.12)

10   Where is the concentration of effort placed when considering the running of high-volume manufacturing systems? (3.44)

Further reading

*   *Operations Management*, Slack, Chambers and Johnston, Chapter 14.

*   *Production and Operations Management*, Muhlemann, Oakland and Lockyer, Chapters 26 and 27.

*   *Operations Management*, John Naylor, Chapter 12.

CHAPTER 8

The Management of Demand

Learning objectives and indicative content

1.3 Compare the different characteristics of products and service operations and analyse how they impact on operations management practice.

- Demand management

4.2 Analyse, select and use basic techniques to forecast demand.

- The use of some basic techniques for forecasting
- Qualitative and quantitative forecasting techniques
- Independent and dependent demand

4.3 Analyse and explain the mechanics of materials requirements planning (MRP), manufacturing resource planning (MRP II) and enterprise resource planning (ERP).

- MRP/MRP II and how they work
- Advantages and disadvantages of MRP/MRP II
- ERP – applications and content

Chapter headings

1 Dependent and independent demand

2 Methods of forecasting demand

3 Materials requirements planning and manufacturing resources planning

4 Enterprise resource planning

1 Dependent and independent demand

The nature of demand for products and services

1.1 The need to accurately assess demand is crucial in today's business environment. Accuracy in forecasting brings with it the opportunities to maximise resources and minimise spend and waste. The increased business emphasis in forecasting and demand management marks it out as an identified aspect of business operations where substantial gains can be made and competitive advantage enhanced.

1.2 Confidence in the predictability of demand enables better decisions at the operational level. When linked to effective inventory management the two areas combine to be greater than the sum of their parts.

The distinction between dependent and independent demand

1.3 Many stock items are subject to dependent demand – that is, the extent to which the item is used depends on the production schedule for a larger item of which it forms part. To estimate the demand for such items requires detailed examination of the product breakdown. For example, if 1,000 units are being manufactured and each unit requires 5 modules, then the order placed is for 5,000 modules. The amount ordered is dependent on the amount being produced.

1.4 The situation is easier in the case of items subject to independent demand. For example, the amount of oil required to maintain a manufacturing machine in working order does not depend on which products are being processed on that machine. It is possible to estimate that a particular amount of oil will be used each day, week or month, regardless of the exact detail of the production schedule.

1.5 As a further example, what items are bought out in a typical service organisation? This will depend on the exact nature of the organisation, but the following are likely answers. Notice that in all cases the items are characterised by independent demand; they are not related to the exact volume and nature of the service organisation's outputs. Clearly these purchases are not limited to service companies but they serve to illustrate the difference between dependent and independent demand.

- Office equipment and supplies such as stationery
- Computer hardware and software
- Motor vehicles
- Advertising and design services
- Maintenance services

1.6 The distinction between dependent and independent demand is important because some inventory control systems (such as MRP) take into account the peculiar difficulties of dependent demand, while the two methods described below are more suited, although not exclusive, to independent demand items. Both methods require good inventory management as the optimum goal is to operate effectively carrying as little stock as possible.

Periodic review systems

1.7 One method of stock control for independent demand items is the periodic review system. The stock level of the product is determined and examined at regular or fixed intervals and, depending on the quantity in stock, a replenishment order is placed. Consideration should be given to when the product period will be reviewed, the form the review should take, and what quantity should be ordered following the review.

1.8 To determine the review period it is necessary to deal one by one with each item of stock, or at least each category of item. However the review period may need to be amended in the light of fluctuation in usage or stockholding patterns.

1.9 The shorter the review period the more trouble is involved. For this reason it is usual to apply an ABC analysis. Items in Category A might be reviewed weekly, those in Category B monthly and those in Category C quarterly. These suggestions are only illustrative, and each organisation must assess the appropriate periods in the light of its particular circumstances and experience.

1.10 The review can be undertaken by physical inspection (staff simply walking around the stores and recording stock held) or by a computerised or manual system that records purchases, requisitions and returns of each item to give a current figure of stock held. This system can be referred to as perpetual inventory as it records every item of stock as it comes in and leaves, providing a current stock figure. There is the danger that mistakes in counting, recording or inputting may occur causing discrepancies in the stock count. The system would usually require supplementing by regular physical stock counts.

1.11 Once the current stock level has been established, the next decision concerns how many units of the item should be ordered to replenish the stock. Experience or forecasting of demand patterns is the main guide. Managers should be able to estimate how much is likely to be required before the next review. Comparing that with the level actually in stock and already on order leads to a decision on order quantity.

1.12 The system assumes that there will be no review of a stock item other than at the stated interval. This has the disadvantage that unusually high levels of demand can cause unexpected stockouts. For this reason, it is usual to supplement a periodic review system with the use of safety stocks.

Fixed order quantity systems

1.13 An alternative approach is a fixed order quantity system. Stock of an item is replenished with a predetermined quantity when inventory falls to a predetermined level. A specific stock level is agreed, at which point a replenishment order will be placed. To determine the order point for a particular stock item, managers rely on past experience of demand patterns, modified by any known changes expected to occur in future.

1.14 Using this data, they fix on a stock level sufficient to keep the business in stock during the supplier's delivery lead time, plus possibly a level of safety stock. Once stock falls to this predetermined level the computer flags the need for action and a new order is placed.

1.15 One common method used is the two-bin system. For each stock item two bins are maintained. The first is in use; the second contains the stock representing the order point. When the first bin is emptied, it is automatic to re-order. While waiting for the order to be delivered the contents of the second bin are used. Both bins are replenished when the order arrives.

1.16 When it is time to re-order, the quantity ordered is the same each time. The order quantity will vary from organisation to organisation in line with their individual needs. In particular, for items of large value it may be sensible to use a more structured approach such as the application of the economic order quantity described later. For small-value items simple decision rules may be more cost-effective.

1.17 The ability to use the economic order quantity is an advantage over periodic review systems. Another advantage is the automatic nature of the process where the computer directs attention on those items where action is needed, and time is not wasted on items where the stock level is satisfactory.

1.18   The fixed order quantity system can be said to suffer from much the same disadvantages as the periodic review system as both accept that a level of stock is inevitable. It also assumes a pattern of stable stock usage and supplier lead times; if these change the order point and order quantities will need to be reviewed.

ABC analysis

1.19   Vilfredo Pareto (1848–1923), an Italian economist and sociologist, made the observation that a large proportion of national wealth tended to be under the control of a relatively small number of individuals. This observation enabled him to formulate the following rule.

'In any series of elements to be controlled a selected small factor in terms of number of elements almost always accounts for a large factor in terms of effort.'

1.20   The Pareto principle (or '80/20 rule') serves as the basis for ABC analysis. ABC analysis can be defined as follows.

'The application of Pareto's principle to the analysis of supply data. If items in a store are arranged in descending order of usage-value and the cumulative number of items is plotted against the cumulative usage value the result would [be expected to] show a curve of the general form associated with Pareto's principle.'

1.21   The Pareto principle suggests that, roughly speaking, 80 per cent of the total value of material will be accounted for by 20 per cent of the items. The ABC analysis is a refinement of this idea by developing the concept one stage further into three stock categories.

- **Category A items**: The 'vital few'. Small in number but high in usage value. Devote most managerial control effort here.
- **Category B items**: 'Normal' items. Medium in number, medium usage value
- **Category C items**: The 'trivial many'. High in number, low usage value. Devote least managerial control here.

Figure 8.1 *Pareto analysis*

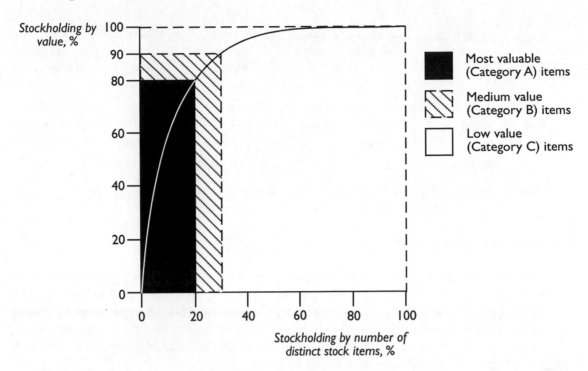

1.22 The procedure for sorting items commences by tabulating stock items in a list by part number. Alongside each part number the unit cost and annual usage rate is then entered. The latter two are then multiplied in order to record the annual usage value.

1.23 The next step is to relist all the items in order of annual usage value starting with the highest, then to record alongside each the cumulative annual usage value and finally each individual percentage of the total.

- **Stage 1: Calculate the annual usage value**

A Part number	B Unit value	C Annual usage	D Annual usage value
	£	Units	(B × C)
300-171	58.00	6,000	348,000
310-060	6.00	10,000	60,000
691-020	220.00	500	110,000
Total			518,000

- **Stage 2: Rank the items in descending order of annual usage value**

A Part number	B Unit value	C Annual usage	D Annual usage value	E Cum. annual usage value	F D as % of total usage value
	£	Units	£	£	%
300-171	58.00	6,000	348,000	348,000	67
691-020	220.00	500	110,000	458,000	21
310-060	6.00	10,000	60,000	518,000	12

1.24 Clearly any stocklist will have many more items than this simple example, but this is sufficient to illustrate the approach.

The economic order quantity

1.25 There are significant costs incurred in acquiring and holding stock. Purchasing managers have a concern for minimising these costs but there is an inherent conflict that has to be overcome. On the one hand, buyers could seek to minimise acquisition costs by placing fewer orders. In this case the orders would have to be for relatively large quantities, which means that high stock levels would be inevitable. Stock holding costs would rise as a result, and the overall objective would be endangered.

1.26 On the other hand, buyers could seek to reduce holding costs. The logical culmination of this approach is just in time purchasing where stock is delivered as and when required, but this approach requires an integrated effort across the organisation and is difficult to introduce in isolation. An intermediate measure is to plan for low stock levels by means of small order quantities. This will mean that the frequency of orders will increase with a rise in acquisition costs as a result.

1.27 Holding costs are simply the cost of holding goods. These costs include the cost of working capital committed, together with the loss of interest on capital tied up in inventory. The costs of storage (such as rent, rates, heating, insurance, wages, machinery etc) must all be considered. High stock holding may lead to outsourcing considerations if an organisation does not have sufficient warehouse space to cover the requirement. Other costs that must be considered include the costs of physical deterioration of goods and obsolescence.

1.28 Acquisition costs are incurred when orders are placed. By reducing the number of orders placed savings in management time and administration can be made. Electronic ordering systems are increasingly used to reduce paperwork and speed up the transaction process.

1.29 Figure 8.2 shows the trade-off between holding and acquisition costs.

- If a higher order quantity is selected, higher stock levels will result, and this leads in turn to higher stockholding costs. This is why the HC line slopes steadily upwards from left to right.

- On the other hand, total acquisition costs are lower if large orders are placed. This is because fewer orders and less clerical work will be needed. This is why the AC line slopes down from left to right.

Figure 8.2 *The EOQ model*

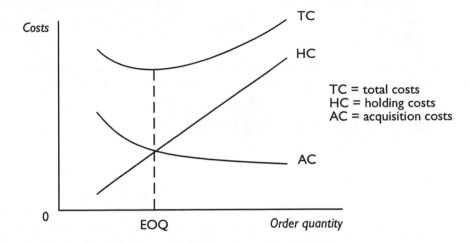

1.30   The TC line is derived simply by totalling the holding costs and acquisition costs at each point along the horizontal axis. We are seeking to minimise total costs and so we look for the lowest point of the TC line. This is marked on the diagram. It is no coincidence that this occurs where the HC and AC lines intersect (ie where total acquisition costs are equal to holding costs).

1.31   This analysis relates to items purchased from external suppliers. For operations managers it is worth noting that a very similar analysis can be applied to internal production costs. In this case the problem is one of minimising total costs of set-up (which are greater if many small production runs are undertaken) and stockholding (which, as before, are greater if production is in large infrequent batches). Instead of the economic order quantity we arrive at an economic batch quantity.

1.32   The mathematical calculation of EOQ is as follows.

$$EOQ = \sqrt{\frac{2cd}{h}}$$

1.33   In this formula, c represents the cost of placing an order, d represents the estimated usage of the stock item in the relevant period, and h represents the cost of holding one unit of the stock item in stock for the relevant period.

1.34   Notice that the EOQ formula makes no reference at all to the largest component of stock costs: the actual purchase price of the stock item. The reason for this is that purchase prices are assumed to be constant regardless of the order quantity. Clearly this is a simplifying assumption, as in practice there may be supplier discounts for larger order quantities.

1.35   The EOQ model is based on assumptions such as consistent demand, consistent order quantities, and constant lead-times. Apart from the artificiality of these assumptions, the model suffers from other limitations.

- It is a cumbersome method to apply and may not always be justified.

- Annual forecast demand may not be accurate.

- The mathematical calculations incorporate some simplifying assumptions (eg that use of the stock item is even over time and that prices remain stable), and these will not always remain valid.

- Some of the costs (such as clerical time, interest rates and order costs) are difficult to estimate.

1.36 Despite these limitations it is successfully employed by many organisations, particularly as a tool that allows for more accurate and informed purchasing decisions.

2 Methods of forecasting demand

Introduction

2.1 Forecasting is an essential part of all planning and decision-making and is of fundamental importance to many areas of operations management. It forms a key element in the long-term management process and the accuracy of long-term forecasts can have a considerable impact on the activities of operations managers at a later date.

2.2 Accurate forecasting can mean that the right resources are available as required. Inaccurate forecasting can mean different degrees of remedying operational activities to bring them in line with strategic plans.

2.3 Forecasts will rarely be 100 per cent accurate as they are based on projections and assumptions. Forecasts involve a number of considerations.

- **What is the forecast for?** As with any project the objectives should be clear from the outset.

- **What is the projected timescale?** Traditionally forecasts are categorised as long-term (two to five years or more), medium-term (six months to two years) or short-term (less than six months).

- **On what data should the forecast be based?** Forecasting is often a combination of 'hard data' ie facts and figures (such as prices, trends, sales, etc) and 'soft data', eg customer feedback, market knowledge, etc.

- **What forecasting techniques should be applied?** These can be divided into two approaches: quantitative (hard data, using figures with the application of statistical analysis) and qualitative (using such techniques as the Delphi method and test marketing that will be discussed below).

- **How accurate is the forecast?** A key requirement of forecasting is to monitor the accuracy achieved.

2.4 Characteristics of a good forecast include:

- **Timely**: have a horizon with time to implement possible changes
- **Accurate**: state the degree of accuracy
- **Reliable**: be reliable and work consistently
- **Meaningful**: be expressed in meaningful units
- **Written**: be expressed in writing
- **Easy to use**: simple to understand and use
- **Consistent**: be consistent with historical data

Simple moving average

2.5 As the name suggests, this is a simple technique. All we do is to look at the demand for recent periods, and assume that demand for the coming period will be the average of that experienced in the past. There is no particular rule about how many past periods we should take into account. If we are trying to estimate demand during July we might, for example, look at the actual demand experienced during January to June, and take the average of those six months.

2.6 Suppose that usage of an independent demand material was as follows in the months of January to June.

Month	Usage in litres
January	450
February	190
March	600
April	600
May	420
June	380
Total usage January to June	2,640

2.7 Using a simple moving average we would simply take the average of these six months: 2,640/6 = 440 litres. This would be our estimate of usage in July.

2.8 The reason for the term 'moving' average is that each month we move along by one step. Thus in estimating usage for August, we discard the January figure above and replace it with the figure for actual usage in July. Our estimate for August is therefore based on the six months preceding August, namely February to July.

2.9 Of course, this procedure is really a bit too simple. It is clear from the figures that demand for this material fluctuates quite markedly. The figures for January to June show a low of 190 litres, and a high of 600 litres. The simple average of such figures does not inspire confidence. The actual figure in July might turn out to be either of these extremes, in which case our estimate of 440 litres will prove wide of the mark. The next method tries to inject greater sophistication into the estimates.

Weighted average method, or exponential smoothing

2.10 The simple moving average gives equal weight to each of the figures recorded in previous periods. In the example, the figure for January contributed exactly as much to the averaging calculation as did that for June. This does not take account of a fact which is very commonly observed in practice, namely that older figures are a less reliable guide to the future than more recent figures. If there is any gradual change taking place in our pattern of usage of the item, it is more likely that the change will be reflected in our usage for June than in the figure for January six months ago.

2.11   To take account of this, the technique of exponential smoothing can be used. This is designed to give greater weight to the figures experienced in recent months, and to reduce the weight given to older figures. Our first step is to settle on a number between 0 and 1 – say 0.2. We then perform the following calculation, using the figures from the example above.

$$\text{July usage} = 0.2 \times 380 + (0.2 \times 0.8) \times 420 + (0.2 \times 0.8^2) \times 600 + \ldots + (0.2 \times 0.8^5) \times 450$$
$$= 0.2 \times 380 + 0.16 \times 420 + 0.128 \times 600 + \ldots + 0.066 \times 450$$
$$= 76 + 67.2 + 76.8 + 61.4 + 15.6 + 29.5$$
$$= 326.5$$

2.12   The factor 0.8 is simply 1 minus our chosen factor of 0.2. How we chose the value of 0.2 – rather than 0.1, say, or 0.95 – is a matter of experience. We look back on known values from the past and we work out what factor would have given the best estimates if we had used it in the basic formula. We deduce that this is the value which best encapsulates the nature of the historical trend, and so we apply it for the future in the hope that it will continue to give good results.

2.13   Notice that this has given a lower estimate for demand in July than the simple moving average. This is because the high values of March and April, being some months ago, have little weight in the calculations above, but were given full weight in the simple average calculation.

2.14   It is very easy to calculate the value of the weighted average from one month to the next, once the initial calculation has been done. This is because the arithmetic of the situation leads to a simple formula. The estimate (E) for the coming period is given by the formula:

$$E = (0.2 \times D) + (0.8 \times A)$$

where **D** is the actual demand experienced in the most recent month (June in our example), and **A** is the average which we calculated last month (when we were trying to estimate the figure for June).

2.15   Of course, this formula uses the value 0.2 that we decided on in the case of this particular material. In the case of another material, we might have settled on a different value and the formula above would have to be amended accordingly.

Time series trend analysis

2.16   A time series is a sequential arrangement of selected statistical data according to their occurrence in time. The objective of a time series trend analysis is to measure the variation of a data set about the average, often for the purpose of data comparison.

2.17   In assessing trends, you can also make meaningful comparisons with comparable organisations in the same industry or related overall industrial averages, the general industrial economy, gross national product, population, and so on. Current data may be compared with past data in the same series, such as sales volume or product costs. Using this approach you can anticipate future trends with greater certainty.

2.18 Projecting the time series into the future is a form of statistical forecasting. Time series analysis is therefore very important to analysts who apply statistics to business activity and economics. An economy's or company's dynamic nature makes the time factor a vital element in analysing sales, product costs, production etc. A time series represents economic data moving through time, and its analysis provides the basis for reviewing the statistics in motion.

2.19 The factors to be taken into account in time series analysis are as follows.

- Trend
- Seasonal variation
- Cyclical changes
- Irregular data series fluctuations

2.20 A trend is a long-term movement, either upward or downward. Time series trends can be attributed to a number of factors, such as the introduction of mass production, technological changes, variations in population growth, development of new products, revisions in product mix, war, inflation, and so on.

2.21 Seasonal variations represent period movements that occur at regular time intervals, particularly during the calendar year. For example, consumer expenditures in retail stores increase at Christmas and Easter, and costs for utilities go up during the winter season.

2.22 Cyclical variations are usually influenced by prosperity, recession, and depression. In periods of prosperity, sales, production, income, and employment are accelerated, whereas the opposite effect is predominant in periods of depression. The cycles of economic activity show no regularity with respect to their occurrence or duration. History has shown that predicting future cycles with any degree of accuracy could be extremely difficult.

2.23 Irregular fluctuations are exactly what the term suggests: no amount of statistical analysis can account for every variation in demand patterns. There will always be variations that are not predicted by the analysis.

Regression analysis

2.24 Regression is a technique for deriving a mathematical relationship between two variables that are thought to be connected with each other. For example, managers might suspect that the level of sales achieved each month is related to the advertising spend in the previous month.

2.25 To investigate this idea scientifically, managers might use one axis of a graph to represent the value of sales achieved each month. The other axis of the graph would represent the amount of advertising spend in the previous month. The actual values might be plotted for each month in a period of, say, a year. Managers would then look at the pattern disclosed by the graph and examine whether it revealed a relationship.

2.26 The mathematical technique involved is called regression analysis. For any two variables – such as sales levels and advertising spend – a relationship can be calculated mathematically. Managers would use the information by predicting the amount of extra sales they might achieve by increasing the advertising spend to a particular level, or the amount of sales they might lose by a defined reduction in advertising spend.

2.27 A variation of this technique (called trend analysis) can be used to predict sales levels over time (which is relevant to calculating usage of dependent demand items). The trick is to treat time itself as the variable to be related to sales levels. The manager can then derive a relationship between sales on one hand and months of the year on the other.

2.28 The mathematics of regression analysis is fairly complex and unlikely to be tested in the examination but you should be aware of the general approach outlined above.

Qualitative approaches to forecasting

2.29 Qualitative (judgemental) approaches to forecasting fall under two broad headings: marketing research and expert opinion.

2.30 **Marketing research** is a common marketing tool used to ascertain potential interest and demand particularly in new products or to help identify trends in sales and the reasons behind them. Processes include focus groups, questionnaires, test marketing and interviewing. Research in the operations environment can mirror these methods and comparable results in terms of applicability to the specific operation may be obtained from suggestion boxes, quality circles, discussion groups, exit interviews etc.

2.31 **Expert opinion** is the gathering and collation of views, judgements and opinions from people regarded as knowledgeable in specific business areas (directors, consultants and business area specialists). The value of the contributors and the judgement made can be called into question, but knowledge and experience will usually provide a sound basis on which to develop a forecast.

The Delphi method

2.32 The method of using experts is frequently criticised. The 'Delphi' method (originally developed in 1944), in essence seeks to impose a statistical rigour and counter the argument of bias that frequently accompanies the gathering and use of 'expert opinion'.

2.33 The term Delphi refers to the site of the most revered oracle in ancient Greece. The objective of the Delphi method is the reliable and creative development of ideas or the production of suitable information to aid decision-making.

2.34 The Delphi method involves group communication by experts who are geographically dispersed. Questionnaires are sent to the selected experts by post or email and are designed to elicit and develop individual responses to the problems posed. The responses are considered and refined with subsequent questionnaires to develop a group response.

2.35 A main consideration of the Delphi method is to overcome the disadvantages of conventional committee action where individuals may dominate, bias may develop or groups polarise in their thinking. The group interaction in Delphi is anonymous, as comments made are not identified to their originator. A panel director or monitor whose role is to focus the group on the stated objectives controls the interaction between group members.

2.36   To operate successfully the participants should understand the process and aim of the exercise although there is some debate on the level of expertise required from the 'sages'. Armstrong and Welty suggest that a high degree of expertise is not necessary while Hanson and Ramani state that the respondents should be well informed in the appropriate area.

2.37   Fowles describes the following ten steps for developing and applying the Delphi method.

- Formation of a team to undertake and monitor the exercise on a given subject
- Selection of one or more panels to participate in the exercise – customarily, the panellists are experts in the area to be investigated
- Development of the first round Delphi questionnaire
- Testing the questionnaire for proper wording (ambiguities, vagueness etc)
- Transmission of the first questionnaire to the panellists
- Analysis of first round responses
- Preparation of second round questionnaires (and possible testing)
- Transmission of the second round questionnaires to the panellists
- Analysis of second round responses (these steps are reiterated as long as desired or necessary to achieve stability in the results)
- Preparation of the report by the analysis team to present the conclusions of the exercise

2.38   The Delphi method has proved useful in answering specific, single-dimension questions. There is less support for its use to determine more complex forecasts that involve multiple factors.

3   Materials requirements planning and manufacturing resources planning

3.1   Materials requirements planning (MRP) developed during the 1970s but is equally applicable today. It operates as an integrated information management, production planning and stock management system that has been enhanced in practicality in recent years as the speed and power of IT systems have increased.

3.2   MRP is also known as MRP I. This differentiates it from manufacturing resources planning (MRP II) which will be addressed later in the chapter.

3.3   MRP enables the advance planning of materials required for manufacture. The system utilises a bill of materials (BOM), in essence a breakdown of all the materials and components that go to make a finished product. The BOM serves to inform purchasing that goods must be ordered to meet an anticipated manufacturing date. Purchasing will then order, taking into account suppliers' lead times and a 'safety margin' (it is not a just in time system but works to allow a practical margin for error, ie an agreed number of days in advance of production). The objective is to ensure that when production commences the goods are available as required and that inventory levels are minimised.

3.4 MRP is defined as 'a set of logically related procedures, decision rules, and records designed to translate a master production schedule (MPS) into time-phased 'net requirements', and the planned coverage of such requirements for each component inventory item needed to implement this schedule'. The elements of this definition are examined below.

- **A set of logically related procedures**: MRP systems follow a logical sequence that incorporates decision rules relating to existing stock held, forecasting etc.

- **Translate an MPS into time-phased 'net requirements'**: time-phased because not everything is required at the same time. If the manufacturing run is extending over six days it may not be until the final day that you require a particular component. By getting delivery later than when the run commenced inventory cost savings can be made. 'Net requirements' because the MRP system takes into account that you may already hold some of the required items in stock and will reduce the ordered quantity accordingly.

- **The planned coverage of such requirements for each component inventory item needed to implement this schedule**: ensuring that each item required, taking into account suppliers' lead times, is ordered correctly.

Principles of MRP

3.5 An MRP system is a **dependent demand** system. For example, suppose you are making 5,000 square-framed prints. You require four pieces of wood cut to the same length and shape for each frame – a total of 20,000 pieces of wood. You require 5,000 pieces of glass to fit the frame, etc. The number of parts you require is dependent on the number of finished units to be produced.

3.6 The approach of materials requirements planning to dependent demand is to start from the end and work backwards. The first step is to estimate customer demand for a finished product, and then to calculate a production schedule to meet that demand. Customer demand will usually include orders received together with forecast estimates of additional customer demand.

3.7 Forecasting is important as it enables longer production runs to be undertaken, thereby gaining in reduced set-up time and economies of scale, where either future sales are predicted or where a justifiable case of manufacturing for stock has been accepted.

3.8 The main elements of the MRP process are shown in Figure 8.3.

Figure 8.3 *The main elements of an MRP system*

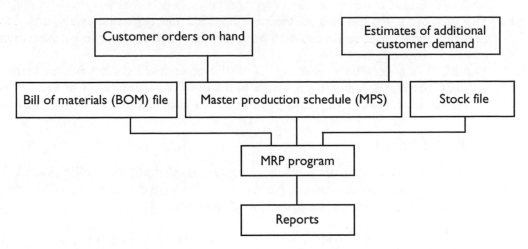

The master production schedule

3.9 Both forecast demand and actual orders on hand are combined in the MPS to decide the quantity to be produced. The role of the MPS is crucial in the MRP system. It provides the specification of the work to be progressed. Linking with the manufacturing availability in the capacity requirements plan (CRP) it brings together what is to be made, assembled or brought in within a specific timeframe.

3.10 The MPS enables us to plan the utilisation of both labour and equipment. In turn this identifies to the purchasing department when delivery is required from suppliers to meet production run requirements.

3.11 The MPS is in effect a summary of customer demand. The MRP program acts on the MPS as follows.

- By reference to the BOM file the program translates details of finished products required into details of materials and components required.

- By reference to the inventory file the program compares what is required with what is in stock.

3.12 The outputs from the program specify not just the amounts required in this process but also the time by which each is required. They also highlight the need for any special action, such as a possible need to reschedule or expedite orders.

3.13 Detailed outputs of the system will include any or all of the following.

- Order releases to purchasing for the current period, including the dates when required.

- Planned order releases to purchasing for future periods, based on current stocks, orders in progress, scheduled requirements and known lead times.

- Order releases for items to be produced in-house, with due dates for completion.

- Feedback on problems such as bottlenecks or lack of availability. This allows schedulers to make adjustments that can then be incorporated in a revised program run.

The bill of materials

3.14 The BOM is a list showing all the raw materials and components required to make a particular product. It specifies which parts go into which product and in what quantity.

3.15 The BOM is a detailed breakdown of all the component parts that comprise the final product. For components this is usually in the form of part numbers or unique identifiers. The breakdown enables purchasing to place orders for the exact quantity required.

The inventory file

3.16 Accurate inventory records are a fundamental requirement of an MRP system. We need to know our 'net requirements'. For example, if we need 1,000 units of X, and we hold 300 units in stock, our 'net requirement' is 700 units.

3.17 It may be that for practical purposes we have decided to hold a minimum stock of 100 units. Our 'net requirement' would be 800 units, allowing for the agreed 'safety stock'

3.18 MRP requires inventory records that describe:

- Each item of stock (part number, part description, supplier's lead time for supply). The information is held on the item master file and requires regular review particularly with regard to supplier lead times.
- Stock location, which is normally held on a location file following delivery. This will often form part of an integrated system covering storage and distribution in this instance.
- Transaction records relating to each stock item. This information is stored on a transaction file and may be linked to a purchasing management system such as SAP or ORACLE.

Capacity requirements planning

3.19 The capacity requirements plan (CRP) estimates the workload of each department or machine in the plant. Its purpose is to anticipate problems in advance to ensure that short-term adjustments can be made in order to meet capacity requirements. The CRP can operate at monthly, fortnightly or daily levels (for example) and can feed back to the MPS to bring forward or delay orders as appropriate.

3.20 CRP will look initially at aggregate plans and seek to meet those needs in a manner consistent with operational protocols. On a shorter timeframe it will look at planned orders and schedule accordingly. Finally, it looks at released orders particularly with regard to short-term remedies and issues such as overtime or idle time to ensure production objectives can be met

3.21 The MPS controls both the MRP and the CRP with the objective of bringing all considerations together to maximise efficiency and effectiveness.

MRP and inventory control

3.22 The MRP program works by 'exploding' the BOM by reference to the production schedule. What this means is that for each finished product on the MPS, the program scrutinises the BOM file and calculates how much of each material will be needed in the manufacture of the required number of finished units. This process is repeated for each finished product.

3.23 The result of this calculation is the gross requirement for each material. This is translated into a net requirement by referring to the stock file for details of stock already on hand or on order. The net requirement is time-phased, ie the program determines when each material must be to hand and consequently when it must be ordered from a supplier or alternatively when internal production must commence.

3.24 This process of time-phasing is crucial to the inventory control process. By using the detailed calculations prepared by the program, buyers can delay ordering until the materials are really required. For example, a seven-day production run may not require a particular item until Day 6. This serves to cut down the amount of stock in the overall system.

3.25 In this respect MRP produces similar benefits to those arising under a just in time (JIT) system. However MRP is not primarily aimed at eliminating stock and it is common in practice to find that a safety margin is allowed. The safety margin accepts that delays and problems will occur (eg suppliers will deliver late, deliver faulty goods or suffer manufacturing problems of their own). This is not to say that these issues are accepted by the purchasing department, who will always seek improvements from their suppliers, but is more practical in the sense that being unable to start a production run as scheduled will be very costly in both financial and customer service terms.

3.26 The safety margin will vary between organisations. The aim will always be to reduce it to the minimum acceptable time. MRP can be viewed as an inventory minimisation process rather than a just in time approach.

Benefits of MRP systems

3.27 The production of the MPS and the running of the MRP program lead to a detailed and timetabled approach to planning orders and production. The system is based on customer demand and software is increasingly capable of responding to such changes in demand by producing revised schedules. The emphasis on end customers is in line with modern management thinking, which stresses that customer needs should shape action throughout the organisation.

3.28 MRP systems emphasise the importance of precise and accurate ordering and production policies, which if successfully followed will lead to reduced inventory levels. By focusing management attention on production schedules well in advance, MRP systems can give an early warning of potential problems in production or hold-ups in the supply chain.

3.29   The MRP system offers the following benefits.

- Provides accurate and timely information to purchasing staff
- A scheduling tool in that it tells planners if due dates remain valid
- Anticipates shortages and/or slow moving stock
- Communicates priorities (what is wanted and in what sequence)
- Professional business discipline with the ability to build on and expand

3.30   An MRP system does not suit all organisations. It is a complex system to introduce and administer successfully. Once launched it may be difficult to make changes. While results are good in batch production and some assembly processes, the application elsewhere is less straightforward.

Manufacturing resources planning (MRP II)

3.31   The disciplined approach introduced by MRP has been further developed over the years. Manufacturing resources planning (MRP II) builds on key areas of MRP by considering all the resources needed for production, not just materials. For example, it deals with manpower, machinery and money.

3.32   The differences are made clear in their respective names. Materials requirements planning concentrates on securing the right materials to enable the production run to go ahead. Manufacturing resources planning examines the manufacturing resources required for the production to go ahead, eg the labour costs involved, the costs of machinery and proportion of overheads attributable etc. MRP II enables materials and work to be costed accurately.

3.33   MRP II is a method for planning manufacture and assessing the costs involved. It draws on the aggregate plans via the MPS not only to develop the areas covered by an MRP system but also to allow for such areas as personnel deployment, maintenance planning, and financial analysis.

3.34   Building on the discipline required for traditional MRP systems the MRP II model has led some to say that MRP II adds the financial function to MRP.

3.35   Managers can determine the dates when suppliers must be paid by studying MRP timing of purchase orders and their due dates. Accurate costing of manufacturing can be obtained as the system can look at machines and personnel used and analyse the information to provide accurate costings on production runs. The analysis can be further used as a benchmark for future production runs in order to seek operational improvements.

3.36   MRP II is often described as a closed-loop system, in that there is an automatic feedback from the manufacturing function to the MPS, leading to changes in the MPS. This in turn leads to adjustments in manufacturing plans, thus closing the information loop as illustrated in Figure 8.4.

Figure 8.4 *A closed-loop MRP II system*

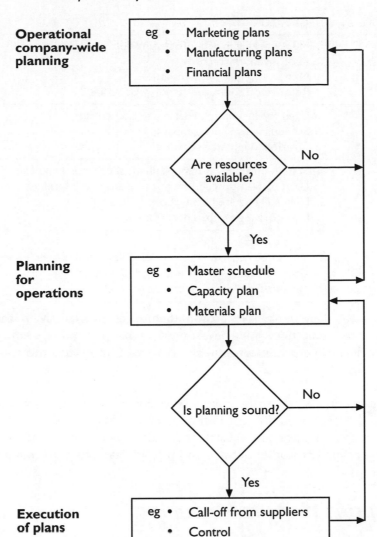

3.37 Closing the loop involves comparing production plans against the availability of resources. MRP makes the assumption that resources required are available. Closed loop MRP II checks whether the required resources are available. If this is not the case then the MPS is modified.

3.38 Oliver Wright has classified MRP/MRP II implementation and effectiveness under four headings. Starting with Class D status they have the ability to graduate to Class A status.

Table 8.2 *Implementation and effectiveness of MRP/MRP II*

Class	Characteristics
D	MRP working in data-processing department only Poor inventory records Master schedule mismanaged Reliance on shortage lists for progressing
C	Used for inventory ordering, not scheduling Scheduling by shortage lists Overloaded master schedule
B	System includes capacity planning, shop floor control Used to plan production, not to manage the business Help still required from shortage lists Inventory higher than necessary
A	Uses closed-loop MRP Integrated capacity planning, shop floor control and vendor scheduling Used to plan sales, engineering and purchasing No shortage lists to over-ride schedules

3.39   MRP and MRP II systems have proven themselves particularly in batch manufacture. Although they require ongoing investment in people and system development the rewards in increased professionalism as the system integrates into the organisation can be impressive.

3.40   Manufacturing on a larger scale brings a new range of issues that goes beyond the design of MRP and MRP II systems. Just in time (JIT) systems can utilise MRP and MRP II, but MRP shows to best advantage in batch production systems where the need is to schedule production around customer demand and supplier lead times. JIT will be discussed as the text develops.

4   Enterprise resource planning

What is ERP?

4.1   Enterprise resource planning (ERP) is the practice of consolidating an enterprise's planning, manufacturing, logistics, supply chain, sales and marketing efforts into one management system.

4.2   To integrate systems across an organisation is a tall order. Each department has its own system designed to meet its particular needs (known as 'legacy' systems). ERP combines them together to form a single, integrated software program that operates off a single database enabling the sharing of information and enhanced communication.

4.3   ERP systems are increasingly being used, at this stage primarily by multinational organisations, to integrate all aspects of the business into one unified database that interfaces across the entire organisation.

4.4   ERP helps the communication between all aspects of a business including human resources, financial accounting, manufacturing, supply-chain management, logistics and sales.

4.5   ERP systems are a development of the MRP approach that enables an examination of the consequences that changes will bring. The same principle forms the basis of ERP systems but on a far wider scale.

4.6   ERP (despite the name) is not a planning system but is more about resources and enterprise. It can have a defined purpose (particularly with supply chain management and financial accounting where resources can be more finely monitored and discrepancies become more apparent), but its main purpose is about gaining competitive advantage for the enterprise as a whole.

Implementing ERP

4.7   When implementing ERP, an organisation must go through a careful period of strategic planning that will involve a strong and ongoing commitment from senior management. Implementation will take from three months to two years and will prove a costly operation. Existing systems (legacy systems) must be integrated into the new software, and packages and features required from the new system will require development.

4.8   ERP systems provide a generic business model for an organisation to follow. This may cause problems, as most businesses will not fit neatly into this model. It may prove necessary to reconfigure or reengineer aspects of the business. Software can be customised to meet requirements but at a price.

4.9   Many companies have successfully integrated ERP software systems. Others have not been as successful. Hershey Foods issued two profit warnings in the run-up to Christmas 2004 as huge distribution problems followed a flawed implementation. In November 1999, domestic appliance manufacturer Whirlpool also blamed shipping delays on implementation problems.

4.10   Clearly the strategic considerations and possible implementation pitfalls of ERP systems require detailed thought. Here are some relevant considerations to ponder.

- Who are our stakeholders?
- Which processes are most important now and why?
- Does the system meet our needs or go beyond them?
- Do we integrate over stages and if we do what sequence should we use?
- Who will be responsible for change management?
- Who will be our change champions?
- What is our business culture and what are its strengths?
- How can we maximise those strengths?
- What are our weak areas and how will we address issues caused by them?
- What will be the toughest changes and how will we address them?

Chapter summary

- An item is subject to dependent demand if its demand depends on the demand for a larger product of which it forms part.

- Independent demand items are goods that are required for an operation in quantities independent of those used in the production process. There are very few independent demands in supply chains.

- With periodic review systems the stock level of the product is determined and examined at regular or fixed intervals.

- Fixed order quantities are based around a fixed point reorder system where inventory is replenished with a predetermined quantity when inventory falls to a predetermined level.

- ABC analysis is a form of Pareto analysis based on the principle that in any series of elements to be controlled, a selected small fraction in terms of numbers always accounts for a large fraction in terms of effect.

- With the EOQ approach the objective is to work out the balance between acquisition and holding costs so as to minimise total costs relating to stock.

- The objective of the Delphi method is the reliable and creative development of ideas or the production of suitable information to aid decision-making.

- The MRP program works by 'exploding' the BOM by reference to the production schedule

- MRP systems emphasise the importance of precise and accurate ordering and production policies, which if successfully followed will lead to reduced inventory levels.

- Manufacturing resources planning (MRP II) builds on key areas of MRP by considering all the resources needed for production, not just materials.

- MRP II is often described as a closed-loop system, in that there is an automatic feedback from the manufacturing function to the MPS, leading to changes in the MPS.

- Enterprise resource planning (ERP) is the practice of consolidating an enterprise's planning, manufacturing, logistics, supply chain, sales and marketing efforts into one management system.

Self-test questions

Numbers in brackets refer to the paragraphs above where your answers can be checked.

1. What is the distinction between dependent and independent demand? (1.3, 1.4)

2. How might a review be undertaken when an organisation is using a periodic review mechanism for stock management? (1.10)

3. What are the limitations of the EOQ approach? (1.35)

4. What are the characteristics of a good forecast? (2.4)

5. What system enables the advance planning of materials required for manufacture? (3.3)

6. Is MRP II a closed loop or open loop system? (3.36)

7. What system combines discrete systems together to form a single, integrated software program that operates off a single database enabling the sharing of information and enhanced communication? (4.2)

Further reading

*   *Operations Management*, Slack, Chambers and Johnston, Chapters 10, 12, 13 and 14.

*   *Production and Operations Management*, Muhlemann, Oakland and Lockyer, Chapter 26.

CHAPTER 9

Just In Time Manufacture

Learning objectives and indicative content

4.2   Analyse, select and use basic techniques to forecast demand.

-    Characteristics of 'push' and 'pull' operations

5.2   Examine and evaluate the philosophy of just in time (JIT) and continuous performance improvement in the context of lean manufacturing

-    The definition and philosophy of JIT
-    JIT as the basis for a continuous improvement programme
-    The advantages of JIT
-    Aspects of lean manufacturing and lean supply chains

5.3   Analyse and explain the different approaches to continuous improvement.

-    Process mapping
-    FMEA
-    The PDCA cycle
-    Different methods for managing and reducing stockholding

Chapter headings

1   Push systems and pull systems

2   The definition and philosophy of just in time

3   Lean manufacturing

4   Detecting and preventing failure

1   Push systems and pull systems

1.1   Inventory control systems fall into two categories: 'push' systems and 'pull' systems.

-    A **push system** provides supplies of materials in anticipation of demand.
-    A **pull system** is one that controls the flow of work through a factory by releasing materials into production when they are needed, and not before.

1.2   Push systems are characterised by stock management methods such as periodic review and fixed order quantity, where demand is anticipated in advance and stock levels are kept to predetermined levels in order to meet anticipated demand. Production is scheduled to meet expected use or sales.

1.3   Pull systems are based on the sale of the manufactured item and here goods are provided only in response to demand. Production scheduling is based on the use or sale of the manufactured item. Pull systems are best demonstrated by just in time manufacturing systems.

1.4   An MRP system is predominantly a push system as it involves supplies of materials in anticipation of demand (ie forecasting) but could be said to contain elements of a pull system in that it responds to customer orders. The reason it could be said to be predominantly a push system is that it responds to customer orders rather than being led by them, as is the case with just in time systems.

1.5   For the operations manager it is important to understand how push and pull systems affect manufacture. The plan of action (loading, sequencing and scheduling) requires monitoring and control. One aspect of control is when problems occur and intervention is required to remedy the situation.

1.6   Push systems are controlled by a central system where the workstations push the completed work from one workstation to the next. Although production schedules and capacity are well planned and co-ordinated there may be practical issues that arise that cause bottlenecks and delays in the production process. Push systems are often characterised by idle time, bottlenecks and storage issues caused by inventory build up during idle time. Management of these issues will be an important aspect of operations management.

1.7   With pull systems the production scheduling is based on the use or sale of the manufactured item. Pull scheduling is usually used to describe a kanban system that we will examine when looking at just in time manufacturing.

1.8   The customer is the catalyst for manufacture in a pull system. The pace of work is dictated by customer demand. Orders are placed with suppliers based on customer demand. Within the manufacturing environment the workstations pull the material from the previous workstation only when they want it.

1.9   Slack, Chambers and Johnston illustrate the differences clearly by using the gravity analogy. With the push system goods pass downhill from one workstation to the next as soon as their processing has been completed. There will often be a build up of stock due to disruptions in the manufacturing process.

1.10   The pull process sees goods travelling uphill and being moved onto the next stage only when required. As they cannot move uphill as easily as downhill they need to be 'pulled' to the next workstation when required. This enables stockholding to be minimised and later deliveries to be made resulting in reduced inventory cost. Greater emphasis is placed on provision of a quality item and there is greater flexibility in satisfying customer demand as goods can undergo late customisation to meet customer requirements.

Case study *Dell Computers*

A good example of a 'pull' system in practice is that developed and operated by Dell Computers. Based mainly on internet ordering, their system, involving both direct sales to consumers and business-to-business dealings, allows the organisation to perform mass customisation to meet customers' individual requirements.

Rather than manufacturing against a sales forecast, goods can now be tailor-made to meet customer requirements.

Making to order transforms the supply chain into a demand chain, in which the trick is not to optimise the chain to fill the warehouse, but to deliver to the customer.

Dell computers are built to order over a short timeframe (target 15 minutes). Orders are placed. A limited number of suppliers are used who have an IT link to the orders received by Dell. Their timed deliveries to Dell's JIT system are dependent on the orders placed. By adopting this approach to supply, Dell minimise stockholding and associated costs and utilise dependent demand to automatically order the latest component or part from their supplier.

The limited number of suppliers allows Dell to develop partnership strategies with their suppliers where both parties work together to enable delivery of the common goals of efficiency savings and high levels of customer service.

To do this effectively means synchronised production schedules between supplier and end manufacturer. It also enables suppliers to be proactive, anticipating the need to make deliveries. Suppliers can be granted access to customer feedback, enabling them to improve their performance. The benefits come not only from greater customer satisfaction but also from pulling higher volumes through the supply chain and not holding stocks of finished product.

Every PC is sold and ready to ship as it comes off the production line.

(Adapted from Institute of Logistics Newsletter, Summer 2000)

2 The definition and philosophy of just in time

Defining 'just in time'

2.1 Just in time (JIT) can be taken to mean exactly what it says: goods arrive at the factory just in time and they are available at the appropriate assembly point just in time. The just-in-time approach challenges the assumption that at least some stock should be held by manufacturers.

2.2 JIT is a Japanese management philosophy applied in manufacturing that involves having the right items of the right quality and quantity in the right place at the right time. Those organisations that have successfully adopted and integrated JIT into their operations have acknowledged increases in quality, productivity and efficiency, improved communication, reduced costs and waste.

2.3 The concept of just in time is more than a stock control approach. To operate successfully, JIT requires the progressive reduction of wasteful activities, a commitment to quality and the effective use of IT systems to analyse, monitor and integrate operations throughout the supply chain.

2.4 A useful definition of JIT is given by Christopher Voss.

'Just in time provides a disciplined approach to improving overall productivity and eliminating waste. It provides for the cost-effective production and delivery of only the necessary quantity of parts at the right quality, at the right time and place, while using the minimum amount of facilities, equipment, materials and human resources. JIT is dependent on the balance between the supplier's flexibility and the user's flexibility. It is accomplished through the application of elements that require total employee involvement and teamwork. A key philosophy of JIT is simplification.'

2.5   Key points of this definition:

- 'A disciplined approach' – structured procedures and processes but ones that can be challenged.

- 'Improving overall productivity' – overall implies the acceptance of 'trade-offs' in the JIT system. The aim is that increases in one area may be more than balanced by reductions in other areas.

- 'Eliminating waste' – JIT has its roots in the Toyota Production System that was headed by Taichi Ohno (of 'seven wastes' fame).

- 'Minimum amount of facilities' – JIT approaches and adaptations include continuous flow manufacture, lean operations and high value-added manufacture all of which seek to maximise available facilities while minimising costs.

- 'The balance between the supplier's flexibility and the user's flexibility' – JIT requires late deliveries often utilising linked IT systems where a close business relationship and commitment between supplier and customer allows for an understanding of each other's business needs to be developed for the overall good of the process.

- 'Total employee involvement and teamwork' – JIT integrates the quality approach to be central to its operations.

- 'Simplification' – keep all processes as simple as possible. If something does not add value, question its validity and purpose.

2.6   The drive to implement JIT lies largely in attaining the gains in quality and productivity evidenced by Japanese manufacturing companies from the 1980's onwards. In today's competitive world organisations that are quick to apply innovative ideas in a thorough way to their manufacturing processes can gain a competitive advantage over those who do not.

2.7   Being a 'pull' system, JIT manufacturing is not adversely affected by economic or other fluctuations as production is readily flexible to meet variable consumer demand.

2.8   JIT focuses on adding value to products. The use of high quality components, assembling of these components and self-inspection of work in progress are all features that add value during the manufacturing process. Operations such as reworking, scrapping materials, holding inventory and excess handling do not add value, only cost. Consequently, closely associated with the concept of adding value is that of reducing waste.

2.9   Waste can be defined as 'anything other than the minimum amount of equipment, materials, parts, and working time essential to production' (Hay). The 'seven wastes' of Taichi Ohno demonstrate the meticulous approach used by Japanese manufacturing organisations. Refer back to Chapter 1 if you have forgotten about Ohno's analysis of waste.

'Inventory is evil'

2.10   JIT is fundamentally different from the more traditional methods of planning and control.

2.11 Conventional production control systems ensure resources are available when required by utilising inventory buffers (such as safety stock) which provide protection from disruptions to the manufacturing process. The approach seeks to ensure that even if one part of the manufacturing process is disrupted then other parts will still be able to continue.

2.12 JIT seeks to eliminate inventory because this merely hides an operation's inefficiencies. If inventory is removed, disruptions will have a major impact. Inventory can be viewed as a 'safety blanket', providing a fall-back when things go wrong. If no inventory is held problems are exposed, recognised and resolved.

Contrasting JIT with traditional systems

2.13 As compared with traditional systems, JIT systems seek reduced stock levels, reduced (and consistent) lead times, higher quality, improved responsiveness and flexibility and better customer service. Effective functioning of JIT depends on close synchronisation of all elements in the system, including external contributors (suppliers). Provided this is in place, the system can run without the need for safety stocks.

2.14 Some of the key differences between JIT and traditional systems are shown in Table 9.1.

Table 9.1 *Differences between JIT and traditional systems*

Just in time systems	Traditional systems
Inventories are reduced or eliminated	Safety stocks and operating stocks are held as a matter of policy
Production runs are short, and switch quickly from one product to another	Production runs are long, and relate to a single product, so reducing set-up and changeover costs
Lead times for both supply and production are consistently short	Long lead times are expected and are built into calculations of order quantities
A target is set of zero quality defects, because the system is so finely tuned that defective inputs can disrupt production	A certain level of defects is expected, and again is built into calculations of order quantities and stock levels
Relationships with suppliers are close and committed, with the objective of mutual benefit	Relationships with suppliers are often based on adversarial tactics, under which one party seeks to gain benefit at the expense of the other

2.15 Of course, the reliability of manufacturing processes is critical. Each stage in the production process is dependent on inputs from previous stages and if these fail to turn up there is no safety stock to fall back on. Reliable forecasting of supply needs is also vital, and this is an area where the purchasing department have an indispensable liaison role between internal production and suppliers. The reliance on integrated IT systems between suppliers and the organisation, coupled with simpler processes, changes the purchasing role to a more strategically led commercial relationship management role.

2.16 Assuming all goes to plan, the improvement in stock turnover periods can be dramatic.

2.17 JIT seeks to constantly improve the operation and requires the improvement in all performance objectives. Key JIT operational objectives are as follows.

- **Quality**. Disruptions to the production operation have a major impact. Consequently it is necessary to ensure that suppliers deliver a quality product consistently. All tiers of suppliers must share the commitment to quality. There is no chance for inspection, rework or rejection of product. The delivered product must be right every time, all the time.

- **Speed**. Within the JIT environment little work in progress is held, with most of the work effectively being made on a make-to-order basis. Speed of manufacture and throughput is therefore essential in order to maximise resources, to minimise stockholding and to be flexible in the delivery of the right finished product.

- **Flexibility**. One advantage of JIT is its ability to react to customers' changing requirements. One way of being flexible is to keep the manufacturing batch size small. In essence, run a number of small batches that meet requirements and maximise flexible systems of manufacture with quick exchange of tools and dies and computer controlled manufacture that can be quickly adapted to meet a new manufacturing configuration.

- **Dependability**. The result of all of the above is the exposure and rectification of problems. The resultant process should encounter an ever reducing number of operational problems resulting in greater predictability and dependability.

2.18 JIT does cause some reduction in capacity utilisation. The flexibility inherent within JIT means that some sacrifices must be made when compared to mass production systems. The benefit in this regard is that the output product can meet customer requirements more precisely.

The importance of zero

2.19 'Zero' is a commonly used word in JIT: not just zero inventory but zero defects (through a commitment to quality), zero lead-time (as suppliers are programmed to be more responsive to demand), zero handling (the elimination of physical handling of goods and those aspects of the operation that do not add value) and zero set-up times (for machines used in the manufacturing process). 'Zero' is difficult to achieve but is an ongoing target.

2.20 Manufacturing related costs are reduced by methods such as design for manufacture or design for assembly techniques where all unnecessary attributes, processes or parts are eliminated. Costs of quality are reduced as inspection and related costs (returns, rework) are eliminated.

2.21 Materials related costs are reduced by a zero inventory approach coupled with a reduction in the number of suppliers an organisation deals with and a commitment to a closer business relationship with the remaining suppliers. This allows for the standardisation of documentary processes, eliminating the need to count individual parts, eliminating expediting, simplifying receiving systems, minimising unpacking and eliminating the costs of excess inventory.

2.22 Just-in-time techniques impact across all related areas of business activities. Procurement requires a 'partnership' approach with suppliers involving greater emphasis being placed on 'relationship management'. Distribution is about working on on-time deliveries and scheduling, optimum loads where appropriate and flexible loads where appropriate. Finance considers payment on delivery via automated systems (goods will not be rejected as quality is guaranteed.)

Kanban

2.23 Kanban is often seen as a central element of the JIT system. The word is Japanese in origin, **kan** standing for card or ticket and **ban** for signal. The concept of cards has been long established in production for visual identification and location of goods and serves to identify the part number and quantity held in a storage box or container. The 'two-bin system' where one bin of parts is replaced by another, the original then being refilled, is established practice for many production operations worldwide. Kanban develops this process further in that it becomes the 'driver' of the manufacturing operation.

2.24 As we have discussed JIT is a 'pull' system. Here the flow of work is controlled by releasing materials into production, as the customer demands them. Kanban is not a scheduling system but a production control system. Scheduling will be planned as we have described earlier in the text but changes or adaptations to the schedule come from customer demand rather than bottlenecks or capacity constraints (features of a 'push' system).

2.25 The kanban process uses two different kinds of cards: transport (conveyance) and production.

- The transport kanban contains information concerning the origin of the part and its destination. When this card only is used it is known as little or simple kanban with a focus on scheduling parts and providing resources when needed. Transport kanban is described by Roos as 'ordering a box when one is left on the line'. One box of components goes to the operator as required. When the box is empty it is returned and this will automatically trigger the delivery of the next box.

- The production kanban schedules to what extent and when work has been accomplished at production stages on the assembly line. The production kanban signals the need to produce more parts to enable this requirement to be met.

2.26 Production ordering is only carried out when an operation signals that it is needed. The signalling can be by the passing of cards, by painted squares on the ground (which when empty need to be refilled), by chalk marks on the wall or by e-signalling (known as e-ban). Production is pulling the goods through the manufacturing process as they are needed.

2.27 To maximise the effectiveness of production, quantities ordered are always the same. Any increases or decreases in production are reflected in the number of production kanbans placed.

2.28 The reality of the production line is that there will be occasions where rush jobs have to be carried out. If this is to be accomplished in a JIT system there needs to be a method of prioritisation. This can be achieved by the use of coloured kanban cards. If an operative has a number of cards to produce to, then the red card is an automatic signal to the operative to prioritise that order. This is sometimes referred to as 'emergency kanban' but also demonstrates how flexibility can be introduced into the system.

2.29 **Roos** lists the following advantages for kanban over traditional push systems such as MRP.

- A simple and understandable process
- Provides quick and precise information
- Low costs associated with the transfer of information
- Provides quick response to changes
- Limit of over-capacity in processes
- Avoids overproduction
- Minimises waste
- Maximises control
- Delegates responsibility to line workers

2.30 He goes on to state that 'Kanban represents an efficient tool to continuously rationalise the production process and find the source of problems'. The kanban system, particularly by delegating responsibility to line workers, means that if there is a problem on the production line then it is easy to spot and then can be rectified.

JIT techniques

2.31 The kanban process is more than a production methodology. To operate successfully on the shop floor it requires a close interaction between workers and management. The empowerment of workers is fundamental. Worker involvement, in particular the use of daily meetings where work practices and methods can be discussed, are a cornerstone of this. Those involved on a daily basis will often see aspects of the job that management will miss. Their contribution should be valued. A US/European development of this process can be seen in 'quality circles'.

2.32 Simple visible controls are a characteristic of JIT operations. JIT factories are often open plan. Visible controls enable workers to communicate with each other easily and help keep the operation simple. Lights indicate the status of machinery (working, idle or broken). Statistical process control data is displayed, as are samples of good and bad output.

2.33 Simple methods are used such as standardised containers replacing irregular sizes (enabling counting of the containers, not the standardised quantities contained in them), chalk marks or marked floor spaces indicating when stock should be replaced and the use of flip charts so that workers can note down problems as they occur for discussion in the next daily meeting.

2.34 Layout of production lines is kept as simple as possible. Modular/cell manufacturing (sometimes referred to as group technology) involves organising machinery so that related products can be manufactured in a continuous flow. This is based on the principle that product focused manufacture is much simpler, with reduced material flows, than where similar processes are grouped together.

2.35 Modular/cell manufacturing can be optimised by U-shaping of processing lines which enables a manageable continuous workflow within the team working concept of JIT.

2.36 The use of multiple small machines (as opposed to larger, efficient machines that require product maximisation) enables enhanced flexibility. Considerable thought is given to machines that 'multi-task' and have little downtime. Set-up reduction times are a key focus as speed of changeover allows increased flexibility and productivity.

2.37 Production smoothing or levelled schedules enable small, regular batch sizes to be integrated into the manufacturing process. For production kanban to operate successfully requires a stable demand for the end product. JIT operates best with predictable, level demand so the JIT route is not applicable for all operations. Production smoothing enables better planning of the 'hourly rate of demand' and 'labour balancing' within the manufacturing environment.

2.38 Total productive maintenance (TPM) encourages operatives or 'process owners' to do their own maintenance whenever possible and to call on skilled engineers only when essential. This empowers the workers to become more involved in the process and frees up the engineer for other tasks. Training needs have to be considered and delivered.

The effects on suppliers

2.39 JIT calls for a closer involvement with suppliers. Suppliers become an integral part of the JIT operation through quality, timed deliveries and effective use of IT.

2.40 The JIT approach to operations management changes the nature of the relationship between supplier and manufacturer. Voss develops the theme of 'high dependency theory'. Both parties become increasingly reliant on each other and this reliance has its own dangers as well as advantages. The role of the manufacturer's procurement team is more one of building and sustaining an ongoing commercial relationship in this regard, one that (dependent on the degree of integration between the two companies) can be difficult to break without severe ramifications.

2.41 This increasing dependency requires a more thorough approach to risk assessment and ongoing risk management in order to ensure continuity of supply in case of the relationship breaking down.

2.42 This relationship or partnering approach offers suppliers the following benefits.

- A long-term guaranteed contract
- Commercial benefits of economies of scale
- Steady demand
- Minimal paperwork
- Payment on-time

2.43 Manufacturers secure the following benefits.

- Quality components
- Guaranteed delivery
- Competitive prices
- Suppliers' commitment from the concept stage onwards
- The ability to develop a lean supply chain

2.44 Supplier selection criteria will include the following.

- Proximity to the manufacturing plant. This enables prompt delivery when required.
- Quality. A commitment to quality process and a supply chain philosophy is a core JIT requirement.
- Good industrial relations. Disruptions caused by trade disputes can have a considerable impact and the need to ensure stability in industrial relations is also a core requirement.
- Reduced total number of suppliers.

2.45 The role of purchasing changes fundamentally when dealing with suppliers. Close relationships are established with a limited supplier base. This is reflected by the emphasis placed on the supply chain management approach and the purchasing emphasis on relationship management.

2.46 The supply chain management approach cascades the demands for quality and on-time delivery through the supply chain ensuring that all tiers of suppliers understand their commitment and work pro-actively to meet it.

2.47 The emphasis on relationship management is encouraged by an increasing mutual reliance by supplier and organisation. The reduced supplier base ensures that the selected supplier gets high levels of work, not only the supply of goods but closer development and IT infrastructure links. This reliance on selected suppliers changes the relationship over time as both organisations become more equal in their mutually beneficial relationship.

JIT and continuous improvement

2.48 The concept of continuous improvement has its roots in the early quality management gurus, particularly Deming and Juran. Deming's initial message was about the need to measure product deviations and to continually reduce them. His message was well received in Japan where a thorough and meticulous approach to manufacture has long been appreciated. Deming's approach was based on the PDCA cycle devised by Walter Shewhart.

- Plan – design or revise business process components to improve results
- Do – implement the plan and measure its performance
- Check – assess the measurements and report the results to decision makers
- Act – decide on changes needed to improve the process

2.49 Continuous improvement is an integral part of the JIT concept and, to be effective, must be adopted by each member of the organisation, not only those directly involved in the production process. Continuous improvement means setting goals and standards to be met and, when these have been achieved, increased in such a way as makes them reasonable and achievable.

2.50 **Kaizen** is the Japanese term for continuous improvement. 'It is both a rigorous, scientific method of using statistical quality control and an adaptive framework of organisational values and beliefs that keep management and workers alike focused on zero defects.'

2.51 The kaizen approach is to increase an organisation's competitiveness on an ongoing basis through a series of small, gradual improvements. If part of the process can be improved every week then the accumulated gains can be substantial. The kaizen approach encourages group working, quality circles and cross-functional teamwork in a way that encourages discussion throughout the organisation. Many ideas for improvement come from those working at an operational level and this includes administrative as well as manufacturing operations personnel.

2.52 The kaizen approach is dependent on the commitment of the entire workforce. Improvements come from those who do the work. The system must encourage workers to contribute by setting time aside, encouraging group working ('kaizen groups') and encouraging suggestions. The Japanese approach has not always travelled successfully to the United States and Europe where the concept does not always mix with Western culture and a financial reward system is often linked to the western approach.

2.53 Although not exclusively linked to JIT systems kaizen is an established Japanese business practice that underpins much of the thinking behind JIT and Japanese business practice in general. It has four stages.

- Establish a plan to change whatever needs to be improved.
- Carry out changes on a small scale.
- Observe and measure the results.
- Evaluate both the results and the process and determine what has been learned.

2.54 Although kaizen offers many benefits it is limited in that it can only improve existing systems. On some occasions radical thinking may be required, particularly if the system is out of date or being surpassed by business developments. This process, known as **business process reengineering** (BPR), differs from kaizen in that kaizen improves on what you have while BPR throws away what you have and starts again! Business process reengineering is examined later in the text.

2.55 The drive to make continuous improvements over time and the statistical approach makes the kaizen approach an integral part of the JIT philosophy. JIT is a philosophy that involves eliminating waste, involving everyone and continuous improvement. By utilising JIT an organisation will not suddenly be transformed but will be on a path that might enable it to effectively deliver world best practices for the benefit of itself, its partners and its customers.

3   *Lean manufacturing*

The origins of lean manufacturing

3.1   Just in time has proven itself over time as an effective approach and philosophy to manufacturing and stock control. The main tenets of just in time have been developed further by 'lean production', an approach that takes the best of modern thinking and integrates it into an overall approach to manufacture.

3.2   The idea of lean production was first analysed in depth by John Krafcik when he and others were working on a motor vehicle programme in the late 1980s. The idea was later popularised in *The Machine that Changed the World* (1990) by Womack, Jones and Roos. They defined lean production as follows.

'Lean production is "lean" because it uses less of every thing compared with mass production: half the human effort in the factory, half the factory space, half the investment in tools, half the engineering hours to develop a new product in half the time. Also, it requires far less than half of the needed inventory on site. The expected results are fewer defects, while producing a greater and ever growing variety of products.'

3.3   Lean thinking can be applied to any organisational type (including services) and can be applied across all areas of the business. It is a three-pronged approach that incorporates a belief in quality, waste elimination and employee involvement supported by a structured management system.

3.4   Implications of this new approach were that high volume production of standard models was no longer enough to satisfy ever more demanding customers, and that higher levels of quality and shorter time to market in new product development were achievable targets.

3.5   Lean production is similar to just in time in that it uses a range of waste saving measures. However lean production differs in that it is a philosophy of production that aims to minimise inputs while maximising outputs. Some of the techniques that can be used to develop lean production are just in time, total quality management, zero defects, kaizen, cell-based production, time-based management and simultaneous engineering. It is not one system but an amalgam of related business disciplines that are brought together in the most effective manner in order to meet the goals of lean production.

3.6   Daniel Jones has identified five principles that characterise lean production organisations.

- As far as possible, tasks and responsibilities are transferred to those who are actually adding value on the production line.

- Discovering defects and problems immediately, and eliminating their cause, is an important objective of control systems.

- A comprehensive information system enables everyone to respond quickly.

- Organisation must be based on empowered work teams.

- This in turn encourages a strong sense of reciprocal obligation between staff and the organisation.

Eliminating waste

3.7 Lean manufacturing uses and further develops the concept of the 'seven wastes' pioneered by Taichi Ohno. The 'new' manufacturing culture is based on concentrating on the value stream, to instil the ongoing discipline to reduce waste, to seek to continually improve, to generate capital, to make profit, and to remain competitive in today's global market.

3.8 The value stream of a business is the sequence of steps that an organisation performs in order to satisfy a customer's need. Lean production looks at achieving a big reduction in the number of steps in the process. The initial step is to identify efficiency gaps and areas for waste reduction. Mapping the value stream provides a tool to staff to enable a structured way of identifying waste, establishing the root cause of that waste, and preparing a plan for its elimination.

3.9 The 'seven wastes' are overproduction, excess inventory, transportation, waiting, unnecessary motion, over-processing and correction. Overproduction is a source of waste to many manufacturing organisations. The reliance of many organisations on the batch and queue mode of operation will mean that overproduction is an unavoidable outcome. It costs more to manufacture an item than to hold its component parts.

3.10 The remaining 'wastes' can all be evaluated by reference to the 'value stream'. If these areas can be identified then we can work on eliminating or reducing them.

3.11 Lean manufacturing focuses on waste elimination, continuous one-piece workflow and customer pull. Focusing these elements in the areas of cost, quality, and delivery can form the basis for a lean production system.

3.12 The lean transformation is directed by a set of guiding tenets.

- Positive, clear communications
- Ensure 'no-blame' culture
- Work through cross-functional teams
- Involve staff at every stage
- Process maps displayed to attract comment
- Remove non-value added steps
- Agree design principles with all
- Fix the root cause, not the symptom
- Ensure the solution supports departmental interfaces
- Incorporate continuous improvement

3.13 Lean manufacturing develops the concept of JIT by integrating other applicable aspects of manufacture. Terms that are frequently used in lean manufacture illustrate the integrated nature of the different proven techniques that can be applied.

- **Set-up time**: the work required to change a machine or process from one to the next.
- **Cycle time**: the normal time taken to complete an operation on a product.

- **Takt time**: from the German for rhythm, takt time is the allowable time to produce one product at the rate the customers are demanding it. The cycle time will be less than or equal to the takt time.

- **Jidoka**: an automated process where machinery inspects each item after producing it, ceasing production if a defect is detected.

- **Heijunka**: a production scheduling tool aimed at levelling production. It is used to distribute kanban cards in the most efficient manner.

- **SMED** (single minute exchange of die): changing a die on a forming or stamping machine within a minute. Extended to mean the ability to perform any set-up activity within a minute.

- **Nagara**: smooth production flow, ideally one piece at a time (requires the synchronisation of production processes and maximum utilisation of available time).

- **Mixed-model production**: the capability to produce a variety of models, that differ in material and work required content, on the same production line. This enables efficient utilisation of resources while providing rapid response to demand fluctuation.

- **Flexible manufacturing system**: an integrated manufacturing capability to produce small numbers of a great variety of items at low unit cost.

- **Pull system**: a manufacturing planning system based on the communication of actual real-time needs from downstream operations through to final assembly or manufacture.

3.14 Lean techniques can be applied in the service sector. The process of eliminating anything that does not add value is a common goal. Techniques such as continuous improvement, smooth flow, provision of a mix of services, cycle time and takt time all have their place.

3.15 The search for lean performance soon spread beyond its origins in manufacturing. Service companies realised that the new model was in many respects just as applicable to their markets. Within organisations, individual functions began to seek ways of becoming leaner. In particular, the idea gained ground that eliminating waste in purchasing activities, and avoiding duplication of effort throughout the supply chain, could bring important cost and quality benefits. The concept of lean supply was born.

3.16 According to Harrison, Swift and Gillespie, lean production is likely to be successful when:

- The management style is democratic
- Employees are empowered
- Employees are motivated
- Communication is effective and two-way

Supplier relations

3.17 Two aspects of supplier relations are particularly important in this respect: working together to remove duplication of effort, and cost transparency.

3.18 Removing duplication means reducing elements within the supply chain that do not add value but do add to costs. Professor Richard Lamming has put forward a model of customer-supplier relationships that illustrates the characteristics of lean supply.

Table 9.2 *Customer-supplier relationships in lean supply*

Factor	Lean supply characteristics
Nature of competition	Global operation, local presence Based upon contribution to product technology Dependent upon alliances/collaboration
How suppliers are selected by customers	Early involvement of established supplier Joint efforts in target costing/value analysis Single and dual sourcing Supplier provides global benefits Re-sourcing as a last resort after attempts to improve
Exchange of information between supplier and customer	True transparency, costs, etc Two-way discussion of costs and volumes Exchange of technical and commercial information Electronic data interchange Kanban system for production deliveries
Management of capacity	Regionally strategic investments discussed Synchronised capacity Flexibility to operate with fluctuations
Delivery practice	True, just in time with Kanban Local, long-distance and international JIT
Dealing with price changes	Price reductions based upon cost reductions from order onwards: from joint efforts of supplier and customer
Factor	Lean supply characteristics
Attitude to quality	Supplier vetting schemes become redundant Mutual agreement on quality targets Continual interaction and improvement (kaizen) Perfect quality as a goal

3.19 Cost transparency means that suppliers should be expected to talk frankly with customers about cost structures. The supplier can benefit from this because greater information frequently means that the customer can suggest improvements for the supplier to exploit.

Agile production

3.20 The future of lean production is often viewed as a move to agile production. Agility is an acknowledgement that we operate in an ever-changing world with constantly changing demands.

3.21 'Agile' is different from 'lean' in that it embraces the philosophy and takes the advantages of lean but seeks to build on them by offering more flexibility built in from a strategic level. Manufacturing will be able to be more responsive, products will go from design through to production more quickly, quality will underpin the processes, the views of the supply chain, business partners and the customer will be more fully utilised, and change will be an accepted part of the operation.

3.22 Agile production is a fast developing concept. You have seen in the last few chapters the evolving approaches to manufacturing from MRP to MRP II to JIT to lean production. Clearly this development does not stop but will continue in order to meet customer demands using the best practices, thinking and technology.

4 Detecting and preventing failure

The definition and causes of failure

4.1 Quality is inherent in any product or service. It is, however, subject to change with the age or acceptability of the offering. The acceptability of a product will depend on its ability to perform satisfactorily over a period of time. The reliability of a product is its ability to meet customer requirements over time.

4.2 Reliability ranks alongside quality in importance to customers. It forms the basis of many purchasing decisions where comparisons are being made. There is clearly a closer inter-relationship between quality and reliability as one of the goals of quality production will be to produce a reliable product. However, every product will eventually fail.

Preventing failure through design controls

4.3 Reliability is an important aspect of the acceptability of a product. There is a need to plan and design reliability into products and services, Earlier in the text we examined the design and development phase of product design. Methods such as failure mode and effects analysis and Taguchi methodology were introduced and discussed. Proven methods of this type enable products to be designed to meet customer needs not only in marketing terms but also in terms of quality and reliability.

4.4 When a product, system, component or service no longer performs its required function, it is said to have failed.

4.5 This definition assumes that the required function is being attained exactly. A car could be described as working or broken down, or something in between (eg the clock is not working or performance has deteriorated over time). Failure can be built in (eg a car headlight may be designed to last three years where the car may have an anticipated life of ten years). The engineering and costs involved in producing a headlight may be excessive, technologically too difficult or perceived as being an acceptable failure by users.

4.6 To understand failure it is useful to consider the various types and causes of failure.

- **Total failure**: is the complete lack of ability of the product or service to perform or fulfil its function
- **Partial failure**: where the item does not work as expected but has not completely failed
- **Gradual failure**: which takes place progressively over time. Gradual failure can often be anticipated or built in.
- **Sudden failure**: occurs unpredictably and is not easily predicted

4.7   Failure may be built-in following an acceptable working life, or it may be caused by misuse or by a weakness in design. Misuse is frequently caused by the stresses caused outside the anticipated design and use. Weakness can frequently be traced back to the design or production stage where the ramifications of use have not been fully evaluated.

4.8   Where failure is 'built-in' this is normally evaluated following extensive testing. An example would be a car seat that is subject to one million machine 'visits' to see how it will wear in everyday use. The failure rate of products is higher at the introduction or 'infant' stage, usually consistent during the normal or adult period, and high again during the 'ageing' period.

Asset maintenance, management and replacement

4.9   The purpose of maintenance is to optimise the performance of equipment by attempting to prevent breakdowns or failures. An understanding of the nature and purpose of maintenance regimes and schedules enables the operations manager to view production schedules with greater confidence as the incidence of delays or breakdowns in production will be reduced. This will be discussed in detail in Chapter 11.

Chapter summary

- A push system provides supplies of materials in anticipation of demand.

- A pull system is one that controls the flow of work through a factory by releasing materials into production when they are needed.

- The customer is the catalyst for manufacture in a pull system.

- The concept of JIT goes further than just stock control.

- JIT seeks to eliminate inventory as this merely hides an operation's inefficiencies.

- Kanban is often seen as a central element of the JIT system.

- Simple visible controls are a characteristic of JIT operations.

- JIT calls for a closer involvement with suppliers.

- Lean production is 'lean' because it uses less of every thing compared with mass production

- Lean manufacturing focuses on waste elimination, continuous one-piece workflow and customer pull.

- Lean techniques can be applied in the service sector.

- The purpose of maintenance is to optimise the performance of equipment by attempting to prevent breakdowns or failures

Self-test questions

Numbers in brackets refer to the paragraphs above where your answers can be checked.

1 Distinguish between push systems and pull systems. (1.2, 1.3)

2 How do Slack, Chambers and Johnston illustrate the pull system? (1.9)

3 What are Taiichi Ohno's 'seven wastes'? (2.9)

4 What are the key JIT operational objectives? (2.17)

5 The kanban process uses what two different kinds of cards? (2.25)

6 How does the procurement department's approach to suppliers change when JIT is introduced? (2.39)

7 Lean thinking is a three-pronged approach that incorporates what? (3.3)

8 How is 'agile' different from 'lean'? (3.21)

9 What are the four different types of failure? (4.6)

Further reading

- *Operations Management*, Slack, Chambers and Johnston, Chapter 14.

- *Production and Operations Management*, Muhlemann, Oakland and Lockyer, Chapters 26 and 27.

CHAPTER 10

Project Management

Learning objectives and indicative content

4.4   Identify and analyse the key roles and objectives of project management

- Definition of project management
- The project lifecycle
- Creating a project network
- Calculating the critical path
- Resource constraints

Chapter headings

1   The nature of project work

2   The project management process

3   Creating a project network

1   The nature of project work

Defining project management

1.1   Project management is a carefully planned and organised effort to accomplish a specific and (usually) one-time effort (for example, to construct a building, refurbish a hotel or implement a new computer system).

1.2   Here are two definitions of project management.

- 'An activity, or usually a number of related activities, carried out according to a plan in order to achieve a definite objective within a certain period of time and which will cease when the objective is achieved.' (Lysons)
- 'A unique set of co-ordinated activities, with definite starting and finishing points, undertaken by an individual or team to meet specific objectives within defined time, cost and performance parameters.' (Office of Government Commerce)

1.3   These definitions highlight areas such as co-ordination, related activities, definite start and finish, plan, specific objectives and achievement which are all key considerations with projects and project management.

1.4   Project management includes developing a project plan, which includes defining project goals and objectives, specifying tasks or how goals will be achieved, what resources are needed, and associated budgets and timelines for completion. It also includes implementing the project plan, along with careful controls to stay on the 'critical path', that is, to ensure the project is being managed according to plan and that project milestones are being met.

Characteristics of projects

1.5   A project is a unique set of co-ordinated activities that has the following characteristics.

- A finite and defined lifespan
- Defined and measurable deliverables or outcomes to meet the specified objectives
- A set of activities to achieve the specified objectives
- A defined amount of resources
- An organisation structure, with defined responsibilities, to manage the project

1.6   There are three main points that are most important to a successful project.

- A project must meet customer requirements.
- A project must be within budget.
- A project must be completed on time.

1.7   Lysons distinguishes four different types of project.

- **Manufacturing projects**: such as prototyping a new product, development work or any discrete application of machinery or equipment to attain a defined end goal.
- **Construction projects**: that are characterised by being based off-site from a headquarters or central location.
- **Management projects**: activities, often utilising cross-functional teams, that have a defined purpose, eg office relocation, simultaneous engineering teams etc.
- **Research projects**: aimed at the expansion of knowledge or the acquisition of new data or information.

1.8   How does project work differ from other tasks in the workplace?

- **A project is an instrument of change**. By their very nature projects will produce a different end result (eg a refurbished hotel). This will induce a change situation for the management and staff involved when they return to work.
- **A project is non-routine**. Projects have a high degree of uncertainty as a result. In most cases, a project will not have been done before and will therefore require careful and ongoing planning.
- **A project is complex**. Many different tasks are involved in order to complete the objective. The inter-relationships between these tasks can be difficult to organise and manage. Controlling these inter-relationships involves planning and adaptability by the project manager.
- **A project is unique**. Even in the case of a 'repeat' project (such as building the same model of a house) there will still be differences in the time taken, resources used, personnel involved, etc.

- **A project is composed of inter-dependent activities.** Each of these must be scheduled so that later activities can begin on time.

- **A project is carried out by people who don't normally work together.** Projects throw people together usually based on their expertise in a specific area (eg plumbers, bricklayers and carpenters on a construction project, or designers, purchasing, marketing and engineers when developing a new product). This can cause problems as it takes time to form personal relationships. However, if the function to be carried out is specific and defined then the joint achievement of common goals can provide a bond.

- **A project is temporary with defined start and end dates.** Projects have a defined beginning and end. This will mean that resources are concentrated for the life of the project and may then be redeployed on the next project.

- **A project is intended to achieve a specific outcome.** Projects have a specification or defined end goal from the outset. Problems can often occur when changes are made to the specification during the project that can cause delays and subsequent additional costs. A recent UK example is the Scottish Parliament in Edinburgh where changes in the design led to spiralling costs.

Critical success factors

1.9 Slack *et al* give a detailed list of requirements for successful project management.

- **Clearly defined goals**: which can include the overall philosophy or mission of the project, and the commitment to those goals from the project team members.

- **Competent project manager**: a project leader who has the necessary blend of interpersonal, technical and administrative skills.

- **Top-management support**: commitment that must be communicated to the project team.

- **Competent project-team members**: the selection and training of project teams who have the right blend of skills to successfully complete the project.

- **Sufficient resource allocation**: in the form of finance, personnel, logistics etc, which are available when required.

- **Good communication channels**: between those involved on objectives, status, changes, organisational conditions and client needs.

- **Control mechanisms**: put in place to monitor actual events and recognise deviations from plan.

- **Feedback capabilities**: all parties concerned are able to review the project status and make suggestions and corrections.

- **Troubleshooting mechanisms**: a system or set of procedures which can tackle problems as they arise, trace them back to their root cause and resolve them.

- **Project staff continuity**: the continued involvement of key project personnel through the project lifecycle. Frequent staff turnover can dissipate acquired learning and damage team morale.

1.10 Successful projects have the following features.

- A well-defined scope and agreed understanding of intended outcome.

- Active management of risks and issues, and timely decision-making supported by clear and short lines of reporting.

- Ongoing commitment and support from senior management.
- A senior individual with personal accountability and overall responsibility for the successful outcome of the project.
- An appropriately trained and experienced project team and in particular a project manager whose capabilities match the complexity of the project.
- Defined and visibly managed processes that are appropriate for the scale and complexity of the project.

1.11 For cross-company projects, there may be nominated senior owners from each organisation involved in the project and its delivery. Where this is the case, there must be a single owner who is responsible for the whole project.

Why projects fail

1.12 Experience has shown that projects are inherently at risk through overrunning on time and cost and/or failing to deliver a successful outcome. Such failures are almost invariably caused by some or all of the following shortcomings.

- Poor project definition by the project's owner, perhaps because of insufficient consultation with stakeholders or their failure to be specific about requirements and desired outcomes.
- Lack of ownership and personal accountability by senior management.
- Inadequately skilled and experienced project personnel.
- Inadequate reporting arrangements and decision-making.
- Inconsistent understanding of required project activities, roles and responsibilities.

1.13 Project management techniques help to reduce and manage risk. It puts in place an organisation where lines of accountability are short and the responsibilities of individuals are clearly defined. Its processes are clearly documented and repeatable, so that those involved in the project can learn from the experiences of others.

1.14 Project management uses various measurement tools to accomplish and track project tasks. These include Gantt charts (described in an earlier chapter), critical path analysis and program evaluation and review technique (PERT).

The project manager

1.15 The inherent difficulty of project work places a considerable emphasis on the management of the project. The project manager must be able to successfully run the project and address barrier issues.

1.16 The role of the project manager is one of great responsibility. The project manager leads the project team and is assigned the authority and responsibility for conducting the project and meeting the project objectives, on time and within budget. It is the project manager's job to direct and supervise the project from beginning to end.

1.17 The project manager must define the project, reduce the project to a set of manageable tasks, obtain appropriate and necessary resources, and build a team or teams to perform the project work.

1.18 The project manager must set the final goal for the project and must motivate his workers to complete the project on time.

1.19 A project manager must have technical skills. These relate to financial planning, contract management, and managing creative thinking and problem solving techniques.

1.20 No project ever goes exactly as planned, so project managers must learn to be flexible and adapt to change.

2 The project management process

Stages in the process

2.1 Development of a project from conception through to fulfilment requires a considerable effort in terms of communication, organisation and control. The uniqueness of the project brings with it a degree of uncertainty to those involved and in consequence requires experienced management control.

2.2 Lysons identifies six stages in the project management process but we should be careful when applying this as all projects are different. Some stages will have more emphasis than others and some may not be prioritised in this order.

- **Definition**: the investigation into the feasibility of the project or identification of a problem that requires a solution. Define the goals and objectives of the proposal and submit the proposal for approval.

- **Planning**: prepare plans to see how the project will fulfil its business needs. Propose budgets and cashflow projections for the duration of the project. Develop planning tools such as CPA, PERT and work breakdown structures.

- **Initiation**: recruiting the correct staff and preparing for the project launch. Placing the infrastructure for the project in place is an important aspect of project management as it eases the potential problems when work commences and has a positive effect on morale.

- **Control**: project management tries to gain control over five variables (time, cost, quality, scope and risk). The control process involves monitoring all these variables against project progress and making changes as necessary.

- **Organisational processes**: with a focus on co-ordinating the resources to ensure delivery of the project's goals on time and within budget.

- **Closure/completion**: bringing the project to a successful close and ensuring that clients are happy with the outcome or ensuring that a change in processes is successfully integrated into the organisation.

2.3 The project objectives triangle is used as a tool to ensure that the requirements of the project are fulfilled. The three objectives of project management are cost, quality and time. The relative importance of each will vary with each project. In essence the triangle is used as a grid where the factors are 'traded-off' against each other.

Figure 10.1 *The project objectives triangle*

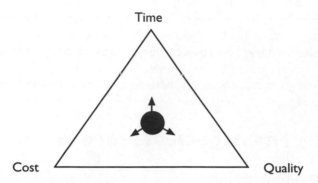

2.4   In order to achieve these objectives managers will use a variety of tools and techniques.

   •   **In relation to cost**: setting of budgets and budgetary control, variance reporting, activity based costing and auditing.

   •   **Quality**: quality assurance, quality control, specifications, quality manuals and quality audits.

   •   **Time**: Gantt charts, and network techniques such as CPA and PERT.

The project environment

2.5   The project environment is influenced by a number of stakeholders and a range of factors that need to be considered. These will vary considerably depending on the type and location of the project. An internal project will need to involve other internal departments as well as suppliers, logistics operators, design engineers etc.

2.6   In the case of an overseas construction project the considerations would be wider in scope.

   •   **Finance**: in terms of fluctuating exchange rates and/or fluctuating commodity prices.

   •   **Shipping lines**: who may need to move oversize items and provide regular sailings.

   •   **Politics**: both national and local. There is an increasing expectation that organisations have a corporate social responsibility to extend good practice through all their projects. In this case an example could be applying UK health and safety rules if it was felt that the international rules were not as rigorous.

   •   **Local businesses**: where the potential may exist to provide local work and look to source some items locally.

   •   **National culture**: developing an understanding of local culture (and particularly work practices) should be considered.

   •   **National and local laws**: which can impact in unforeseen ways on projects if not fully understood. Labour laws in particular require careful scrutiny.

2.7   The list would be extensive. An understanding of the project environment determines many aspects about the project and the approach taken.

Project definition

2.8 A project requires a clear and unambiguous statement that encompasses three aspects.

- **Its objectives**: the end result that the project is trying to achieve. The objectives provide a focus to the project team. Good objectives will be clear, measurable and quantifiable. This may be made easier if they are broken into smaller staged sets of objectives that will come together to meet the overall objective at the end. Common objectives would be cost, time and quality.

- **Its scope**: the exact range and responsibilities covered by project management. The scope of the project serves to identify the work content and outcomes. This helps to set boundaries and will be set out in a specification. The scope of the project helps to define contractors or part of the organisation involved, time periods including start and end dates, commercial and legal responsibilities of those involved and the resources to be employed.

- **Its strategy**: how the project management role will ensure that the objectives will be met. The strategy enables an overview of the project and allows for phases of the project to be identified which then allows for milestones to be set. These can then be conveyed to those involved so as to provide a common understanding.

2.9 A **specification** is the definition of the project. The specification will initially contain errors, ambiguities and misunderstandings. In consequence, the specification will usually need clarification with everyone concerned with the project (from originator, through the workers, to the end-customer) to ensure everyone is working with the same understanding. The outcome of this deliberation should be a written definition of what is required, by when; and this must be agreed by all involved.

2.10 The agreement upon a written specification has several benefits.

- The clarity will reveal misunderstandings.
- The completeness will remove contradictory assumptions.
- The rigour of the analysis will expose technical and practical details which may otherwise be overlooked.
- The agreement forces all concerned to read and think about the details.

2.11 The work on the specification can be seen as the first stage of quality assurance since you are looking for and countering problems in the very foundation of the project. From this perspective the creation of the specification clearly merits a large investment of time. The specification will change as the project progresses but deviations will be agreed rather than imposed.

The project management plan

2.12 The project management plan is a document that embodies the project. It is the most important document in the overall planning, monitoring, and implementation of the project and should be 'owned' by the project manager and his team.

2.13   The plan should include the following elements.

- A definition of the objectives
- Statements as to how these will be achieved and verified
- Estimates of the time required
- Financial budget
- Safety, health and environmental policies
- Quality policy
- Risk management strategy
- Related items concerning technical, commercial or organisational aspects

2.14   The project management plan is a key document in establishing why, what, how, who, how much and when.

2.15   Project planning has four main purposes.

- It identifies and determines the duration and cost of the project. This enables decisions to be made regarding whether the project will commence and provides the basis for further development of specific activities.
- It determines the resources that will be required. This enables planning ahead to ensure the resources are available when required and gives time for an examination of costs quoted.
- Linking with the project strategy, it helps in allocating work, in setting phases and milestones, and in defining responsibilities.
- It forces those involved to consider potential risk areas and the possible impact on the project. The example of the Scottish Parliament showed the risk when the specification was changed on more than one occasion. The result was a project both over time and over budget. The risk was always present but to estimate the impact was difficult.

2.16   Most projects are too involved and complex to be planned effectively unless they are broken down to a manageable size. By instigating smaller projects as a series of work packages then each work package can be given its own objectives that can then be monitored appropriately.

2.17   This process is referred to as the work breakdown structure and is a key component of project management. The discrete work packages can then be monitored and managed more effectively by the project manager whose role will be to ensure that these work packages meet the key objectives in terms of quality, cost and time. The work breakdown structure also assists in scheduling the project, as smaller work packages can be more easily brought forward or put back allowing a greater degree of flexibility.

Project control

2.18   Project control is the administrative interface that ensures that the project is progressing as intended. Project control is there to make sure that the criteria detailed in the project plan are being met and (if not) to instigate remedial action.

2.19   Project monitoring means that the progress of the project must be continually measured against the established schedule. Monitoring does not mean holding to the schedule rigidly. Circumstances change and as the project develops new information becomes available that may require a change in plans. The schedules serve as a yardstick against which to measure progress, to show where and how plans must change. The schedule is a tool to keep attention on the final objective and goal.

2.20   Although monitoring against the schedule is of paramount importance it is not the only measure that can be applied. Monitoring against the main performance objectives of quality, time and cost is equally appropriate. Inspection rejection rates, costs against budget and activities not started on time are examples. The project manager must ensure that the monitoring infrastructure is in place and that prompt and accurate feedback is given. Monitoring is the only way to ensure that resources can be reallocated effectively and judiciously when required.

2.21   Control comprises those administrative measures that must be undertaken to get and keep a project on schedule. Controlling is the adjustment of the work when needed so the overall commitments are maintained or at least optimised. Controlling means taking the appropriate action in the light of the information gained from monitoring. The whole purpose of scheduling and monitoring is to permit intelligent control.

2.22   There are two key elements to the control of a project.

- Milestones (clear, unambiguous targets of what needs to have been achieved and by when)
- An established means of communication

2.23   For the project manager milestones are a mechanism to monitor progress and for those involved in the project they are short-term goals that are far more tangible than the distant completion of the entire project. The milestones maintain the momentum of the project and encourage effort. They allow the team to judge their own progress and to celebrate achievement throughout the project rather than just at its end.

2.24   Project planning and control is greatly aided by the quantitative tools already mentioned (Gantt charts, CPA, PERT).

The project lifecycle

2.25   Every project has a lifecycle: the four sequential time periods through which any project passes. Each period can be identified as a phase and further broken down into stages that will typically reflect the area of project management and the size and complexity of the specific project.

2.26   The **concept** or **definition phase** provides the foundation and initial evaluation of the viability of the project. This is the questioning phase of the project (purpose, benefits, feasibility and overall objectives). Answering relevant questions relating to the project will enable the preparation of the project specification.

2.27   The **planning phase** will generally involve resourcing and scheduling of the project. This role involves identification of activities, sequencing, identifying critical activities and obtaining and allocating resources.

2.28 At the **implementation phase** monitoring and control are the important considerations.

2.29 The **closure phase** is where the project is terminated, hopefully because the objectives have been achieved and the completed project is handed over. This stage may see inspection of the final work before acceptance.

Resource constraints

2.30 Project managers will often have to cope with a constraint in resources (or possibly a bottleneck in the system generally). One approach to dealing with this is known as the **theory of constraints** (TOC).

2.31 According to TOC, a five-step plan is required to deal with constraints.

- Identify the constraint – obviously!

- Exploit the constraint – this means making a virtue of the problem. For example, if the constraint is a certain type of machine, try to ensure that a back-up machine of the same type is available in case of breakdown.

- Subordinate everything else to the constraint – it is pointless having everything else in top condition if the constraining factor is active. Therefore it is necessary to focus on the constraint, and make it the point around which schedules are based.

- Elevate the constraint – this means increasing the flow through this part of the system, in effect removing the constraint.

- Repeat the process.

Contracts in project work

2.32 Forms of contracts used in projects vary according to the complexity, nature and risk involved. The project plan and the agreements on specifications will provide the basis for the contract but areas of risk and contingency may need to be considered and incorporated.

2.33 The choice of contract can be between a tailor-made one to fit individual circumstances or a standard form contract, which will usually relate to a specific business sector. Standard form contracts have usually been agreed by the industry and its professional body and are designed to be balanced contracts. The principal is often in a dominant position when it comes to the awarding of contracts and it is often a case of the contractor accepting the contract offered with little negotiation.

2.34 There are three main categories of contract: lump sum contracts, measured form contracts, and turnkey contracts.

2.35 In a **lump sum contract**, the principal and contractor agree a fixed sum for completing a specified programme of work by a given date. This type of contract may include a contract price adjustment clause (CPA), usually based on agreed cost indices to take account of price fluctuations outside an agreed limit through factors such as exchange rate movements, fluctuations in commodity prices or high levels of inflation etc.

2.36 The role and accuracy of the specification is paramount in awarding lump sum contracts as it forms the basis for the contract. The lump sum approach ensures a high degree of contractor motivation but can lead to quality concerns if attempts are made to cut corners or if time becomes an issue toward the contract end. The contractor carries the greatest risk during the operational phase. The project manager needs to monitor progress carefully (particularly on quality issues) but is freed from the daily work scheduling and costing task.

2.37 **Measured form contracts**. If the contractor is unable to draw up a detailed enough specification to base the contract on then he can agree rates associated with aspects of the anticipated work. Payment is then made against actual quantities (hours or volumes used) applying the agreed rates.

2.38 **Turnkey contracts**: by definition 'turn the key and it works'. When using this style of contract the entire project is placed in the hands of one contractor who will carry the project through to conclusion. The contractor (who may be a consortium in the case of a large infrastructure project) will then organise and operate the project. Quality issues can be a concern as can after-project support and these considerations require both monitoring and specifics included in the contract.

3 Creating a project network

Network analysis

3.1 Projects frequently comprise a large number of separate activities which are related to each other in terms of their timetabling. For example, it may be that Activity C can only be commenced after Activities A and B have been completed. Network analysis is the process of analysing the relationships between activities and exhibiting them in a diagrammatic form. In order to draw a network diagram it is necessary to have estimated durations of each activity.

3.2 Nowadays, the creation of a network diagram invariably involves the use of a computer. The project planner can enter data about the activities (eg the duration of Activity C, and the fact that it can only begin after completion of Activities A and B). The computer program can then draw the network diagram, as well as producing various items of management information useful to the planner.

The benefits of network analysis

3.3 An important benefit of using network analysis is the enforced need to think clearly about the project activities. Once this is done, the computer software can calculate, for example, which activities are on the **critical path**. These are the activities where any delay will lead to a delay in the overall completion of the project. Similarly, the computer can calculate which activities have **float** (ie the activities which take less time than is actually available) and how much float they have. Network analysis, or one particular form of network analysis, is often referred to as **critical path analysis** (CPA) or **critical path method** (CPM).

3.4 This kind of analysis allows the planner to focus attention on the critical activities. It may be worthwhile to pay extra in order to get critical activities completed in time, whereas premium rates would be wasted money if an activity is non-critical. Similarly, it may be possible to shorten the total project timetable by directing extra resources to critical activities in order to complete them more quickly (known as 'crashing' the activities – see later). Again, it would be wasted effort and cost to do this in the case of activities that already have float.

3.5 Another benefit of network analysis is that planners can maintain a constant check on project progress. If a critical activity appears to be overrunning its time allowance urgent measures may be required to rectify the situation. On the other hand, if a non-critical activity is slipping the planners may be able to identify that there is sufficient float to keep the overall project on schedule.

3.6 A final benefit of this technique is the scope for using probability theory to cope with uncertainties in the estimated activity durations. Instead of estimating a definite duration for each activity – which is very prone to error – planners can define an optimistic duration, a pessimistic duration and a most likely duration. The software can then calculate probabilities that particular activities will overrun, and/or that the project as a whole will overrun. This is useful information for planners. This method of network analysis is sometimes referred to as **project** (or **programme**) **evaluation and review technique** (PERT).

Preparing a network diagram

3.7 There are various notations that may be used in the preparation of a network diagram. In this section we will use an arrow diagram, in which each activity is represented by a line (or arrow) joining two circles (usually called nodes). The duration of the activity is written by the arrow representing it. This is illustrated in Figure 10.2.

Figure 10.2 *A basic arrow diagram*

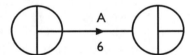

3.8 Figure 10.2 indicates that Activity A has a duration of six (days, say, or hours or whatever). The nodes representing the beginning and end of Activity A are divided into three parts; the reason for this is explained later.

3.9 The best way to understand the preparation of network diagrams is to do an example.

3.10 Project Alpha consists of nine activities, named as A, B, C, D, E, F, G, H, J. The table below shows which preceding activities must have been completed before each activity may begin, and also the estimated durations of each activity.

Activity	Preceding activities	Duration in days
A	–	3
B	–	3
C	–	7
D	A	1
E	D, J	2
F	B	2
G	C	1
H	E, F, G	1
J	B	1

3.11 This information can be shown in a skeleton network: see Figure 10.3.

Figure 10.3 *A skeleton network for Project Alpha*

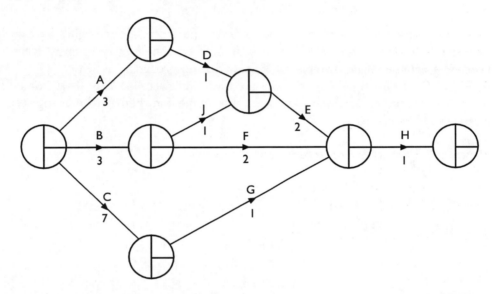

3.12 Next, we number the nodes, beginning at the left with number 1, and moving across the page to the right: see Figure 10.4.

Figure 10.4 *Project Alpha: numbering the nodes*

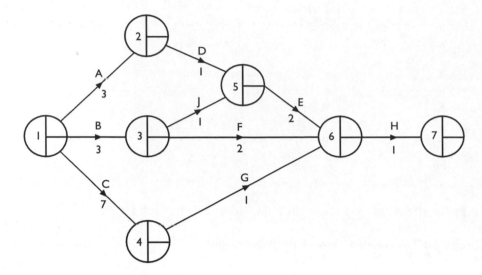

3.13 We now work forward through the network (ie from left to right) to calculate the **earliest starting time** (EST) for each activity. An activity cannot start until all preceding activities have completed. If there are no preceding activities (eg for Activities A, B and C in our example) the EST is conventionally called Day 0 (ie immediately). If there are preceding activities, we must allow time for them to be completed. This is illustrated in Figure 10.5.

Figure 10.5 *Project Alpha: earliest starting times*

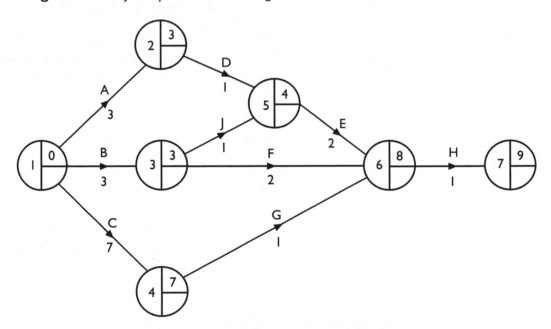

3.14 The EST is entered in the upper quadrant of the node. Where there is more than one activity coming into a node, it is the **largest** accumulated time that must be entered, because all activities ending on the node must be completed before the next activities can begin. For example, the EST on node 6 is Day 8. Although it only takes six days to reach node 6 via node 5, the route via node 4 takes eight days, which means that Activity H cannot begin until after Day 8.

3.15 We now work backwards through the network (ie from right to left) to calculate the **latest finishing time** (LFT) for each activity. This is the time by which all activities ending at a node must be completed if the schedule is to remain on target. This is illustrated in Figure 10.6.

Figure 10.6 *Project Alpha: latest finishing times*

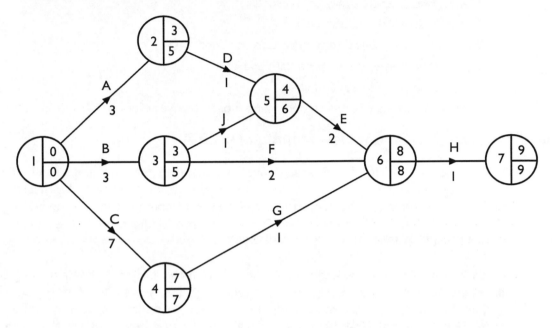

3.16 Care is needed where more than one arrow is emerging from a node, as in node 3. To go from node 3 to node 6 requires two days, so it may look as though the LFT for node 3 is Day 6; that leaves time for Activity F to complete by Day 8. But that is not quite good enough, because if node 3 has LFT of Day 6, and we have already calculated Day 6 as the LFT for node 5, that would leave no time for Activity J. To leave one day for Activity J, we must fix Day 5 as the LFT for node 3.

Analysing the network diagram

3.17 Once the network diagram has been drawn, we can derive useful information from it. For example, it is at once clear that the project will take nine days to complete (assuming no slippage).

3.18 Another key piece of information is derived by comparing the EST and LFT at each node. Where the EST and the LFT are identical, we are looking at activities on the critical path. There is no float in these activities, which means that any delay to the activity will mean delay to the overall project. In our example, it is clear that the critical path goes from node 1, through nodes 4 and 6, to node 8. This means that Activities C, G and H are critical to achieving the nine day project timetable.

3.19 By contrast, the EST and LFT at node 2 differ by two days. This implies that there is float of two days in Activity A. Although we are expecting that activity to take three days, it could take as much as five days without damaging the overall schedule.

3.20 This simple example is enough to show how a network diagram can be prepared and how to analyse the information it discloses.

'Crashing' activities

3.21 Sometimes the network diagram will reveal that the project is taking too long. We then need to consider how to 'crash' activities, ie to shorten their duration by applying additional resources. The procedure is as follows.

- Identify activities that may be 'crashed'
- For each activity, establish cost
- Estimate activity duration with resources added
- Determine revised completion date and cost
- Recalculate critical path and costs
- Compare various options to determine most effective solution

Program evaluation and review technique (PERT)

3.22 In our discussion of critical path analysis we have assumed that the times required for each activity are known. In practice, these times are obviously subject to uncertainty. This causes problems for the project manager, which to some extent can be addressed by statistical analysis. The aim is to establish within probable limits what the actual time may be for each activity.

3.23 One approach to this has already been referred to in this chapter: program evaluation and review technique, or PERT. To apply this technique, we estimate three possible durations for each activity: a most likely duration (*m*), an optimistic duration (*a*) and a pessimistic duration (*b*). These are used to calculate the mean time (*μ*) and the standard deviation (*σ*), using the following formulae:

$$\mu = \frac{4m + b + a}{6}$$

$$\sigma = \frac{6 + a}{6}$$

3.24 By appropriate statistical analysis we can then extend our use of CPA to cater for the uncertainties inherent in our estimates of activity durations. For example, we can calculate the probability that an activity on the critical path will overrun its allotted time and therefore endanger the timely completion of the project as a whole.

3.25 As always, this kind of calculation is invariably carried out using appropriate computer software. All you need for the examination is general awareness of the underlying principles.

Chapter summary

- Project management includes developing a project plan, which includes defining project goals and objectives, specifying tasks or how goals will be achieved, what resources are needed, and associated budgets and timelines for completion.

- The increased application of 'cross-functional teamwork' throughout business recognises the success of the team approach in delivering results.

- Project management helps to reduce and manage risk.

- Project management uses various measurement tools to accomplish and track project tasks. These include Gantt charts, critical path analysis and program evaluation and review technique (PERT).

- Project control is the administrative interface that ensures that the project is progressing as intended.

- Project monitoring means that the progress of the project must be continually measured against the established schedule.

- Every project has a lifecycle (the four sequential time periods through which any project passes): concept (or definition) phase; planning phase; implementation phase; closure phase.

- Network analysis is the process of analysing the relationships between project activities and exhibiting them in diagrammatic form.

- Advantages of network analysis: encourages clear thinking about project activities; enables constant checking on project progress; enables use of probability theory to improve estimates of project duration.

- Activities on the critical path are those for which earliest start time and latest finishing time are identical. Where EST and LFT differ, the activity is not on the critical path and the difference is the amount of float.

- PERT is a refinement of CPA, enabling statistical analysis of the uncertainties surrounding activity durations.

Self-test questions

Numbers in brackets refer to the paragraphs above where your answers can be checked.

1   What are three main points that are most important to a successful project? (1.6)

2   Lysons distinguishes four different types of project. What are these different types? (1.7)

3   Give four critical success factors of projects. (1.9)

4   What is the role of the project manager? (1.16)

5   A project requires a clear and unambiguous statement that encompasses what three aspects? (2.3)

6   What details should be included in the project plan? (2.13)

7   The majority of projects are too involved and complex to plan effectively unless they are broken down to a manageable size. What terminology is used to describe the smaller units? (2.17)

8   What is meant by activities on the critical path? (3.3)

9   What is meant by EST and LFT? (3.13 and 3.15)

10   What does it mean when EST and LFT for an activity are not identical? (3.19)

11   Describe briefly what is meant by PERT. (3.21*ff*)

Further reading

•   *Operations Management*, Slack, Chambers and Johnston, Chapter 16.

CHAPTER 11

Quality Planning and Control

Learning objectives and indicative content

3.4   Evaluate the techniques used to plan and control quality.

- Definition of quality
- Dimensions of quality
- Cost of quality management tool
- Quality management and quality management principles
- Techniques used to plan and control quality in products and processes

3.5   Develop an asset maintenance and replacement strategy.

- Differences between preventative and repair maintenance
- Time to replace an asset calculation

3.6   Analyse and explain the complexity surrounding facility location decisions.

- Reasons for complexity
- Demand side decisions
- Supply side decisions
- Location analysis tools

Chapter headings

1   Definitions and dimensions of quality

2   The costs of quality

3   Techniques for planning and control of quality

4   Asset maintenance and replacement strategies

5   Facility location

1   Definitions and dimensions of quality

Defining quality

1.1   In recent years the issue of product and service quality has assumed overwhelming importance in the search for competitive advantage. Partly this is a natural development as Western economies have become wealthier, and consumers more discriminating and demanding. Partly it is a reaction to trends in Japanese manufacturing that have caused European and American organisations to look afresh at their principles and practices particularly in regard to quality issues.

1.2   Initial definitions of quality focused on product quality. Generic definitions such as 'fitness for use', 'fitness for purpose' and 'meeting specification' have their roots in the early stages of the quality movement. The movement to total quality management brought together the 'quality triangle' advocated by Juran in a definition by Armand Feigenbaum that extended quality definitions to include customers: 'an effective system for integrating the quality development, quality maintenance and quality improvement efforts of the various groups in an organisation so as to enable production and service at the most economical levels which allow for full customer satisfaction'.

1.3   There remains a debate on what exactly constitutes quality, and this is reflected in the variety of definitions that can be found in the literature. Most definitions with wide acceptance emphasise the central position of the customer. That of IBM is cited by Arjan J van Weele: 'Quality is the degree in which customer requirements are met. We speak of a quality product or quality service when supplier and customer agree on requirements and those requirements are met'.

1.4   These requirements relate not only to technical specifications of a product, but to the whole range of benefits that the customer is purchasing. For example, they might include ease of use, after-sales service, short delivery lead-time and so on. Supplying products and services that meet the definition of quality is a task that calls for a wide-ranging management effort.

Dimensions of quality

1.5   David Garvin lists eight main dimensions for quality. (Later in this chapter we look at the Servqual approach, which identifies five such dimensions in a service context.)

- **Performance**: the operating characteristics of the product or the delivery of the service.

- **Features**: aspects such as customer care policy, availability of spare parts and credit facilities. Features assist the marketing effort in differentiating one product from another.

- **Reliability**: the ability of a product or service to perform with consistency and certainty over a period of time.

- **Durability**: the length of time a product will last without deterioration under stated conditions of use.

- **Conformance**: the degree to which agreed standards are met

- **Serviceability**: the time between service periods and the ease and availability of service support.

- **Aesthetics**: how the overall product is perceived by the customer in regard to its design, shape, texture, taste etc.

- **Perceived quality**: the subjective view a customer develops from the influence of advertising, brand image and price etc, that indicates the level of quality the customer anticipates.

1.6   Quality means different things in different operations. A motor manufacturer is looking for parts and components that meet the specification, an assembly operation that is automated to reduce human error in order to produce a product that is reliable and meets customer needs and wants. A contrasting view would come from a hospital: patients require the correct treatment within an acceptable time-frame (which could be quite varied), patients want to be kept informed, the staff to be knowledgeable and the hospital to be clean.

1.7 Professor David Garvin considered the various definitions of quality and the different approaches to it and categorised the various perspectives into his 'five approaches' to quality.

- **The transcendent approach**: this view equates quality with excellence.

- **The user-based approach**: concerns the making of a product that is fit for purpose and use (Juran). Quality is designed to meet the needs of the customer. This does not necessarily mean to excel: it means to produce a product or service that meets customers' needs. The two are not the same.

- **The product-based approach**: the product-based perspective sees quality as precise and measurable. For example, the product will travel 12,000 miles between oil changes or will download data three times faster. The assessment of quality is based on measurable factors.

- **The manufacturing-based approach**: quality is the manufacture of a product that precisely meets specifications. The product is free of errors as a result. It is a product that will do the job.

- **The value-based approach**: develops the manufacturing perspective further by incorporating both cost and price. This involves a trade-off in the customers' mind of what represents value. As an example I could fly direct to Orlando with British Airways, or get the flight cheaper with Delta via Atlanta, but with a six-hour transfer delay.

Customers' expectations

1.8 Customers' views and expectations will all be shaped by a variety of factors such as product knowledge, personal history, lifestyle, etc. Customers may perceive quality in different ways.

1.9 Quality must be understood from the customer's perspective. The customer's view of quality is what they expect the quality to be. The expectations are based on a range of factors that have been communicated to them. If we fail to meet those expectations we are either putting our message across wrongly or are failing operationally to match customer expectations.

1.10 As an example, call centres are one of the most rapidly growing industries in the world today as many service providers are seeking to lower the cost of providing services and increasing the time period during which customer access is available.

1.11 Call centre operators are often required to answer a great number of calls and they are sometimes judged on how quickly they deal with the call, regardless of the quality of the call (eg satisfaction of the customer).

1.12 The performance statistics relating to this become an efficiency measure rather than an effectiveness measure. In a service industry the 'product' is often the employee's service. The rapid growth of call centres emphasises the importance for service delivery in this context. It is important to attain the correct balance between efficiency and effectiveness.

The Servqual approach

1.13 Quality and customer service have been identified as critical strategic issues in today's business environment. The research evaluated the Servqual approach to the measurement of service quality first introduced by Parasuruman *et al* (1995).

'The approach starts from the assumption that the level of service experienced by customers is critically determined by the gap between their expectations of the service and their perceptions of what they actually receive from the service provider.'

1.14 The Servqual model puts forward five **dimensions** on which customers evaluate service.

- **Tangibles**: the appearance of the physical facilities and materials related to the service. There is little tangible about a call centre with the exception of voice contact.

- **Reliability**: the ability to perform the service accurately and dependably. A consideration is the number of operators to receive calls and the need to address operational issues such as scheduling operators to be available at peak times.

- **Responsiveness**: the willingness to help customers and provide a good level of service. Clearly this is compromised by an emphasis on the number of calls answered rather than other performance measures such as problems resolved or customer satisfaction.

- **Assurance**: confidence in the competence of the operation, its systems, security and credibility. This is not easy to develop, particularly at first call.

- **Empathy**: approachability and individual attention to customers. This can be achieved by a knowledgeable operator who is aware of the surrounding issues.

1.15 The Servqual method can serve as an operations management tool in a wide range of operations. To operations managers in the service sector it is useful to have a widely accepted tool to help analyse their operation. If your role is primarily service based consider applying the five points of the model to your organisation and see what the results tell you.

1.16 The purpose of understanding perceived quality is that it can be used to diagnose quality problems. Slack *et al* identify four distinct areas that could explain a perceived quality gap between customers' perceptions and expectations.

- **The gap between the customer's specification and the operation's specification**: the customer's perception of quality could be poor as the operation's specification is lower than he expects or requires.

- **The gap between concept and specification**: the perceived quality could be poor as the product or service was not conceived and developed with adequate consideration being given to customer expectations.

- **The gap between quality specification and actual quality**: perceived quality may evidence a mismatch between the actual product or service quality and its internal specification (eg the product may suggest to the customer a higher level of after-sales support than is actually available).

- **The gap between actual quality and communicated image**: there may be a mismatch between what is actually delivered and what the customer expects, particularly following positive advertising and promotion.

1.17   The key consideration with quality gaps is to understand why they exist. Once this has been established, action can be taken to reduce or eliminate the gap areas.

1.18   More recent definitions of quality reflect this more rounded approach and consider both the production and customer service aspects but also look to place quality in a modern business context. Philip Crosby stated that 'quality is free'. His meaning is that if effective quality systems are in place then production will continually improve and customer service will meet or exceed expectation leading to repeat business and a philosophy that will continue to drive the business forward. The idea of 'zero defects' puts forward a quality objective for companies to aspire to.

2   The costs of quality

Categorising the costs of quality

2.1   We have seen that the main objective of quality is to meet customer requirements. If these requirements are not met for any reason there are possible repercussions, most notably a decrease in sales and a loss of future business.

2.2   The cost of quality is defined (BS 6143) as: 'The cost of ensuring and assuring quality, as well as the loss incurred when quality is not achieved'. It is the latter part of this definition that prompts quality control measures; losses incurred as a result of poor quality are generally perceived to be higher than the costs of securing quality in the first place.

2.3   Quality related costs are the expenditure incurred in defect prevention and appraisal activities and the losses due to internal and external failure of a product or service through failure to meet agreed specifications. Quality related costs can be classified as failure costs (internal and external), appraisal costs and prevention costs.

Figure 11.1 *The costs related to quality*

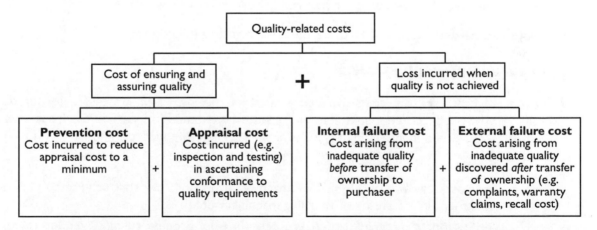

2.4   Operations management needs to produce a competitive product based on achieving an acceptable balance between quality and cost factors. This balance will vary between organisations and with the emphasis placed on producing a high-quality product. The analysis of these costs provides a method of assessing the overall effectiveness of the management of quality and acts as a means of problem spotting and prioritisation.

Failure costs

2.5 Failure costs can be categorised under two headings: internal and external.

2.6 **Internal failure** costs are those that arise from inadequate quality before transfer of ownership to the purchaser.

- Loss or reworking of faulty items discovered during the production or inspection process
- Scrapping of defective products that cannot be repaired, used or sold
- The re-inspection cost of output that has been modified or corrected
- Downgrading of products with the subsequent loss of income
- The waste incurred in holding contingency stocks, providing additional storage and duplicating work
- Failure analysis and the cost of those activities required to establish the causes of internal product failure

2.7 **External failure** costs arise when products or services fail to meet the standards expected of them, perhaps because of poor design, inadequate materials, or production errors.

- Repair of products (either returned products or the costs of servicing in an outside location)
- Guarantee and warranty claims
- The administration of complaints and refunds
- Potential liabilities arising from claims
- Possible loss of customers and contracts
- Loss of goodwill, which may have a long-term effect on the organisation's business
- The physical handling of returns and the costs involved in the returns process
- The cost of either returning repaired goods to stock or writing stock off

2.8 Both internal and external failures are the cost of getting things wrong.

Appraisal and prevention costs

2.9 Appraisal costs are the costs incurred as part of the inspection process in order to ensure that products meet specification. This can be extended to include the inspection of parts and components being delivered from suppliers for incorporation into a more refined product.

- The costs involved in physical or machine inspection; the staff required and the investment in measuring or weighing machinery etc
- Verification of incoming material, process set-up, process running, vendor rating and performance appraisal against specification
- Quality audits to check that the quality system is performing as intended

2.10 Prevention costs are those incurred in order to reduce appraisal costs to a minimum. Costs include investment in machinery, technology and training programs designed to reduce the number of defective products during production. The resources invested in prevention are aimed at getting it right first time.

- The determination of quality requirements and the establishment of specifications for suppliers
- Investment in improved production equipment and processes
- Customer research and surveys
- Supplier appraisal and reviews
- Quality circles
- Quality engineering
- ISO 9000 approval

2.11 Traditionally failure rates, scrap and reworking were included within the costs of production while other aspects of poor quality were accounted for in either production or marketing overheads. Quality management aims for a continuous improvement in quality, efficiency and effectiveness and will develop methods and processes that help to achieve these objectives. It does not accept the cost of poor quality as inevitable and requires that the cost is highlighted in management reports and remedial action taken.

2.12 The impact of an analysis of quality-related costs is that quality related issues are not intangible; they translate directly into money lost and saved. An important operations management role is to measure the costs of quality, because until something is measured it is very hard to control and improve.

3 Techniques for planning and control of quality

Online and offline controls over quality

3.1 Quality is a philosophy that organisations embrace as part of their work culture. Quality assurance puts in place systems and procedures that ensure that quality standards will be met. Quality controls are the operational activities that are used to meet quality requirements.

3.2 In a quality control and improvement process the measurement or examination of data will form the basis for decisions and actions. The control of quality is achieved by some form of inspection or by the application of processes that lead toward reducing the need for inspection.

3.3 Quality control techniques can be divided into two main types.

- **Online controls**: these are controls of quality when the product is in the supply chain or on the production line. Examples include inspection and statistical process control (SPC).
- **Offline controls**: these are designed to prevent failure from occurring by intervening early in the design process. Examples include Taguchi methodology and failure mode and effects analysis (FMEA).

Online controls: the reactive approach

3.4 Inspection forms an integral part of most quality control systems (with the possible exception of just in time production systems). Inspection is usually based on the statistical process of **sampling**: a smaller number is considered as representative of a higher number. For example, from 1,000 items delivered 50 selected at random will be inspected. These 50 will be assumed to be representative of the whole.

3.5 This is not only a process that has proven statistical rigour (if carried out correctly) but clearly reduces inspection costs and speeds up the inspection process.

3.6 Inspection can be categorised under four headings.

- **Receiving inspection**: where materials, parts or components from suppliers are inspected for conformance to agreed specifications. This should be part of a formal process where records are kept.
- **Classification inspection**: the inspection of materials, parts or components into separate categories according to specifications. This allows for the inspection to be more tailored and specialised.
- **Control inspection**: the inspection of work in progress in order to correct variations from those expected (statistical process control).
- **Audit inspection**: the audit of procedures and processes such as ISO 9000.

Statistical process control

3.7 Statistical process control (SPC) is one of the most influential quality processes developed, in that its use and application aided Japan to become a major trading nation. Developed primarily by W Edwards Deming it involves the measurement of a production run, comparison against expectations, an investigation into why variations have occurred and a gradual reduction of variations. In essence, every time you do a production run, measure it and do it better next time (continuous improvement).

3.8 SPC is a technique for identifying the possibility of quality defects at an early stage of production. It is designed:

- to impose **control**
- over **processes**
- using **statistical methods**.

3.9 Complete uniformity is not to be expected in the output from any manufacturing process. Even in the most accurate and highly automated process for producing, say, steel rods it would be possible, given sufficiently accurate measuring instruments, to detect differences between one rod and the next. If the process is working well these random differences will usually cause no concern: it would take very accurate measurements to detect them, and they are probably well within the allowed tolerances.

3.10 The situation is different if the process is out of control. Perhaps the cutting tools have become blunt, or the machine has gone out of adjustment. In this case the variances from specification are potentially very serious, and (even worse) unpredictable. It is this kind of fault that SPC can detect to enable remedial action to be taken. By testing samples of output again and again throughout the production run, an operator skilled in the use of SPC can detect when the pattern of variances indicates a fault in the process.

3.11 The principles are relatively simple. Quality assurance and/or maintenance specialists determine that the process is working the way it should be. The operator begins production and takes samples of output for inspection at short time intervals. The measurements are recorded and, by using statistical analysis, it is established what average measurement is expected for all units of output. A determination of the expected range of measurement is provided. If the measurements taken from samples cluster around this predetermined measurement or average within expected parameters then the process is in control. If the results are outside the expected parameters then they are not.

3.12 This is the strength of the SPC concept, because at this stage the operator can halt production to seek and rectify the fault. Few defective units will have been produced. Once the fault is remedied, production begins again.

3.13 Fortunately the operator does not need to be an expert in statistics in order to perform these tasks. For the most part SPC relies on computer-based systems applying control charts. The control limits are determined after the operator's first few samples. These are taken just after the quality assurance team have ensured that the process is in control, so they provide reliable benchmarks for what should be expected throughout the production run. Control charts vary, but typically the operator will be concerned with two measurements.

- The average diameter, weight, length etc, of each sample
- The range of variation in each sample (the idea being that a narrow range of variation should be expected, while a wide variation around the average is a bad sign)

3.14 The average measurement of units in a sample is often denoted by the symbol $\overline{X}$, while the range of measurements within a sample is denoted by R. As the operator measures the units in a sample and calculates their average value ($\overline{X}$), the result should fall within defined limits, the upper and lower control limits, around the expected value. Similarly, the value computed for R should not exceed the expected value by more than a certain amount, marked by an upper control limit.

3.15 All of this is illustrated in Figure 11.2.

3.16 SPC is a mathematical technique that is applicable under defined conditions. It works best in situations where the production task is continuous and repetitive. It is a technique for ensuring that the production process remains in control (operating within its normal level of precision). The refinement that Japanese manufacturers added to the process was to work to tighter and tighter tolerances, over time. This led to a gradual and sustainable improvement in product consistency.

Offline control: the proactive approach

3.17 Offline (off the production line) approaches are based on ensuring that quality considerations are considered from the concept stage through to delivery of the final product. They involve planning, teamwork and measurement. The most influential of the offline processes (but by no means all) are: Taguchi methodology, quality function deployment (QFD) and failure mode and effects analysis (FMEA). Of these, the first two have been discussed in earlier chapters; FMEA is discussed below.

Figure 11.2 *SPC charts*

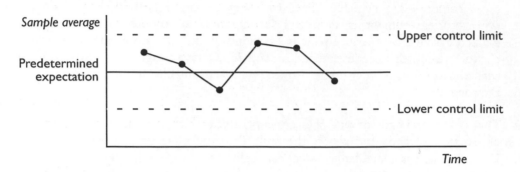

x̄ chart

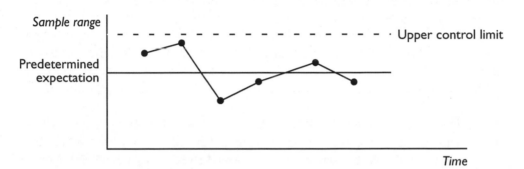

R chart

Failure mode and effects analysis

3.18 Failure mode and effects analysis (FMEA) is a technique for determining the different ways (modes) in which a product can fail, and assessing the seriousness of the effects in each case. By using appropriate numerical parameters, the different modes can be ranked in order of how critical they are. (The term FMECA, or failure mode, effects and criticality analysis, is sometimes used.) Attention can then be concentrated on the most critical areas.

3.19 The most appropriate time for applying FMEA is at the design stage. However, examples of its use at other stages of the product life cycle are not uncommon. To provide the basic data, inputs are required from a variety of different departments: marketing, customer service, design and engineering, purchasing, operations and others. In light of their experience in buying in parts and components from suppliers, purchasing staff have an important role to play in identifying parts that have given rise to problems in the past.

3.20 To conduct the analysis, the following steps are required.

• Identify the components forming part of the product.

• For each component, list the different ways in which failure may occur and the causes of each.

• For each failure mode identified, list the effects on the overall product.

• Assess the probability (**P**) of each failure on a scale of 1 (not very probable) to 10 (extremely probable).

- Assess the seriousness (**S**) of each failure mode by considering its effects, again, on a scale of 1 (not very serious) to 10 (extremely serious).

- Assess the difficulty (**D**) of detecting the failure before the customer uses the product, on a scale of 1 (easy to detect) to 10 (very difficult to detect).

- Calculate the criticality index (**C**) for each failure mode by use of the formula:

$$C = P \times S \times D$$

3.21 A low figure for C indicates that the failure mode is less important, ie it may have a low probability of occurrence, or a low seriousness level, or may be of such a nature that discovery is likely before the customer uses the product, or all three of these. If C has a high value it would indicate that urgent attention is required.

3.22 Finally, the means of correcting the problem should be indicated in each case.

3.23 By this stage, the required actions should be reasonably clear. Where the means of correction are simple and inexpensive they should normally be adopted in all cases. On the other hand, if correction is complex and costly management must carefully consider the criticality of that particular failure mode before determining what to do.

4 Asset maintenance and replacement strategies

The objectives of maintenance

4.1 The purpose of maintenance is to optimise the performance of equipment by attempting to prevent breakdowns or failures. An understanding of the nature and purpose of maintenance regimes and schedules enables the operations manager to view production schedules with greater confidence as the incidence of delays or breakdowns in production will be reduced.

4.2 There is a close correlation between maintenance and quality as only those machines that operate within anticipated parameters will be able to deliver the required quality of product. Without effective maintenance there will clearly be concerns relating to product quality.

4.3 Muhlemann, Oakland and Lockyer cite the following objectives of maintenance.

- To enable product or service quality and customer satisfaction to be achieved through correctly adjusted, serviced and operated equipment

- To maximise the useful life of the equipment

- To keep the equipment safe and prevent the development of safety hazards

- To minimise the total production or operating costs directly attributable to equipment service and repair

- To minimise the frequency and severity of interruptions to operating processes

- To maximise production capacity from the given equipment resources

4.4 In the operations environment the objectives of maintenance must be balanced against the objectives of production. This is explained below.

Differences between preventive and repair maintenance

4.5 There are two approaches to repairs and maintenance: repair maintenance and preventive maintenance.

4.6 **Repair (or breakdown) maintenance** is involved with failures and related problems as they occur. This is reactive in nature. The operations manager must have in place details with regard to guarantees, warranties or specialists to call on.

4.7 Unscheduled maintenance of this type can be highly disruptive to any production process and consideration should be given to the appropriate level of after-sales support in this area at the time of unit purchase. The availability of spares, response times and costs should all be fully evaluated prior to purchase.

4.8 **Preventive maintenance** requires a proactive approach and is concerned with the reduction of failure by the implementation of a rigorous preventive regime.

4.9 Preventive maintenance is defined as 'a system of daily maintenance, periodic inspection, and preventive repairs designed to reduce the probability of machine breakdown'.

Preventive maintenance

4.10 When maintenance is delayed, one risks premature equipment failure, product damage and production delays.

4.11 The primary reason for preventive maintenance is to reduce unexpected downtime and repair costs caused by machine breakdown. Preventive maintenance is largely precautionary and will be undertaken according to a predetermined and regular schedule.

4.12 A regular schedule should be established for items that have manufacturers' maintenance guidelines, predictable reliability or known breakdown characteristics. Preventive maintenance will also be undertaken where there is evidence of a reduction in manufacturing capability of a unit.

4.13 Preventive maintenance plays an important role in operations management with benefits ranging from cost reductions and decreased downtime to safety and improved performance. It involves routine machine inspection, servicing, cleaning, and keeping accurate maintenance records.

4.14 Preventive maintenance will normally be undertaken when the operating facility is idle. This allows for work to be planned with the minimum amount of disruption to production schedules. This may not always be possible and, apart from any unscheduled maintenance requirements, it is inevitable that some maintenance will be required during production hours.

4.15 The total cost curve demonstrates that increased effort in preventive maintenance should reduce the cost of repair.

Figure 11.3 *Cost effects of preventive maintenance*

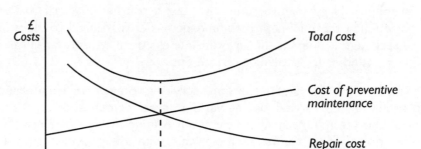

4.16 The more frequently preventive maintenance is carried out then the less need there should be for repair or breakdown maintenance. With no preventive maintenance the cost of repair would be substantial. However, often a balance must be struck between the operating needs of the production system and the scheduled maintenance requirement. The short-term production requirement may win over the longer-term objectives of preventive maintenance.

Maintenance decisions

4.17 To establish a maintenance policy for an operation we consider three linked aspects.

- Which machines, items or facilities, etc, are to be maintained?
- What is the appropriate maintenance in each case?
- How will the maintenance work be organised?

4.18 There is often an interdependence between machines of similar capacities. These are often operated together in a production run. If one is undergoing preventive maintenance it will often make sense to carry out maintenance on the other at the same time.

4.19 The development of a maintenance policy that meets the needs of the organisation (eg both operations staff and maintenance staff) is difficult. Clearly there are conflicting needs and these must be addressed by a mutual understanding of each other's aims and objectives.

4.20 Preventive maintenance policy should consider the alternative approaches that can be used and decide on the appropriate mix of approaches. The options available are as follows.

- **Work-based**: where maintenance is carried out after a set number of operating hours or usage. Usage can be gauged by counting (eg after 10,000 miles, 5,000 units or 50,000 copies).

- **Time-based**: where maintenance is based on time intervals irrespective of usage. This system is easy to schedule and monitor but often neglects the problems that may become apparent if high usage in an area is not recognised.

- **Opportunity-based**: where maintenance takes place outside work hours (evenings and holidays) or when machine breakdowns provide downtime on other machines that can then be used for maintenance.

- **Condition-based**: often relies on planned, visual or measured inspection in order to ascertain the need for maintenance (eg when brakes wear down to a 1mm minimum). Many manufacturers will use a tougher material that causes audible noise when the minimum recommended level is reached to alert operatives that replacement is due. Or they may include electrical systems (as in cars) that indicate when maintenance should be carried out.

4.21 Maintenance, which involves inspection, servicing, preventive maintenance and repair maintenance, can be carried out at various levels of operation. In certain cases the operators who use the machine can carry out routine maintenance tasks as part of their role. The organisation can supplement this with their own team of maintenance engineers, and/or external maintenance personnel can be brought in either on contract or as provided by machine manufacturers under a guarantee, warranty or after-sales arrangement.

4.22 Total productive maintenance (TPM) is a development from total quality management thinking and is designed to encourage the unit operative and those linked with the production process to take 'ownership' of their role. The key features are as follows.

- To optimise the use and effectiveness of equipment and eliminate unplanned failures
- To involve the operator in maintenance activities where appropriate in order to develop a sense of ownership, involvement and responsibility
- To encourage employees to be involved in continual improvements in machinery and equipment operation

4.23 The replacement of worn, defective or damaged parts is an integral part of preventive maintenance. When the cost of repair is becoming substantial a new approach may need to be taken. A common method is to set a repair limit and if the estimated cost of repair exceeds this limit then the machine is due for replacement.

Asset replacement

4.24 The costs involved in operating machinery and equipment will normally increase with the age or high usage of the piece. These costs (eg the cost of maintenance necessary to keep the piece operational and the obsolescence of the equipment particularly in the light of technological advances) will together eventually present an economically viable case for replacement.

4.25 Asset replacement is dependent on a number of factors. One of these factors is the repair limit but other considerations are dependent on the nature and value of the item to be replaced. This can include replacement cost and whole life costing, cashflow implications, downtime costs, obsolescence, and projected long-term production requirements. These factors are discussed in turn below.

4.26 Replacement cost and whole life costing. Asset replacement will be considered before it is immediately necessary. If a high-value unit is being replaced a case must be put forward by the operations team and discussed with other business functions (most notably finance and purchasing). Finance will need to evaluate the implications of future purchase and consider options such as hire or leasing. Purchasing are the specialists in supply and increasingly have a wider remit. They will evaluate the purchase over the whole life of the unit. This includes such areas as running costs, power usage, emissions and recycling and/or disposal costs, which are very much a feature of the modern view of purchasing when buying capital equipment.

4.27 Cashflow implications. Organisations should have a structured replacement plan with anticipated replacement dates and cost estimates in order that funds will be available when required. The role of finance will involve a full appraisal of alternatives to purchase (such as leasing and hiring) and they will need a fully justified case for the purchase of a major unit. Purchasing will negotiate with an aim of spreading the payment period over time. This is often linked to scheduled payments related to hours used, output or reliability.

4.28 Downtime costs. These can be minimised by careful planning that allows for linked machines to be maintained in the same time interval. Maintenance outside normal work hours is often the preferred option as it causes minimum disruption to the production process.

4.29 Obsolescence. This is an increasing concern to modern business, owing largely to the rapid advances in technology that are taking place. Particularly with computer-based equipment, consideration should be given to the ease and effectiveness of upgrades during the product's life. The impact of fast-moving technology can be seen in the way that many organisations handle their office PC requirement: by outsourcing supply, maintenance and upgrades to a specialist or by leasing equipment where upgrades are an essential part of the renewal arrangements. Similar decisions will be relevant to the operations manager.

4.30 Projected long-term production requirements. As discussed earlier in the text, the purchase of high-value items, in particular, should be viewed and costed over the long term. Consideration should be given to strategic aims and objectives to justify the purchase decision. Other aspects such as compatibility, future product plans, and possible requirements for increased output will all be areas for discussion and evaluation.

4.31 Advances in technology have enabled the development of systems that reduce the overall cost of maintenance while improving production performance. The impact of technology can be compared to that found in modern cars (warning lights indicate problems, interval times are flagged-up, temperature sensors indicate status, vibration sensors indicate a machine operating outside acceptable parameters, etc).

4.32 Computers can analyse the feedback from units to give an early warning of possible maintenance requirements. **Predictive maintenance** can work alongside preventive maintenance as an additional way of ensuring maintenance objectives are met.

4.33 The role of modern maintenance is broadening in scope and sophistication. Failure of any one part can cause major problems in manufacturing and the maintenance role is crucial in ensuring that failures of this type are minimised and that machines continue to work accurately within the parameters laid down for the operation.

5   *Facility location*

Supply side and demand side decisions

5.1   Location decisions are essentially to do with placing an operation relative to those who supply it with inputs and relative to those who derive benefit from its outputs or services. With the move to globalisation and overseas manufacture these location decisions may take on a much wider perspective and include viewing customers, culture and logistics as areas of increased importance.

5.2   There are two main criteria that cause organisations to make or reconsider location decisions.

- **Changes in the demand for goods and services**. An increase in demand for the organisation's product or service may require greater capacity. Steps such as outsourcing parts of the business or subcontracting manufacture help to alleviate these issues. However, substantial growth may cause an organisation to strategically re-evaluate in the light of the need to meet customer requirements. The organisation may consider: whether to expand present capability and facilities; whether to seek locations for additional facilities; whether to close down and move to larger premises.

- **Changes in the supply of inputs into the operation**. A policy that stresses the cost element of the operation may consider reduction of stockholding and closeness in proximity to suppliers as an overriding prerequisite. To take the example of moving to a just in time manufacturing system, one of the key requirements is responsive delivery in small lots from suppliers. A change in the operating process may require a re-evaluation of location decision.

5.3   With an existing location, operations managers will be familiar with controlling input – transformation – output relationships and will have experience relating to the capabilities and limitations of the existing operation. An initial evaluation relating to facility location would have been carried out and changes in business demands will first be re-evaluated in light of the current operation and its ability to meet the changes being asked of it.

5.4   Circumstances over time may cause the original decision to be reconsidered in the light of current and predicted future events.

5.5   A wide range of factors will be considered including those in Table 11.1.

Table 11.1 *Factors influencing choice of location*

Appropriate region	Appropriate area	Site selection
Location of markets	Costs, land, construction, grants etc.	Labour availability
Location of suppliers	Communication links	Access by staff and customers
Location of existing facilities	Related industries	Site characteristics
Road, rail, port and airport infrastructure	Required amenities and utilities	Expansion potential
Transport costs	Availability of sites	Services available
Skills base	Local taxes, rates etc.	Environmental issues
Management preferences	Local development plans	
Costs, labour, legislation, etc		

5.6 Manufacturing operations tend to focus on cost-minimisation issues in making location decisions. Service providers, while not ignoring cost issues, will also look for greater 'presence' in order to add value to enhance revenue generation.

Tools of location analysis

5.7 The location decision can be aided by a number of location analysis tools that bring a more scientific and detailed approach to the decision.

5.8 **Factor rating** (if you are familiar with vendor rating you can apply the same thinking). Here relevant factors are identified and weighted according to importance. A weight is assigned to each factor indicating its importance relative to other factors and these are multiplied together to attain a factor weight. The option with the highest score should be selected. Weights may be assigned objectively, such as weighting the factor for utilities costs based on its percentage of total costs of the organisation, or they may be based on the judgement of the decision makers involved.

5.9 **Breakeven analysis** can also be applied to help make or support the location decision. Initially the relevant fixed and variable costs are determined for each proposed location. Then the total cost curves for each alternative are plotted on a single graph. Then, based on the forecast level of activity, the location with the lowest total cost is selected.

5.10 **The centre of gravity method.** This is based on a mathematical model but in essence examines the ideal position for a warehouse based on factors such as distances travelled, loads carried, traffic considerations and fuel usage to arrive at the optimum location to place the warehouse.

5.11 **Simulation.** This is an increasingly effective tool, using specialist modelling programmes to weight relevant factors and to consider a number of potentially viable situations before making the final decision. Simulation can include both factor rating and centre of gravity factors plus any other viable considerations to thoroughly appraise location decisions. Although specialist and relatively expensive, the costs should be weighed against the ramifications if a poor final decision is made.

5.12 **Linear programming**. A form of linear programming known as the transportation method is particularly relevant for the organisation that has multiple plants serving multiple warehouses. This quantitative method will evaluate each proposed site in terms of its impact on the cost of the entire system, particularly the transport and distribution costs. The analysis provides the optimal distribution of products from the manufacturing base to warehouses.

5.13 The decision to locate a facility depends on a combination of many factors; customer location, customer service, distribution costs, road and rail links, facility costs among them. The use of the various tools of analysis relevant to a given situation provides a structured approach that analyses and weighs the various factors. Often these tools will be used together, with their results balanced out against each other. The decision will mean a long-term commitment and in consequence needs to be addressed in a thorough and professional business manner.

Chapter summary

- Quality is the degree in which customer requirements are met.

- Customers may perceive quality in different ways.

- The key consideration with quality gaps is to understand why they exist.

- Quality related costs can be classified as failure costs (internal and external), appraisal costs and prevention costs.

- Quality management aims for a continuous improvement in quality, efficiency and effectiveness and will develop methods and processes that help to achieve these objectives.

- Quality management is about doing things right first time.

- Quality assurance puts in place systems and procedures that ensure that quality standards will be met.

- Quality controls are the operational activities that are used to meet quality requirements.

- Quality control techniques can be divided into two main types: online controls and offline controls.

- Location decisions are essentially to do with placing an operation relative to those who supply it with inputs and relative to those who derive benefit from its outputs or services.

- An organisation will only seek to re-locate if the costs involved and the inconvenience caused are less than the gains to be made from moving to a new location.

Self-test questions

Numbers in brackets refer to the paragraphs above where your answers can be checked.

1   Define quality. (1.2, 1.3)

2   What are David Garvin's eight main dimensions for quality? (1.5)

3   What is the name of the management tool developed by Parasuruman *et al*, which looks at the 'gap' between customer expectations and what is delivered? (1.14)

4   How is the cost of quality defined? (2.2)

5   Failure costs can be categorised under what two headings? (2.5)

6   What are the two main quality control approaches? (3.3)

7   Define statistical process control. (3.8)

8   What is the purpose of a failure mode and effects analysis? (3.18)

9   Define 'preventive maintenance' (4.9)

10   Asset replacement is dependent on a number of factors. Name four. (4.26ff)

11   What are two main criteria that cause organisations to make or reconsider location decisions? (5.2)

12   Explain three tools of location analysis (5.8ff)

Further reading

•   *Operations Management*, Slack, Chambers and Johnston, Chapter 20.

•   *Production and Operations Management*, Muhlemann, Oakland and Lockyer, Chapters 19 and 20.

CHAPTER 12

Total Quality Management

Learning objectives and indicative content

3.4   Evaluate the techniques used to plan and control quality

- Quality management and quality management principles

5.1   Explain the cultural change required to implement total quality management.

- Total quality management (TQM) as a philosophy
- The development of TQM by Deming, Crosby and Juran
- Benefits of TQM
- Criticisms of TQM

Chapter headings

1   Total quality management

2   The quality gurus

3   The benefits and criticisms of TQM

1   Total quality management

The TQM philosophy

1.1   For an organisation to be effective each part of it must integrate and work together. With the modern views of supply chain management and closer supplier relationships this role of integration and working effectively together will often extend outside an operation and cascade through the supply chain. Total quality management (TQM) is conventionally a commitment to quality adopted by an organisation but with the increasing drive toward supply chain management the TQM philosophy is one that impacts along the supply chain as suppliers strive to meet customer needs in relation to quality.

1.2   TQM is an extension of quality thinking. Quality has long been achieved by inspection of products to check that they meet the required specifications. As we have discussed earlier in the text there is an increasing emphasis placed on building quality in to new products, processes or services from the beginning. The customer is at the heart of this thinking. Terms such as 'satisfying customer needs' or 'delighting the customer' are not only marketing terms – they are the drivers for delivering quality.

1.3   Recognising customers and discovering their needs is a crucial aspect of quality thinking. Designing processes that lead to the cost-effective meeting of those needs underpins the quality process. Management have a responsibility for setting the guiding philosophy and supporting it over the long term, providing motivation through leadership and equipping people to achieve quality. TQM is as much a philosophy as a set of techniques; it requires everyone in the organisation to view everything in terms of meeting customer needs.

1.4 Customers are becoming increasingly intolerant of poor goods and services and the delivery of a quality product and/or service gives organisations a competitive edge over the opposition. TQM is a philosophy that must be introduced, integrated, supported and continually improved. Those in the organisation, and those supporting the organisation, need to see the tangible and intangible benefits that a TQM approach can bring and need to see this continuing over time and leading to noticeable quality improvements. TQM thrives on its own success.

1.5 John S Oakland in *Total Quality Management* puts forward a ten point plan for senior management to adopt when implementing a TQM approach.

- The organisation needs long-term commitment to constant improvement with constancy of purpose fully supported by senior management.
- Adopt the philosophy of zero errors/defects to change the culture to right first time.
- Train people to understand the customer-supplier relationships.
- Do not buy products and services on price alone – look at the total cost.
- Recognise that improvement in the systems must be managed.
- Adopt modern methods of supervision and training – eliminate fear.
- Eliminate barriers between departments by managing the process – improve communications and teamwork.
- Eliminate: arbitrary goals without methods; all standards based on numbers; barriers to pride of workmanship; fiction – get to the facts by using the appropriate tools.
- Constantly educate and retrain – develop the 'experts' in the business.
- Develop a systematic approach to manage the implementation of TQM. It requires a carefully planned and fully integrated strategy.

1.6 TQM requires a 'core' of management: appropriate systems, tools for analysis and corrections, and teamworking. These underpin the 'softer' aspects that involve the organisational culture, communication and commitment.

1.7 Business culture has put quality at the heart of competitiveness over recent years and new ways of thinking and considering quality issues have been developed.

- Quality control has developed a more refined and systematic approach, particularly with the increasing impact of information technology across all operations, and this has led to recognisable gains and improvements for many organisations.
- Quality assurance has widened the concept and responsibility for quality management by introducing a formalised approach that extends beyond production and encompasses the service element of organisational operations.

1.8 TQM has been developed as a way of management that seeks to improve the effectiveness, flexibility, reputation and competitiveness of a business overall. TQM can be defined as 'a continuous improvement in quality, efficiency and effectiveness' and has the following features.

- It aims towards an environment of zero defects at a minimum cost.
- It involves measuring and examining all costs that are quality related.

- It requires awareness by all personnel of the quality requirements involved in supplying the customer with products that meet the agreed specification.

- It is a philosophy that involves all parts of the organisation and everyone working in it.

- It aims at the elimination of waste, where waste is defined as anything other than the minimum essential amount of equipment, materials, space and workers' time.

- It must embrace all aspects of operations from pre-production to post-production.

- It involves an emphasis on supply chain thinking (working with suppliers to improve quality along the supply chain).

- It works toward a continuous process of improvement.

1.9 TQM will seek changes in methods and processes that will help in achieving these objectives and lead to measurable quality improvement.

1.10 TQM comprises three major components.

- A documented and auditable quality management system such as ISO 9000 and derivatives

- The application of relevant online and offline controls

- The development of cross-functional teams

The three components are complementary and support each other. They share the same requirement – a commitment to quality.

1.11 TQM is designed to include everyone in the organisation. It is designed with the 'internal customer' very much as a focus. The concept of 'total quality' is just that. No one, no part of the organisation, is excluded. All have a role to play in attaining total quality.

1.12 TQM develops this concept by stressing the role of 'micro-operations'. To use purchasing as an example: internal customers could be marketing, operations, quality control or warehousing; external customers would be suppliers, logistic operators and supplier reference agencies etc. The purchasing department has a role to manage all these relationships by defining as clearly as possible their customers' requirement and how they are going to meet it.

Quality circles

1.13 An important element of TQM is that every one in the organisation should be involved and that anyone with an idea should be heard. One approach is to form groups of managers and employees into 'quality circles'. These groups (normally consisting of around 10 people) meet on a regular basis to discuss quality issues and put forward ideas. The mix and nature of the team will vary, depending on individual circumstances.

1.14 Based on the Japanese model the quality circle approach has met with mixed success in Europe and the United States, perhaps because many organisations continue to operate them beyond their useful life. Quality circles must be flexible in membership and skills in order to meet changing situations.

1.15 Other approaches that are adopted include quality councils, quality improvement teams and corrective action teams. The approach will depend on the organisation and its needs.

ISO 9000

1.16   ISO 9000 was launched in 1987 and comprises a group of quality management standards laid down by the International Organisation for Standardisation (ISO). Although not an essential within the philosophy of TQM the integration of ISO 9000 standards provides a quality assurance structure that ensures good practice is applied and is seen to be applied.

1.17   The ISO 9000 standards are built around business processes, with an emphasis on improvement and on meeting the needs of customers.

1.18   The ISO 9000 model contains eight quality management principles, on which to base an efficient, effective and adaptable quality management system. The principles reflect best practice and are designed so as to enable continual improvement in the business.

- **Customer focus**. Customer needs and expectations must be determined and converted into product and/or service requirements.

- **Leadership**. Good leaders establish a direction and a unity of purpose for an organisation. They formulate an acceptable and appropriate quality policy and ensure that measurable objectives are set for the organisation.

- **Involvement of people**. The role of people in the organisation and their full involvement in the quality ethos enables their abilities to be used for the organisation's benefit while also enhancing their own personal role. Management must act as the enablers of this process.

- **Process approach**. A desired result is achieved more efficiently when related resources and activities are managed as a process. In consequence a quality management system must have, at its core, a process approach, with each process transforming one or more inputs to create an output of value to the customer.

- **Systems approach to management**. Identifying, understanding and managing a system of inter-related processes for a given objective contributes to both the efficiency and the effectiveness of the organisation. These processes must be fully appreciated and understood in order that the most efficient use is made of them.

- **Continuous improvement**. This is a permanent and ongoing objective. Customer satisfaction is a moving target and the quality management system must take this into account. Monitoring of customer feedback and proactive research supported by the measuring and monitoring of performance delivery must be an integral part of the system.

- **Factual approach to decision-making**. Effective decision-making is based on the logical, intuitive analysis of data and information. This requires that a system is in place that provides current and relevant information to managers to assist in the decision-making process.

- **Mutually beneficial supplier relationships**. These types of relationships between an organisation and its suppliers (commonly known as 'win-win' relationships) enhance the ability of both organisations to create value. Each organisation is just one of the links in a much larger supply chain. In order to serve the longterm needs of the community and the organisation itself, mutually beneficial relationships must exist at all points in the supply chain.

1.19   The most recent family of ISO standards for quality management systems comprises:

- **ISO 9000: 2000**: Quality management systems – fundamentals and vocabulary.
- **ISO 9001: 2000**: Quality management systems requirements. This specifies the key requirements of an efficient, effective and adaptable quality management system.
- **ISO 9004: 2000**: Provides guidelines and focuses on performance improvement.

1.20   The ISO 9000 and ISO 9004 standards are designed to be used together but can be operated separately if required. The year 2000 standards are intended to be generic and adaptable to all kinds of organisations including those that are primarily service based.

1.21   The ISO 9001: 2000 standard specifies the requirements for a quality management system that can be used by organisations for internal application, contractual purposes, or certification. The standard identifies quality management systems as comprising four processes: management responsibility, resource management, product realisation and measurement, analysis and improvement.

1.22   The majority of organisations who adopt the ISO 9000/9001 route will have their systems approved by an independent certification body to reinforce in-house disciplines and to demonstrate compliance to customers and purchasers. A number of other potentially relevant standards (such as ISO 10012 measurement systems and ISO 10014 managing the economics of quality) are also in place. For more information visit www.iso.org.

2   The quality gurus

The development of TQM

2.1   The philosophy of TQM has evolved over the years both through practical experience and through the researches of certain influential authorities on the subject (who are often referred to as the 'quality gurus'). Your syllabus specifies three such gurus (Deming, Crosby, Juran) and we look at each of them in turn.

W Edwards Deming

2.2   Deming was a statistician who worked with Walter Shewhart at Bell Laboratories in the 1920s. Shewart pioneered the statistical measurement of product deviation from an accepted norm – the process that Deming developed further to become statistical process control. After a period of considerable success in the US Census Office, Deming was sent to Japan as one of the consultants that supported the Marshall Plan following the Second World War.

2.3   Deming's initial message was about the need to measure product deviations and to continually reduce them. This message, now known as the 'Deming Cycle' (Plan-Do-Check-Act), forms the basis for **kaizen** or **continuous improvement**. His message was well received in Japan where a thorough and meticulous approach to manufacture has long been appreciated.

2.4 Deming placed considerable importance on the role of management, both at the individual and at the company level, believing managers to be responsible for 94 per cent of quality problems. His view was that inappropriate systems, processes and procedures were the root cause of many quality concerns and that workers could do little to influence these issues unless they were empowered to do so.

2.5 In his 1986 book *Out of Crisis* he published his 14 points for management (although these had been published in Japan much earlier).

- Create constancy of purpose towards improvement of product and service.
- Adopt the new philosophy for the new economic age. We can no longer live with commonly accepted levels of delay, mistakes and defective workmanship.
- Cease dependence on mass inspection. Instead, require statistical evidence that quality is built in.
- End the practice of awarding the business on price; instead minimise total cost and move to single suppliers for items.
- Improve constantly and forever the system of production and service to improve quality and increase productivity.
- Institute modern methods of training on the job.
- Institute modern methods of supervision of production workers. The responsibility of foremen must be changed from numbers to quality.
- Drive out fear, so that everyone may work effectively for the company.
- Break down barriers between departments.
- Eliminate numerical goals, posters and slogans for the workforce asking for new levels of productivity without providing methods.
- Eliminate work standards that prescribe numerical quotas.
- Remove barriers that stand between the hourly worker and their right to pride of workmanship.
- Institute a vigorous programme of education and retraining
- Create a structure in top management that will push towards the transformation.

Philip Crosby

2.6 Philip Crosby is one of the most highly regarded of the modern quality gurus. His two leading publications *Quality is Free* (1979) and *Quality Without Tears* (1984) help to expound his philosophy. In these books he defines quality as 'conformance to requirements' and develops (some already existing) themes such as 'quality is free', 'zero defects' and 'do it right first time'.

2.7 In these publications Crosby laid down his original four absolutes for quality.

- Quality is conformance to requirements.
- The system of quality is prevention.
- The performance standard is zero defects.
- The measurement of quality is the price of non-conformance.

2.8 Crosby also published a 14-step plan to quality improvement.

- Management must commit to a formalised quality policy.
- Form a management level quality improvement team with responsibility for quality issues.
- Determine where current and potential quality issues are.
- Evaluate the cost of quality and explain its effectiveness as a management tool to measure waste.
- Raise quality awareness and involvement amongst all employees.
- Take corrective actions, using formal systems to expose the root causes.
- Establish a zero defects committee and programme.
- Train all employees in quality improvement.
- Hold a zero defects day.
- Encourage groups and individuals to set improvement goals and targets.
- Encourage employee communication.
- Give formal recognition to those involved.
- Establish quality councils for information dissemination and sharing.
- Do it all over again – the quality process never ends.

2.9 Quality management is not easy to achieve. Crosby offers his Quality Management Maturity Grid, a five-stage progression in awareness and application of quality and quality thinking in an organisation.

- **Stage 1: Uncertainty**. 'We don't know why we have problems with quality.'
- **Stage 2: Awakening**. 'Is it absolutely necessary to always have problems with quality?'
- **Stage 3: Enlightenment**. 'Through management commitment and quality improvement we are identifying and resolving our problems.'
- **Stage 4: Wisdom**. 'Defect prevention is a routine part of our operation.'
- **Stage 5: Certainty**. 'We know why we do not have problems with quality'.

Dr Joseph M Juran

2.10 Juran, a former co-worker at Bell Systems, followed Deming to Japan and developed the **quality trilogy** (quality planning, quality improvement and quality control), the implementation of which requires management actions and processes to be planned, measured, managed and continuously improved.

2.11 Juran's approach is more formal than Deming's with a greater emphasis on a structural approach within the organisation. Juran defined quality as 'fitness for use' in which he categorised quality under four headings with three subheadings for each.

- **Quality of design**: market research, product concept, design specifications.
- **Quality of conformance**: use and application of technology, human resources, management.
- **Quality of availability**: distribution (perhaps more correctly logistics with the modern understanding), reliability and maintainability.
- **Field service**: promptness, competence and integrity.

2.12   In 1951 he published the highly influential *Quality Control Handbook* which encouraged top management involvement, introduced the Pareto principle into quality, defined quality as 'fitness for use' and propounded a project-by-project approach to quality improvement.

2.13   His later **quality planning map** provides a stage process for understanding quality.

- Identify the customers both internal and external.
- Determine the needs of these customers.
- Translate those needs into our language.
- Develop a product designed to meet those needs.
- Optimise the product features so as to meet both our needs and our customers' needs.
- Develop a process that is able to produce the product.
- Optimise the product.
- Prove that the process is effective under operating conditions.
- Transfer the process to operations.

3   The benefits and criticisms of TQM

3.1   The evolution of the quality movement has led to dramatic changes in product and service delivery. The increased emphasis on meeting customer needs is a business essential in a competitive world. Quality, often viewed as a tool that would help organisations gain competitive advantage, is now a 'given' in many industries. Those who do not offer quality products or services are increasingly at risk.

3.2   The phrase 'quality is free' (Philip Crosby) demonstrates the main benefit gains of a TQM approach. Quality is gained over time. The Deming Cycle underpins many of the quality processes. The PDCA cycle ensures continuous improvement. It ensures that processes and procedures are scrutinised with the objective of improvement (better manufacturing techniques, tighter tolerances, improved customer communications, reduced waste etc), and when integrated into an organisation's culture the philosophy brings intangible benefits to staff and stakeholders.

TQM implementation

3.3   Implementation of TQM can be seen as time-consuming, bureaucratic, formalistic, rigid, impersonal and the property of one group within the organisation. The implementation of TQM requires good management practice particularly in regard to change management and communications in order to introduce and then embed TQM within the organisation.

3.4   There are two main approaches to TQM implementation. The 'blitz' approach introduces TQM very rapidly with mass education and communication programs. This can lead to problems in not knowing what to do next (or even first!) and can prove highly disruptive to existing business. The second approach is more measured and gradual, requiring a commitment to change to be identified, supported and communicated at a strategic level and integrated into strategic and business plans.

3.5   Criticism of TQM differs over time. Initially the introductory phase may be poorly communicated or managed, perhaps seen as another 'management fad' rather than a long-term commitment. During the implementation phase the TQM process may be seen as under the ownership of a particular group rather than the whole organisation and when implemented it may be seen as inflexible and too bureaucratic.

3.6   The challenge for management is to understand TQM and how the implications of fundamental change will impact on the organisation.

3.7   TQM offers a comprehensive approach to improving competitiveness, effectiveness and planning throughout the organisation but requires long-term commitment and organisational policies to succeed. TQM starts at the top where a serious long-term commitment to quality should be demonstrated. Chief Executives must accept responsibility for commitment to a quality policy that encompasses organising for quality, understanding customer needs, appreciating the abilities of the organisation, developing suppliers, education and training and on-going review of manufacturing and management systems.

3.8   TQM takes time to implement and embed successfully. The introduction of this new approach will change the culture of an organisation. The culture of an organisation is formed by the traditions, beliefs, behaviours, norms, values, rules and approach. The introduction of a TQM philosophy is concerned with allowing and encouraging individuals to take 'ownership' of their role and responsibilities and having the means to communicate their respective issues in a way that leads to 'micro-improvements' and in turn to overall improvement.

3.9   Individuals require to understand the TQM process, its purpose, the reasoning behind it and why it is important for the organisation. A key word in successful implementation is 'empowerment'. The empowerment of individuals lies in their ability to put forward ideas, discuss issues and influence changes in their area or over the organisation as a whole.

3.10   Building a quality culture is of crucial importance and, if achieved successfully, is a major intangible benefit that can serve to drive an organisation forward. Management commitment and cohesion are created as processes develop.

- Employees are more involved in managing.
- Managers are obligated to recognise the operational difficulties that employees work under.
- TQM demonstrates management commitment to quality by deed rather than words.

3.11   TQM is difficult and time-consuming to implement. It requires long-term cohesive commitment from senior management that must be successfully cascaded throughout the organisation. Quality thinking must be embedded in the organisation. Manufacturing gains are measurable and a clear benefit. Cultural change is less measurable but can be of equal or greater benefit.

Chapter summary

- Total quality management (TQM) is an extension of quality thinking
- Recognising customers and discovering their needs is a crucial aspect of quality thinking.
- TQM is designed to include everyone in the organisation
- ISO 9000 standards are built around business processes, with an emphasis on improvement and on meeting the needs of customers.
- Deming's initial message was about the need to measure product deviations and to continually reduce them. This message, now known as the 'Deming Cycle' (Plan-Do-Check-Act), forms the basis for kaizen or continuous improvement.

Self-test questions

Numbers in brackets refer to the paragraphs above where your answers can be checked.

1 What ten point plan for senior management does John S Oakland in *Total Quality Management* put forward to adopt when implementing a TQM approach? (1.5)

2 TQM comprises what three major components? (1.10)

3 The ISO 9000 model contains what eight quality management principles? (1.18)

4 What makes up the 'Deming Cycle'? (2.3)

5 What criticisms have been made of TQM implementation? (3.5)

Further reading

- *Operations Management*, Slack, Chambers and Johnston, Chapters 20 and 21.
- *Production and Operations Management*, Muhlemann, Oakland and Lockyer, Chapter 8.

CHAPTER 13

Mock Exam

THE EXEMPLAR PAPER

The exam paper below was published by CIPS as an illustration of what might be expected under the new syllabus. If you are able to make a good attempt at this you should be very well prepared for the live examination.

SECTION A

You are strongly advised to carefully read and analyse the information in the case study before attempting to answer questions 1 and 2.

Domplas

Background

John Smith looked out of his office window into the rural countryside. In all the years of being managing director of Domplas he had never had to deal with problems on this scale before. He and his father had gained a good living from this manufacturing company, and it had kept them more than comfortable over the last 50 years. He was preparing himself to meet his newly appointed operations director, who had started this morning. This position had been vacant for over a year because he had decided not to replace Ron Jones, who had retired due to ill health. He had decided to take on this role himself for a period in order to avoid the burden of another large director's salary, and also because he felt it was not such a difficult job. The state of things on the shop floor was almost the same as it had been 20 years ago, and while some improvements had been made, he felt that, if anything, Domplas was now falling behind its competition. He accepted now that not replacing the operations director was perhaps not the best of decisions, but it had seemed the right one at the time.

The struggling business

The business was struggling. Historically the business had fairly consistent year on year sales of around £18m, but these had declined over the last three years down to the figure of £14m for the last financial year. The company's employee numbers were steady at 220 and so far he had not had to make any redundancies. Stock was at an all time high and WIP was also increasing.

Domplas produced a variety of small domestic appliances such as electric kettles, coffee percolators and kitchen processing equipment. Competition from the Far East was more intense than ever, and Domplas was finding it difficult to compete on cost. As a result profits were well down to just a few percent, and the way things were going the next financial year would be a loss-making year. John was aware that, although he could not compete on cost his main customers valued his products, as they were of very good quality and his lead times were quite reasonable at around two to three weeks. Domplas was also good at innovating; his design and development team continually came up with new ideas for products that were significantly different. The only issue was that he felt it took too long to convert these ideas into actual saleable products. The designs were there, but the manufacturing equipment and machinery appeared to be incapable of producing what was required. For example, Domplas could have done with knowing how to produce soft touch controls on its appliance keypads, but somehow its injection moulding department had not been able to deliver what was needed.

John was aware that the company was very vertically integrated. Its core competencies were in the areas of injection moulding and assembly, which John had always considered to be key to producing a good appliance. The only issue with this department was that as volumes for each moulding reduced or as the variety of moulding options increased, staff had to manage a larger number of machine setups. He had managed this issue by keeping some of the older machines and leaving tools in them, and only running them when needed. The company also stamped out all its own metal pressings, and even had a number of small welding cells that manufactured some of the smaller metal components. The volumes of these had also declined significantly due to lack of demand, but John liked the idea of being in control and self-sufficient.

Other items such as heating elements were also made in-house, although John acknowledged that the equipment was quite old, and quality problems continually delayed despatch of some of the lower volume batches to customers. However, the culture of his workforce was very positive. All the staff were prepared to work overtime in order to get orders out at the month end.

John felt that the current real business problem was that of the breakeven point for his company. Discussions with his financial director suggested that sales of £14m were around the breakeven point, and he had some interesting ideas about how they could reduce the business overheads. Conveniently the site was split into roughly two halves. He had had conversations with a local businessman who was interested in moving in to one half of the site, which would effectively halve the overhead, with the result that the business would become profitable again almost overnight.

The new operations director had been recruited because of his expertise in the philosophy and practices of lean manufacturing. John was hoping that this expertise would help him in reducing the footprint of the site by fifty percent and bring the business back into profitability.

You are to take on the role of operations director of Domplas and answer the questions below.

The information in this case study is purely fictitious and has been prepared for assessment purposes only.

Any resemblance to any organisation or person is purely coincidental.

SECTION A

Questions 1 and 2 relate to the case study and should be answered in context of the information provided.

Question 1

Demonstrate how lean manufacturing principles might be applied within Domplas in order to achieve John Smith's objectives. **(25 marks)**

Question 2

(a) Discuss the terms 'core competencies' and 'vertical integration' in the context of the above case study. **(10 marks)**

(b) Appraise which of Domplas's manufacturing processes might be outsourced as part of the company's new approach to manufacturing. **(15 marks)**

SECTION B

Answer **TWO** questions from Section B.

You are strongly advised to carefully read all the questions in Section B before selecting **TWO** questions to answer.

Question 3

(a) Describe the design process for either products or services, and appraise the anticipated benefits of using this process in an organisation with which you are familiar. **(13 marks)**

(b) Examine the benefits of using cross-functional teams within the design process in order to deliver better value. Provide examples from your own experience or from course material. **(12 marks)**

Question 4

(a) Define the term 'total quality management' (TQM) both as a system and as a philosophy. **(6 marks)**

(b) Compare and contrast the different approaches to TQM as proposed by Juran, Crosby and Deming. **(19 marks)**

Question 5

Compare and contrast the challenges facing operations managers who operate in increasingly complex global markets for goods and services. **(25 marks)**

Question 6

(a) Explain the stages you would go through in order to benchmark a function or process within an organisation of your choice. **(10 marks)**

(b) Discuss the benefits and limitations of benchmarking. **(15 marks)**

CHAPTER 14

MOCK EXAM: SUGGESTED SOLUTIONS

THE EXEMPLAR PAPER

Some general observations

Make sure that you have read the 'Instructions for Candidates' section at the front of the Mock Exam, in order to be quite clear as to what is required.

Please bear in mind that our solutions are lengthier than you would attempt in an exam, in order to cover the wide range of points that might be included – and to reflect the full (and rather demanding) suggestions given in the CIPS Answer Guidance.

SUGGESTED SOLUTIONS

SECTION A

Solution 1

Recommended answer structure:

- *Introduction to lean, including a definition*

- *Main body: discuss main lean targets for Domplas using the lean definition as defined by Womack, Jones and Roos*

- *Reflective summary*

The just in time (JIT) philosophy was first introduced by the Toyota organisation in the 1960s. JIT is now a proven approach in manufacturing environments for increasing operational efficiency. The main tenets of JIT have subsequently been further developed via the concept of 'lean production'. Lean production is an approach to operations management that takes the best of modern thinking and integrates it into an overall approach to manufacture.

The idea of lean production was first analysed in depth by John Krafcik when he and others were working on a motor vehicle programme in the late 1980s. The phrase 'lean manufacturing' was subsequently popularised in the publication *The Machine That Changed the World* (1990) by Womack, Jones and Roos. In this book lean production was defined as follows.

> *'Lean production is "lean" because it uses less of every thing compared with mass production: half the human effort in the factory, half the factory space, half the investment in tools, half the engineering hours to develop a new product in half the time. Also, it requires far less than half of the needed inventory on site. The expected results are fewer defects, while producing a greater and ever growing variety of products.'*

Lean thinking can be applied to any organisational type (including services) and can be applied across all areas of the business. It is a three-pronged approach that incorporates a belief in quality, waste elimination and employee involvement supported by a structured management system.

Implications of this new approach were that high volume production of standard models was no longer enough to satisfy ever more demanding customers, and that higher levels of quality and shorter time to market in new product development were achievable targets.

Lean production is similar to just in time in that it uses a range of waste saving measures. However lean production differs in that it is a philosophy of production that aims to minimise inputs while maximising outputs. Some of the techniques that can be used to develop lean production are just in time, total quality management, zero defects, **kaizen**, cell-based production, time-based management and simultaneous engineering. It is not one system but an amalgam of related business disciplines that are brought together in the most effective manner in order to meet the goals of lean production.

The original definition of lean as devised by Womack et al would provide an ideal outline structure for the new Domplas operations director to achieve the objectives of John Smith. Specifically, this definition brings focus to the following operational themes.

- Half the human effort in the factory

- Half the factory space

- Half the investment in tools

- Half the engineering hours to develop a new product in half the time

- Less than half of the needed inventory on site

The above themes will now be developed further to demonstrate how lean principles could assist in reducing the overall footprint of the Domplas operation whilst also aiding increased productivity and profitability.

Half the factory space

One of the main tenets of the lean philosophy is to eliminate waste. Specifically, facility layouts can be notoriously wasteful due mainly to the evolving nature of facilities. What was perhaps an efficient layout originally has often been subsequently modified to accommodate numerous changing business circumstances.

Business process reengineering (BPR) concepts could be used to perform a complete review of the current manufacturing process. For example, a useful initial approach for Domplas would be to conduct a value stream mapping activity for the purpose of highlighting where value is being added within the current process and where wasteful activities are being incurred.

The lean philosophy uses the concept of cellular manufacturing to minimise wasteful activities such as material and operator movement together with product transportation.

In addition to cellular layouts, the lean optimal approach is to achieve unidirectional flow, ideally for a batch size of one. The application of a cellular layout supported by the concept of unidirectional flow can result in a considerable reduction of required floor space.

Other possible considerations for Domplas that would assist in further reducing the required floor space might be the outsourcing of operations such as the moulding department. It is apparent from the case study that there appears to be a manufacturing problem somewhere along the internal supply chain operation. This could possibly be due to:

- Lack of design for manufacturing awareness

- Lack of operator skills

- Lack of fitness for purpose of the moulding machines

Outsourcing, if a viable business case can be made, would considerably assist in many of these issues. In addition, outsourcing could further contribute to increased profitability when financial issues such as company asset maintenance and replacement are taken into account.

Inventory reductions

The purpose of inventory along the supply chain is to assist in managing operational variation. Variation can exist in many forms.

- Customer demand variation

- Supplier delivery variation

- Quality variation etc

In addition, the lack of any balanced material flow through the facility causes WIP and operational inefficiencies. WIP invariably occupies floor space whilst also attracting operational costs.

In the lean philosophy excess inventory is viewed as waste and considerable effort should be made to progressively reduce existing stock levels. However, it is dangerous to remove inventory without first addressing the operational variations at source. The reduction of inventory needs to be done in a very structured manner which might be supported by:

*   Six sigma process performance measurement

*   Demand/supply network considerations (eg consideration of where inventory might be kept along the supply chain to gain maximum commercial advantage)

*   Planning and controlling quality initiatives

*   Supplier development targets (eg VMI)

*   Setup reduction initiatives coupled with subsequent small batch manufacture

As inventory is progressively reduced there will be financial benefits (reduction in the costs related to holding inventory) as well as the related reduction in facility storage requirements. However, the balance between the costs of holding inventory and the costs of not holding inventory is a delicate one and therefore needs to be approached in a considered manner.

Half the human effort in the factory

Doing operations right first time moves considerable cost from the overall operation whilst improving productivity. Lean principles embrace several techniques for addressing the root causes of problems. Considerations might include:

*   Process mapping of business processes

*   Automation possibilities within the supply chain that might embrace both materials handling and manufacturing processes

*   Progressive removal of process variation using continuous improvement techniques such as six sigma

Half the investment in tools and halving the engineering hours to develop a new product in half the time

Reduction in both the time-to-market and the associated costs should be high on the Domplas agenda. Rapidly changing markets now demand innovative products and services at competitive prices. As with many of the lean concepts this means addressing the root causes, which in this case traces back to the design and engineering processes.

The basic problem with traditional product development processes is that most of the cost is built in even before the product is manufactured. For example, overly complex designs often require an inefficient transformation process. This can also extend the time-to-market for new products which will impact on the Domplas profitability.

Applying lean tools to the new product development process will help to reduce development lead-time but this would entail Domplas taking a broader view of their new product development. Each new product design must be considered in the context of both existing and future products. Typical lean initiatives that Domplas could consider include the following.

*   Standardisation of parts and processes

*   Platform designs that leverage design efforts from one product to many other related products. This allows them to have highly flexible product lines that require less overall engineering and manufacturing effort.

Each new product design should be viewed by Domplas as an opportunity to reduce overheads by reusing existing equipment, floor space, personnel, and systems (eg developing new products without the need for new production equipment). They should target removing waste from the transformation process at every opportunity by designing products to ensure lean production ideally with six sigma capability before product launch.

Domplas has already identified a sales breakeven point of £14m. This is based on the examination of current fixed and variable costs and identifies a breakeven point where revenues are equal to costs.

The recent trend in many manufacturing environments has been to progress through a business cycle that includes price competition, cost reduction, a proliferation of new products, higher fixed costs, increased breakeven points and lower profits. To counter this cycle effectively the application of operations philosophies such as lean production has been successfully deployed both to decrease operational costs but equally to provide a viable approach to production systems design where costs are more sensitive to changes in demand.

Solution 2

Part (a)

Outline solution

- *Define core competencies and vertical integration*

- *Briefly discuss in the context of Domplas*

Organisations face decisions regarding processes and process management. A key decision surrounds the concept of 'core competence' – the distinctive, value-creating skills, capabilities and resources in an organisation. This decision in turn determines whether processes are accomplished in-house, or outsourced or subcontracted. Make or buy decisions will often relate to the strategic objectives of the company.

Vertical integration can be viewed as the potential within an enterprise to incorporate all aspects of management, production, sales and distribution into the business operations. In theory, the greater the level of vertical integration, the less vulnerable an organisation is to external forces.

In the context of Domplas, John Smith assumes that the core competencies of the business are in the areas of injection moulding and assembly. However, this assessment appears to be made using an historical perspective.

The changing dynamics of today's markets have meant that innovative solutions are more likely to be the norm than the exception. As a consequence, historical process skills are often found wanting in producing more technical requirements as is evidenced with the problems being encountered by Domplas in producing soft-touch control mouldings. In addition, the need to produce smaller volumes of mouldings in a cost effective manner will potentially jeopardise profit margins owing to the adverse impact on profitability.

Domplas is currently very vertically integrated. This is not uncommon with many traditional manufacturing organisations where the idea of being in control and self sufficient had obvious appeal. However, as manufacturing volumes have diminished and the need for customer responsiveness has increased the resultant operating complexities have intensified. Retaining full control of the manufacturing process via in-house operation now means a substantive increase in process and financial risk.

Part (b)

Outline solution

- *Outline the reasons for the emerging popularity of outsourcing*

- *Analyse the Domplas options*

- *Reflective summary and recommendations*

The popularity of outsourcing has significantly increased as organisations react against the once popular strategies of spreading risk by diversifying into a number of different business areas.

At the micro level the complexities of coping with today's operational demands has meant that past core competencies are sometimes not capable of being sustained because of technical and operational advances.

Domplas currently considers that its core competencies revolve around injection moulding and product assembly. In addition it is also manufacturing in the following areas.

- Metal assemblies

- Welding cells producing heating elements

The reality of the injection moulding area is that much of the current machinery is old and therefore may not be technically capable of handling the specifications needed such as the soft touch control mouldings.

Domplas must urgently review the way forward with the injection moulding area. They either need to have a capital and people investment for this area or should consider the option of outsourcing. However, the current low levels of production would probably mean that making a viable business case for investment would be somewhat difficult. Outsourcing could also result in a substantive space and energy saving for Domplas.

The metal assembly manufacturing area is faced with lower and lower volumes. This kind of low-skill assembly work could easily be outsourced to a specialised third party who would probably produce these assemblies at a lower unit cost. In addition, outsourcing this work would also have the added benefit of saving the storage space that is being currently occupied by the supporting raw materials/components required for the assemblies.

The Domplas welding cells that produce the heating elements could hardly be described as a core competency of the business. However, owing to lack of investment in equipment for this area production and quality problems are beginning to emerge. These problems are now beginning to have an adverse effect on customer service.

Similar to the metal assembly section, the welding cells are a prime candidate for outsourcing. Again, this would also free up both production and storage areas to assist in the Domplas rationalisation objective.

In contrast, Domplas could conceivably consider its design capability as a new emerging core competency. It is consistently developing innovative designs to meet market needs even though the current Domplas manufacturing operation cannot support their innovative ability.

In summary, there would appear to be a justifiable case for outsourcing the peripheral Domplas manufacturing activities of metal assembly and welding. This would immediately assist in reducing the required facility size as well as reducing the employee overheads.

The case for outsourcing the injection moulding department is less clear cut. In its current state it is fast becoming a non-core competency of the business. With appropriate investment it might be possible to resurrect this manufacturing area to its former status. However, the current financial status of Domplas might restrict this option and if this is the case outsourcing would again be recommended.

Changing business pressures have led to many organisations reviewing their activities and deciding to concentrate on core activities. Domplas is no exception to this. The strategic view – as discussed by Hamel and Prahalad in *Competing for the Future* – encourages organisations to identify their core business, the parts of their business that are at the heart of their operation and where they excel, and build on this. In the case of Domplas this might now mean a progressive migration away from its vertically integrated manufacturing operation to one that maybe focuses on developing innovative designs and producing final assembly products.

Solution 3

Part (a)

The dictionaries give a variety of definitions for design. 'The act of producing a drawing, plan or pattern showing details of something to be constructed', 'the arrangement of elements of a work of art' and 'a decorative pattern', are three. The term is wider than all three. It is a blend of concept, taste, style and practicality from a business perspective.

The purpose of design, in a business sense, is to satisfy the needs of customers. For example, a product is designed to meet customer requirements. While this is of great concern to both designers and marketing, the view of operations is more pragmatic. The main operational concern is whether the product can be made to specification at an acceptable cost. To put it another way: is it designed for manufacture?

There are various models that specify recommendations for the sequence of the design process. In general these models tend to embrace much of the same content but for the purpose of this response the model proposed by Slack *et al* in their book *Operations Management* will be used. This model states that every design programme should pass through five phases.

Concept generation

Ideas for concept generation can come from a variety of sources both internal and external to the organisation. Within the organisation ideas can be generated by staff, R&D, sales personnel etc whilst external sources can include the customer, competitors, market surveys etc.

Screening

Not all generated concepts will be viable for further development. The screening stage effectively acts as a filtering process where concepts are evaluated against criteria such as the following.

- Feasibility
- Acceptability
- Vulnerability
- Competitor analysis
- Price performance targeting
- Financial analysis

Preliminary design

With the preferred concept already established this stage is focused on developing a specification for the product or service together with defining the process to create the package. This stage of the design process will normally require multi-functional inputs from within the organisation.

Evaluation and improvement

Prior to the product or service being exposed to the market the preliminary design is analysed to see where it can be improved both from a product and a process point of view. This analysis and evaluation can be supported by techniques such as the following.

- Quality function deployment
- Value engineering
- Taguchi methods

Prototyping and final design

Before progressing to full manufacture or release it is usual to carry out a pilot run or test marketing. Only after full evaluation and approval of pre-operational testing should the project move to implementation.

Here are some benefits of following the above approach to developing products and services.

- Provides a structured approach to developing products and services and also reduces the problem of individual bias overly influencing the final entity. There are many examples where the influence of an individual has ended with a marketing disaster (eg Sinclair C5 vehicle).

- Improved time to market for new products is critical for many organisations and can be a key factor in competitive advantage. This need is further highlighted by the fact that the lifecycle of products and services is diminishing as the competitive pressures in many markets intensify. For example, in the automotive market it was usual in the 1980s for vehicles to remain in production in excess of ten years without any serious design alterations (eg Ford Sierra). Today the lifecycle of a typical vehicle is 3–4 years and the time required from concept to market must reflect this time base.

- The structured and multifunctional approach to design is also important in reducing design and development costs. In other words, the developed product or service is more likely to be 'right first time' when compared to developing designs via a fragmented, departmental approach – often referred to as the 'over the wall' technique. For example, the development of historical products in manufacturing was often plagued by expensive and time consuming debugging activities where problems only became evident when bulk manufacture was attempted.

- Finally, a structured approach to the design process ensures that the 'voice of the customer' (both internal and external to the organisation) is successfully captured at all stages of the process. For example, products and services should be designed in such a way that they can be manufactured or prepared effectively. Ideally the processes that will transform the product or service should be flexible enough that new demands can be integrated into existing systems without major changes to the operation.

Part (b)

Cross-functional teamwork brings all relevant concerns into open discussion during the formative phase of development and allows for discussion and clarification. This integrated approach helps ensure that all potential areas are discussed by the team who become increasingly familiar with the project and, in consequence, gain a wider understanding and perspective on the issues raised by other team members.

The traditional product/service development process is often constrained by the functional personnel involved. Thus the use of a multifunctional team breaks down traditional barriers within the organisation as well as providing an excellent opportunity to improve transparency and communications.

Marketing staff have responsibility for bringing the new product successfully to market. This involves an awareness of changing tastes and requirements. Increasingly, capturing the 'voice of the customer' is critical in today's global and competitive markets. For example, the voice of the customer is now embedded within the ISO 9001 quality management standards.

Designers are normally looking for the freedom to develop innovative designs for products and services. However, multifunctional involvement achieves the realisation of the practicalities involved at all stages of the supply chain. This realisation of other supply chain needs will therefore positively influence the manner by which customer needs are transformed into the end product or service.

Finance staff are responsible for financing the research and development that is involved in new product introduction and for monitoring and approving the spend as the new product progresses. It can be quite easy for the cost implications of new products and services to be overlooked in the excitement of developing design concepts and processes.

Purchasing staff have an increasingly important role in new product development. If purchasing staff are involved early in the design process they can advise on different materials, potential costs and supply problems. They can also involve potential suppliers early in the process if specialist research, involving the skills of suppliers, is called for.

The non-involvement of suppliers can be potentially embarrassing. For example, it is quite common for design concepts to be well advanced to the prototype testing stage before problems emerge. Involvement of the suppliers at an early stage to provide specialist advice and guidance can often save both time and costs.

Operations staff have a central role in the new product development process. Whereas purchasing has a crucial role as the external interface between an organisation and suppliers the role of operations has more of an internal focus through the development stages. The concern of operations is the integration of design into the practicalities of production. For example, the input of shop floor expertise can guide and advise when deciding appropriate radius dimensions that will be needed for robust tooling design.

In summary, the cross-functional approach can bring many advantages to the development of new products and services. It encourages 'buy in' by all parties concerned and improves the overall cost and time effectiveness of the design process. The use of techniques such as simultaneous engineering encourages concurrent development of product and services as opposed to the historical linear 'over the wall' approach that is more costly and time consuming in nature.

Solution 4

BS 7850:1 1992 defines the total quality management philosophy and system as follows.

> *A management philosophy and company practices that aim to harness the human and material resources of an organisation in the most effective way to achieve the objectives of the organisation.*

The TQM philosophy is a set of beliefs and general concepts that embrace practices of continuously improving every aspect of organisational activity.

The TQM system is an integrated system of principles, methods, and best practices that provide a framework for organisations to strive for excellence in everything they do.

TQM can be described as an extension of quality thinking. Traditionally, quality has been predominantly achieved by inspection of products to check that they meet the required specifications. Increasingly the emphasis is placed on building quality in to new products, processes or services from the beginning. The customer is at the heart of this thinking. Terms such as 'satisfying customer needs' or 'delighting the customer' are not only marketing terms – they are the drivers for delivering quality.

For an organisation to be effective each part of it must integrate and work together. With the modern views of supply chain management and closer supplier relationships this role of integration and working effectively together will often extend outside an operation and cascade through the supply chain.

Part (b)

The philosophy of TQM has evolved over the years both through practical experience and through the researches of certain influential authorities on the subject (who are often referred to as the 'quality gurus'). Three such pioneering gurus in the field of TQM are Deming, Crosby and Juran.

W Edwards Deming

Deming was a statistician who worked with Walter Shewhart at Bell Laboratories in the 1920s. Shewhart pioneered the statistical measurement of product deviation from an accepted norm – the process that Deming developed further to become statistical process control.

Deming worked for some time in post world war Japan as a consultant to assist in the economic recovery of the nation. One of his key messages to the Japanese related to the importance of measuring process deviations and the need to continually reduce them. This message, now known as the 'Deming Cycle' (Plan-Check-Do-Act), forms the basis for *kaizen* or continuous improvement. His message was well received in Japan where a thorough and meticulous approach to manufacture had long been appreciated.

Deming placed considerable importance on the role of management, both at the individual and at the company level, believing managers to be responsible for 94 per cent of quality problems. His view was that inappropriate systems, processes and procedures were the root cause of many quality concerns. Workers could do little to influence these issues unless they were empowered to do so.

Deming published many authoritative books on the subject of quality. For example, in his 1986 book *Out of Crisis* he introduced the now famous 14 points for management which effectively provided a framework by which organisations could embrace total quality management.

Philip Crosby

Philip Crosby is one of the most highly regarded of the modern quality gurus. His two leading publications *Quality is Free* (1979) and *Quality Without Tears* (1984) help to expound his philosophy. In these books he defines quality as 'conformance to requirements' and develops (some already existing) themes such as 'quality is free', 'zero defects' and 'do it right first time'.

In these publications Crosby laid down his original four absolutes for quality.

- Quality is conformance to requirements.

- The system of quality is prevention.

- The performance standard is zero defects.

- The measurement of quality is the price of non-conformance.

Like Deming, Crosby also published a 14-step plan to quality improvement. Crosby recognised that quality management is not easy to achieve within organisations and therefore developed his **quality management maturity grid**, a five-stage progression in awareness and application of quality and quality thinking in an organisation.

Stage 1: Uncertainty. 'We don't know why we have problems with quality.'

Stage 2: Awakening. 'Is it absolutely necessary to always have problems with quality?'

Stage 3: Enlightenment. 'Through management commitment and quality improvement we are identifying and resolving our problems.'

Stage 4: Wisdom. 'Defect prevention is a routine part of our operation.'

Stage 5: Certainty. 'We know why we do not have problems with quality'.

Dr Joseph M Juran

Juran, a former co-worker at Bell Systems, followed Deming to Japan and developed the quality trilogy (quality planning, quality improvement and quality control), the implementation of which requires management actions and processes to be planned, measured, managed and continuously improved.

Juran's approach is more formal than Deming's with a greater emphasis on a structural approach within the organisation. Juran defined quality as 'fitness for use' in which he categorised quality under four headings.

- Quality of design: market research, product concept, design specifications.

- Quality of conformance: use and application of technology, human resources, management.

- Quality of availability: distribution (perhaps more correctly logistics with the modern understanding), reliability and maintainability.

- Field service: promptness, competence and integrity.

In 1951 Juran published the highly influential *Quality Control Handbook* which encouraged top management involvement, introduced the Pareto principle into quality, defined quality as 'fitness for use' and propounded a project-by-project approach to quality improvement.

In addition, Juran developed a quality planning map which provided a staged process by which organisations could understand quality. This mapping introduced many key concepts that are key considerations for management in the 21st century such as identifying both internal and external customers and determining the needs of these customers.

Each of these three quality gurus has his own distinctive approach to TQM. However, whilst their approaches to TQM are not totally the same, they do share some common themes.

Management responsibility

- Provide commitment, leadership, empowerment, encouragement, and the appropriate support.

- Determine the environment and framework of operations within an organisation.

The participation of the employees in quality improvement

The importance of developing a quality culture by changing perception and attitudes toward quality

The importance of employee education and training

The need for employee recognition

The organisational emphasis needs to be on the prevention of product defects, not inspection after the event

Quality is a systematic company-wide activity from suppliers to customers

Equally, whilst there is much agreement from these gurus as to the key themes of TQM, there are also marked differences as to the journey towards TQM. The following examples support this conclusion.

- Deming's approach to TQM is quite revolutionary in nature whilst Juran's approach is more evolutionary.

- Deming refers to statistics as being the language of business while Juran says that it is money.

However, Juran does agree with Deming on topics such as the following.

- In excess of 80 percent of defects are caused by the organisation systems rather than the workers.

- Worker motivation is a non-solution to quality problems.

All three gurus stress the importance of management commitment and removal of the causes of error. However, there are some aspects of Crosby's approach to quality that are quite different from Deming's. For example, the concept of 'zero defects' is central to Crosby's philosophy but is criticised by Deming. Deming reasoned that the focus of 'zero defects' was directed at the wrong people (workers) and subsequently generated worker frustration and resentment when these targets could not be achieved.

There are also differences of opinion between Crosby and Deming with regard to goal and target setting. Crosby sees these as central to continuous improvement whilst Deming considers that targets can lead to negative accomplishment. Specifically, Deming was very much against the inappropriate uses of management slogans and goals within the organisation, which he viewed as nothing more than cosmetic gestures.

The fact that the concept of quality is so difficult to define probably explains much as to why there are contrasting views and attitudes related to the subject of quality management. However, many of the key underpinning thinking related to TQM is shared by these three pioneering individuals. Whilst there might be different opinions as to the road to be taken to achieve TQM there is no argument about the ultimate destination.

Solution 5

The question is difficult to understand as it stands. Compare and contrast the challenges with what? The official answer guidance suggests that we are meant to compare challenges arising today in an era of increasing globalisation with those of past eras, less globally based.

A recommended approach to this question is as follows.

- *Introduction*

  - *Brief historical context of globalisation and associated issues*

- *Main body*

  - *Discuss key areas of relevance such as:*
  - *Technology*
  - *Marketing and global markets*
  - *Increased competition*
  - *Shorter product lifecycles*
  - *Free markets*

- *Reflective summary*

The period since the Second World War has seen a considerable growth in the numbers, size and spread of multinational companies who have benefited from factors such as the reduction in tariff barriers, the growth in technology, the impact of worldwide communications, the increasing standardisation of trade-related documentation and the harmonisation of customs tariffs.

Organisations confront a challenging set of problems in the form of global competition, emergence of developing economies, formation of trade blocs, environmental neglect, economic stagnation and recessions, and low labour skills. Alongside this, new opportunities are being offered in the form of larger global markets, environmental clean-up operations, infrastructure regeneration and reconstruction, and the ongoing development of the worldwide financial and telecommunications markets.

Technology

The impact of technology and the development of new service markets, programmes for upgrading human skills and the survival of lean producers and lean marketers are all part of the modern trading environment. The ability to succeed in today's economic community will require much more awareness of global issues and the global market place than has previously been the case.

The globalisation of business has been enabled by the impact of enhanced communications. Systems can be integrated within organisations, ignoring international boundaries, and can add value to a firm's performance by reducing stockholding, ensuring efficient materials usage and cost effective manufacture, and saving on labour costs amongst other areas.

With developments in IT and communications, particularly the internet, smaller organisations can now cost-effectively start to view the world in a similar way, as a global market for their products or services. International communications and other developments enable marketing, in particular, to be viewed in the global context.

Marketing and global markets

The convergence of global consumer markets has been emphasised by the widening of marketing from a national or pan-national approach to a highly developed global perspective being taken by organisations. Factors that have enhanced this global approach include the following.

- Branding
- Market positioning
- Promotion
- Distribution
- Pricing

Global marketing requires a different approach from traditional exporting in that it aims towards economies of scale in production and distribution and towards a gradual convergence of customer needs and wants on a global basis.

The global corporation seeks competitive advantage by identifying worldwide markets and then developing a manufacturing strategy that supports the marketing strategy. To the operations manager within this global concept there is the need to gain competitive advantage in manufacturing. This advantage can then be used to underpin the global marketing strategy by delivering goods of the appropriate quality, on time and in a manner that meets customer needs.

Globalisation has been defined by Ruud Lubbers as 'a process in which geographic distance becomes a factor of diminishing importance in the establishment and maintenance of cross border economic, political and socio-cultural relations'. The definition highlights the way in which communications are reducing geographic issues and enabling an approach that can view the world as one market.

The industrialised world has over recent years seen much of its manufacturing base move to overseas markets. The reasons are often discussed but the reality is that many overseas countries offer lower production costs because of lower rates of pay and overheads and can often match or improve on quality.

Globalisation has affected operations management as the operations manager, whether in goods or services, needs to deliver the efficiencies and effectiveness called for in a diverse mix of markets.

The management of overseas operations, whether outsourced or company-owned, calls for a wider appreciation of cultural, ethical and communication issues than is the case when operating only in the domestic market.

Many organisations throughout the world are now taking a global perspective on their strategies to take advantage of the current situation. The globalisation of production has opened new opportunities for countries such as China and Indonesia. The globalisation of services has opened new opportunities for India, in particular as high computer literacy coupled with English language skills have led to a growing IT support and call centre industry.

World best practice demonstrates that organisations should take commercial advantage of these opportunities in order to meet the increasing demands of customers in terms of quality and cost. The role of the operations manager may involve training and updating certain providers to ensure expected standards are met but in many cases the provider may be more advanced because of their ability to specialise and their knowledge of the requirements of global companies.

Increased competition

The globalisation of business coupled with the economic growth in global economies has combined to lead to a highly competitive global environment. Organisations must be sure of their strategies and be responsive to customer needs in order to survive. Professor Michael Porter identifies five competitive forces in the environment of an organisation. The impact of globalisation is serving to widen the impact of these factors.

- The threat of new entrants to an industry. A new entrant will bring extra capacity and poses a threat as established organisations may lose market share and economies of scale. With the increased globalisation of business new entrants may often mean established international firms looking for new markets.

- The threat of substitute products or services. Substitutes pose a threat as they limit the ability of an organisation to charge high prices for its products so that demand for products becomes relatively sensitive to price.

- The bargaining power of customers. Customers will look for better quality products and services at lower prices. Factors such as differentiation by adding value in areas such as delivery or customer service, the ability to switch between products and the importance of the spend, can reduce this strength.

- The bargaining power of suppliers. This depends on a number of factors including the business relationship, the number of suppliers, the importance of the supplier's product and the cost of switching from one supplier to another.

- The rivalry amongst current competitors in the industry. The intensity of competitive rivalry will influence the profitability of the industry as a whole.

With the aid of Porter's five forces model companies need to consider their competitive position. Competitive position describes the market share, costs, price, quality and accumulated experience of an entity or product relative to its competitors.

Competition forces most organisations to look for cost savings or value-added activities that enhance marketability. One of the key roles of operations management is to make improvements in efficiency and effectiveness in order to increase productivity. Operations managers will seek to increase productivity but also to enable value-added production through areas such as design, flexibility in manufacture and late customisation of product.

Shorter product lifecycles

Increased competition, when linked to increasing customer demands, forces companies to review their product offerings more frequently. Product lifecycles are shortening in response to increased competition, advances in technology and customer demand.

The use of computer aided design and manufacture enables faster product development and manufacture. Organisations that can bring new and innovative quality products to market can gain a substantial competitive edge over the competition. CAD/CAM systems permit faster times (from concept through to manufacture) while permitting simulation of use where appropriate. Simulation means that, often, models and mock-ups are not required as computer-generated information can carry out testing on a virtual model. This not only saves money but also speeds up the product development to launch process.

Globalisation widens the remit of the operations role. Greater emphasis is placed on adopting world best practice. This can be achieved through monitoring technical developments and applying benchmarking where appropriate. The operations role is to understand the manufacturing and service development needs of globalisation and apply the benefits to work practices.

Free markets

Free trade means the reduction or elimination of barriers between markets such as import tariffs, duties and taxes, quota restrictions, documentary requirements and technical standards.

Free trade enables a country's consumers or purchasers to seek out the best bargain they can find by not restricting their ability to choose overseas suppliers when they offer a better deal than domestic competitors in terms of quality and/or price. This enhances competition and profitability by enabling consumers and purchasers to seek out the optimum deal.

In summary, the revolution of global markets has changed the role and scope of operations managers forever. The attributes required by today's operations managers cover a diverse range of dynamic and complex issues both within and outside of organisational boundaries. For organisations to survive operations managers need to strive to achieve innovative solutions and a constant refocusing on core competencies and beliefs. As such there is now a critical need for operations management to constantly evolve their business acumen from a global perspective.

Solution 6

Part (a)

Benchmarking is a business discipline that has been utilised over many years. It has gained widening appeal as technology has enabled performance measures to be compared, contrasted and evaluated within tight time-frames and with greater accuracy.

A dictionary definition gives the basic concept of a benchmark.

> 'A standard point of reference against which things can be assessed'

This definition suggests using an acceptable reference point to assess against. In storage and distribution this reference point could be deliveries on time, warehouse space allocated or order fill, as examples.

A further definition of benchmarking from Rank Xerox serves to demonstrate that benchmarking can have a significant role in improving supply chain and logistic performance by identifying and learning from best practice in other organisations.

> 'The continuous process of measuring products, services, and practices, against the toughest competitors or those companies recognised as industry leaders'.

There are many different types of benchmarking that can be used by organisations.

- Internal benchmarking within an organisation (eg between business units)
- Competitive benchmarking with competitors
- Functional benchmarking against similar processes within a business sector
- Generic benchmarking between unrelated industries
- Collaborative benchmarking between groups of companies

During the 1980s Rank Xerox found that its dominant position in the photocopier market was increasingly under threat from Japanese companies. Rank Xerox responded by developing and using benchmarking to identify areas of weakness and opportunities for improvement.

Rank Xerox developed a five-phase approach to benchmarking that suited its needs.

Planning

- Form benchmarking team
- Identify benchmark outputs
- Identify best competitor
- Determine data collection method
- Collect data
- Determine performance measures

Analysis

- Determine current competitive gap
- Project future performance levels

Integration

- Establish functional goals
- Develop functional action plans

Action

- Implement specific actions
- Monitor results/report progress
- Recalibrate benchmarks

Maturity

- Leadership position obtained
- Processes fully integrated in organisational practices

Rank Xerox developed benchmarking by incorporating it into a total quality strategy ('Leadership Through Strategy') that converted benchmarking into a process of continuous improvement. This represented a long-term commitment to benchmarking supported at strategic level.

Many organisations will not become as committed to benchmarking as Rank Xerox and may use it at a tactical level without the perceived need to integrate benchmarking fully into the organisation. However individual organisations use benchmarking it is a powerful tool for continuous improvement and performance breakthroughs.

Part (b)

The process of benchmarking is but one of a number of techniques that can be used by organisations to support continuous improvement initiatives. However, it is not a cure for all ills and organisations need to be aware of both potential benefits and the limitations of the benchmarking technique.

Benchmarking brings a range of benefits. If developed as an integrated process, it becomes a tool for continuous improvement. Benefits quoted by the Public Sector Benchmarking Service include the following.

- Learning from others who have enjoyed success and gaining greater confidence in developing and delivering new approaches
- Greater involvement and motivation of staff engaged in benchmarking and change programmes
- Heightened awareness about performance levels
- Increased willingness to share solutions to common problems
- Wider understanding of the strategic implications
- Increased collaboration and enhanced working relationships

Benchmarking aids an organisation in its understanding of competitors and the methods by which they operate. They bring successful ideas from proven practice that can be adapted or built upon. With benchmarking more options become available as different approaches are introduced and these can help lead to superior performance over time.

Benchmarking is a proactive approach that establishes credible goals and objectives enabling a considered understanding of real problems and issues supported by proven business responses.

There are also limitations and drawbacks to benchmarking.

Benchmarking is complex and time-consuming to implement properly. To succeed requires a high level of consistent commitment over the long term. Clear systems and procedures must be put in place and followed.

In accord with the complexity and the resources required to conduct a professional benchmarking programme associated costs can often be expensive. It is therefore important that businesses compare projected benefits and costs to justify the commencement of such programmes.

Competitive sensitivity often prevents the free flow of information to properly support many competitive benchmarking activities. This can easily lead to benchmarking projects stalling with related staff becoming both frustrated and demotivated.

Benchmarking is copying and adapting what other organisations have successfully achieved. As such benchmarking can stifle creativity and original thought. In other words, companies follow and therefore don't lead. This is an important consideration when attempting to gain competitive advantage because often it is about establishing future, as well as current, customer needs and expectations.

Finally, it is often difficult to establish the real parameters for the success of the target company. Often it is not simply about process efficiency but also success is directly attributable to such complex factors as strategy, organisational size and culture.

Subject Index